Mozart Studies 2

Cultural, historical and reception-related contexts are central to understanding Mozart, one of the greatest and most famous musicians of all time. Widening and refining the lens through which the composer is viewed, the essays in *Mozart Studies 2* focus on themes, issues, works and repertories perennially popular among Mozart scholars of all kinds, pointing to areas primed for future study and also suitable for investigation by musicians outside the scholarly community. Following on from the first *Mozart Studies* volume, internationally renowned contributors bring new perspectives to bear on many of Mozart's most popular works, as well as the composer's letters, biography and reception. Chapters are grouped according to topics covered and collectively affirm the vitality of Mozart scholarship and the significant role it continues to play in defining and re-defining musicological priorities in general.

SIMON P. KEEFE is James Rossiter Hoyle Chair and Head of Music at the University of Sheffield. He is the author of three books on Mozart, including most recently *Mozart's Requiem: Reception, Work, Completion* (Cambridge, 2012), which won the 2013 Marjorie Weston Emerson Award from the Mozart Society of America for the best book or edition published in 2011 or 2012. He is the editor of a further five volumes, all published by Cambridge University Press, including *Mozart Studies* (2006). In 2005 he was elected a life member of the Academy for Mozart Research at the International Mozart Foundation in Salzburg. He is General Editor of the Royal Musical Association Monographs series and a 'Late Eighteenth-Century Composers' series, and chairs the Royal Musical Association Publications Committee.

Mozart Studies 2

EDITED BY

Simon P. Keefe

CAMBRIDGE
UNIVERSITY PRESS

University Printing House, Cambridge CB2 8BS, United Kingdom

Cambridge University Press is part of the University of Cambridge.

It furthers the University's mission by disseminating knowledge in the pursuit of
education, learning and research at the highest international levels of excellence.

www.cambridge.org
Information on this title: www.cambridge.org/9781107044234

© Cambridge University Press 2015

First published 2015

Printed in the United Kingdom by TJ International Ltd. Padstow Cornwall

A catalogue record for this publication is available from the British Library

Library of Congress Cataloging in Publication data
Mozart studies 2 / edited by Simon P. Keefe.
   pages   cm
Includes index
ISBN 978-1-107-04423-4
1. Mozart, Wolfgang Amadeus, 1756–1791 – Criticism and interpretation.
I. Keefe, Simon P., 1968–   II. Title: Mozart studies 2
ML410.M9M7332   2015
780.92–dc23

                                                            2015021139

ISBN 978-1-107-04423-4 Hardback

Contents

Figures

Tables

Contributors

DAVID BLACK, Visiting Lecturer, Australian National University

EMILY I. DOLAN, Gardner Cowles Associate Professor of Music, Harvard University

DAVID WYN JONES, Professor of Music, Cardiff University

SIMON P. KEEFE, James Rossiter Hoyle Chair and Head of Music, University of Sheffield

ULRICH KONRAD, Professor and Executive Director, Department of Musicology, Institute for Music Research, University of Würzburg

RUPERT RIDGEWELL, Curator of Printed Music, Music Collections, British Library, London

STEPHEN RUMPH, Associate Professor, School of Music, University of Washington

IAN WOODFIELD, Professor of Historical Musicology, School of Creative Arts, Queen's University Belfast

Preface

At the beginning of 2011, with no significant anniversary for the composer in sight, the UK's leading classical music station, BBC Radio 3, staged a twelve-day festival entitled 'The Genius of Mozart'. In spite of a specious advertising strapline, airing 'every note he wrote', the breadth of extra-musical coverage – inter alia 'A History of Mozart in a Dozen Objects' by Cliff Eisen, a re-broadcast of Peter Shaffer's *Amadeus* with the original theatrical cast, and a debate on the nature of genius with perspectives from mathematics, science and literature as well as music – was at least as noticeable as the imperative towards musical comprehensiveness. A scholarly article of faith was foregrounded in the media: cultural, historical, contextual and reception-related interrogation is central to understanding a composer's music.

In the fullness of time, traces of the primary thrust of scholarly activity from recent years, namely widening and refining the lens through which Mozart's *oeuvre* is viewed, will hopefully become embedded in the consciousness of performers and musical public. *Mozart Studies 2* contributes to the process by focusing on themes, issues, works and repertories perennially popular among Mozartians of all stripes, pointing to areas ripe for future scholarly study and also suitable for investigation by others. Ulrich Konrad subjects Mozart's letters, one of the most famous bodies of correspondence associated with a musician, to close syntactic and semantic scrutiny, revealing the composer's linguistic and narratological playfulness, sophistication and creativity. My own chapter on Mozart's six-month stay in Paris in 1778 uses the letters to inform a new approach to biography, a cornerstone of Mozart research and popular interest. I establish that Mozart immersed himself in music even during one of the most troubled periods of his life and propose a re-orientation towards music-dominated biography grounded in Mozart's engagement with performers and performance issues. David Black moves the biographical discourse on to Vienna, examining Mozart's six appearances at concerts mounted by the Tonkünstler-Societät, which span his entire decade in the city (1781–91). Drawing on detailed archival evidence, Black refines understandings of both Mozart's relationship with the society and the society's activities in general.

Chapters 4, 5 and 6 situate Mozart's chamber music in broad musical contexts. Stephen Rumph deepens understandings of Mozart's instrumental style, another standard subject of scholarly and general interest, by looking at manifestations of the hymn topic. He discusses its mixture with other topics and styles, such as the sarabande, march and fanfare, and pays special attention to rarely investigated topical *figurae*. Rupert Ridgewell turns to editions of Mozart's music from the 1780s, an issue clearly relevant to modern-day performers. Specifically he identifies the operatic ensembles 'Dite almeno in che mancai' K. 479 and 'Mandina amabile' K. 480, arranged for flute quintet and located in the Czech Republic, as a missing edition from Viennese publisher Anton Hoffmeister's subscription series initiated in late 1785. Ridgewell concludes that Mozart was almost certainly aware of the edition, but that Hoffmeister or one his associates most probably carried out the arrangements. My chapter on the ever-popular quartets dedicated to Haydn, set against the backdrop of critical interest in Mozart's compositional refinements rather than performance-related orientations, uses differences between the autograph and first published edition (Vienna: Artaria, 1785) as a springboard for re-examining and re-evaluating the quartets. I show that alterations from autograph to Artaria edition capture the 'live' nature of these works for Mozart, his views about the performance of them evolving over time.

Chapters 7, 8 and 9 look at issues surrounding the genesis and modification of one of Mozart's best-loved operas, at substantive arrangements of his instrumental and vocal works made by a prominent nineteenth-century admirer, and at the ways Mozart's music is heard and processed. Ian Woodfield accounts for the problematic nature of Cherubino's risqué behaviour in *Le nozze di Figaro*, relating it both to sources connected to Da Ponte's fashioning of the libretto (including Johann Rautenstrauch's *Der närrische Tag*), and to libretto sources for productions elsewhere in the Habsburg empire in the years after the premiere in 1786. David Wyn Jones documents Ignaz von Seyfried's lifelong interest in, and reception of, Mozart's music. Seyfried's adventurous arrangements are often stylistically incongruous with Mozart and demonstrate Beethoven's influence; they capture in microcosm the nineteenth century's fascination with Mozart. Finally, Emily Dolan probes the uncanny in the music of Mozart and others, discussing issues of familiarity, recognizability, lyrical melody and song. She concludes that late eighteenth-century music captures not the uncanny itself, but pre-conditions to it – thus representing the 'pre-uncanny'.

Abbreviations

LMF Emily Anderson (ed. and trans.), *The Letters of Mozart and His Family*, 3rd edition (London and New York, 1985).

MBA Wilhelm A. Bauer, Otto Erich Deutsch and Joseph Heinz Eibl (eds.), *Mozart: Briefe und Aufzeichnungen, Gesamtausgabe*, 7 vols. (Kassel, 1962–75); Ulrich Konrad (ed.), vol. 8 (Kassel, 2006).

MDB Otto Erich Deutsch, *Mozart: a Documentary Biography*, trans. Eric Blom, Peter Branscombe and Jeremy Noble (London, 1965).

MDL Otto Erich Deutsch, *Mozart: Die Dokumente seines Lebens* (Kassel, 1961).

NMA Wolfgang Amadeus Mozart, *Neue Ausgabe sämtlicher Werke* (Kassel, 1955–2007).

NMD Cliff Eisen, *New Mozart Documents: a Supplement to O.E. Deutsch's Documentary Biography* (London and Stanford, CA, 1991).

1   Mozart the letter writer and his language

Ulrich Konrad

Translated by William Buchanan

I

Mozart was an eminent letter writer, the most eloquent among musicians of his time, of almost unparalleled vitality of word and clarity of formulation. Anyone who now expects, on the basis of this statement, to find among the correspondence of the composer well-rounded literary entities, stylistically honed and sublimely argued, will be disappointed. Classical epistles of the kind and rank of his German contemporaries Goethe and Schiller were never written by Mozart, examples of poetry in their sense hardly ever, and of literature not at all. The hardly decipherable handwriting and the very free handling of orthography alone, even by the standards of the eighteenth century, hinder the impression that these pieces of correspondence might have been written with intentions beyond their immediate context. (On 29 December 1778 Mozart indeed admits that he had 'bad handwriting by nature' because he had 'never learnt to write'.[1]) Mozart's letters captivate the receptive reader less for their disclosures of worldviews or aesthetic maxims than for the breath of ongoing life that they exude. It is usually the hasty exhalation of a person hardly able to catch his breath, not the marble respiration of an idealized, fictitious figure. To look for the latter and to wish to see it confirmed in the letters is a vain undertaking, and many a gentlemanly connoisseur of the arts or culturally zealous reader of previous generations has turned away from them in irritation. Not infrequently, later critics have taken their own life experience and worldview as the measure by which to understand what was once Mozart's present. The reading that then takes place is not one which accepts insight into circumstances different from one's own (with at least minimal prejudice), but a reading that serves primarily to confirm the reader's own standpoint, *ex negativo* if necessary. For interpreters of this kind, Mozart's letters have served as testimonies of absurd ineptness; creating distance from the ineptness may appear to be evidence of intellectual superiority – a strategy used successfully time and again in neutralizing 'unsettling' forces. Such

[1] MBA, vol. II, p. 529.

1

projections from the present onto past epochs are nothing unusual and, in fact, are common. But they say more about the time of origin than about their object.

This finding is clearly confirmed by differing reactions to the so-called *Bäsle-Briefe* ('Letters to his cousin'), which comprise nine of at least eleven once-extant pieces of writing sent by Mozart to his cousin Maria Anna Thekla Mozart between 1777 and October 1781.[2] They contain effervescent and unbridled verbal buffoonery, draw sustenance from all processes associated with the digestive system and include detectable erotic nuances. In the *Bäsle-Briefe*, Mozart sets up the stage of the jester and verbal acrobat, adopting principally the role of uninhibitedly bragging jokester. What had no doubt been produced, quasi improvisatorily, in front of his cousin in direct interaction and had been tested for immediate effect, now continues in letters – not as an audibly perceptible, but rather a written linguistic game. We know nothing of the addressee's reactions – she will no doubt have been entertained – but the judgement of posterity speaks volumes.

In 1799 Constanze Mozart considered that 'the clearly tasteless, but nevertheless very witty letters to his cousin',[3] although unworthy of publication in complete form, were deserving of mention in excerpts at least; less than twenty years later, Mozart's son Carl Thomas even thought of destroying them[4] and Georg Nikolaus von Nissen, in his Mozart biography of 1828, only touched in passing on the much 'too childish and common pieces of fun'.[5] Until the twentieth century, a general sense of propriety forbade publication *in toto* of 'Wolfgang's *Bäselbriefe*, notorious for their sordidness (and which are only known to the initiated in their full glory)'.[6] Whatever reasons are given for suppressing them – esteem for Mozart's genius, contravention of respectability or aesthetic considerations – emphasis was always placed on the attitude of posterity towards these unusual works of Mozart's youth rather than on the letters themselves. When they finally became generally accessible via the complete edition and special publications, the perception of them turned from moral reserve to enthusiasm, inspiring fervently psychological interpretation. Suddenly, the *Bäsle-Briefe* were put

[2] In MBA the numbers are 361, 364, 371, 384, 432, 511, 525, 531, 635.

[3] Letter to Breitkopf & Härtel, 28 August 1799; MBA, vol. IV, p. 269.

[4] As explained to the composer Wilhelm Speyer in 1818; see Edward Speyer, *Wilhelm Speyer der Liederkomponist 1790–1878. Sein Leben und Verkehr mit seinen Zeitgenossen dargestellt von seinem jüngsten Sohne* (Munich, 1925), pp. 24ff.

[5] Georg Nikolaus von Nissen, *Biographie W. A. Mozarts* (Leipzig, 1828), p. xxiv.

[6] Arthur Schurig, *Wolfgang Amadeus Mozart. Sein Leben und sein Werk auf Grund der vornehmlich durch Nikolaus von Nissen gesammelten biographischen Quellen und der Ergebnisse der neuesten Forschung dargestellt*, 2 vols. (Leipzig, 1913), vol. I, p. 330, fn. 1.

to service as evidence of an entirely new profile of Mozart's personality – in the popular Mozart films of the 1980s the screen teemed with adolescents constantly reverting to childish stages of basic impulses – and occasionally the question of whether the composer and his cousin had their first sexual experiences together seemed to assume the dimensions of a central problem in Mozart biography. All of this can be easily traced back to the societal and value-related changes in the Western world since the late 1960s. But seeing in the *Bäsle-Briefe* the basis for a meaningful psychogramme of Mozart's personality will convince almost no one today.

One thing, however, can be detected in these nine letters: the verbal cascades can be attributed to ideas triggered in Mozart by the distant addressee. That she alone was capable of revealing precisely this side of the letter-writer Mozart was a fact of which she was probably unaware. Nowhere else in his correspondence did he strike this exuberant tone of unrestrained language, or allow this faecal–erotic babble of voices to emerge; comparable passages are encountered only occasionally in the later letters to his wife Constanze. Mozart was – as expected from an artist profoundly inspired by the theatre – an exceptional judge of character. What he had instinctively gathered about the nature of the other person determined his letter-writing behaviour. This statement may be of only limited relevance in view of the fact that he wrote to no more than twelve addressees in his entire preserved correspondence; the only constant correspondence he conducted as an adult, furthermore, was with his father (1777–9, 1780–7). In addition there are sporadic or situation-related letters to his mother, sister and cousin, to Constanze and to Johann Michael Puchberg. But the whole manner in which Mozart addressed these people and others, such as Joseph Bullinger, Martha Elisabeth von Waldstätten and Gottfried von Jacquin, reveals his ability to meet a correspondent as an individual human being. In this process, he never, or only seldom, dissembled (and then rather unskilfully), as far as a judgement of this kind can be made. In the course of the psychological interpretation to which the letters were subjected, it was now and again claimed that Mozart veiled the truth or sometimes disregarded it.[7] Distrust of statements in parts of Mozart's letters and understanding them in ways contrary to the transmitted wording, however, succeeded in opening easy paths to interpretations that are more superficially striking than convincing. This is in no way to deny that Mozart, particularly in unpleasant

---

[7] See, for example, David Schroeder, *Mozart in Revolt: Strategies of Resistance, Mischief, and Deception* (New Haven, CT, 1999).

circumstances and under pressure to justify himself, embellished the truth for his father or gave him undertakings without any deep inclination and inner conviction. But what is so remarkable about behaviour of this kind in situations of extreme stress? In particular, the constantly observant, clear-sightedly strict Leopold hardly ever allowed himself to be deceived by such attempts on Wolfgang's part – at most, they temporarily distracted him. And the insidious alienation of father and son, which started in the Mannheim winter of 1777–8 with the 'affair' involving Aloysia Weber, and which the sensitive reader today can still detect in the letters, was noticed very early on by Leopold. The way he sought to counteract this process, including in the spring of 1781 in Vienna, desperate and powerless, certainly makes harrowing reading – in letters full of unadorned openness.

When reading these true records of life, subsequent generations have allowed themselves as a matter of course to peer inquisitively, indiscreetly and (only too often) with an air of superior knowledge into the private matters of other people – peering that these people would not usually have tolerated in person. Only historical distance justifies a conscious partaking of these personal documents, which are sometimes documents of the most intimate kind. But what does conscious partaking mean? Any proximity to persons of a long-gone age can only be superficial, and nothing is more laughable than a pretended camaraderie with them, even if motivated by the greatest and most genuine veneration. Reading roughly 250-year-old letters and seeking to meet Mozart in them can only be meaningful if, on the one hand, the circumstances of their time and origin are respected – laying such circumstances bare from under the rubble of history is the historian's task – and if, on the other hand, constant reminders are issued that later readers, with their current capacity for understanding and their epistemic interests, see a reflection of themselves in the old documents. We read Mozart in his letters, but we also read ourselves in them in that we deliberately make them our own. This is inevitable and in no way disreputable, but should warn us against interpretational appropriations – enticements of this kind are particularly seductive.

Mozart's letters and those of his family are not exotic discoveries suitable for being marvelled at in a display cabinet, but are bearers of communications that are still awaiting answers. Today, we are the addressees who can be inspired to react monologically to these historical messages-in-a-bottle. There are a number of hindrances to accessing the content of the letters, above all relating to the forms of language used. It is a major simplification to categorize the language without further ado as 'German'. The German of the eighteenth century is particularly marked in both oral and written usage by a broad palette of dialects, forming a closely meshed net of extremely varied morphological, phonological, semantic and syntactic characteristics. They occasionally depart so substantially from the regulated High German of the twenty-first century that even native speakers have difficulty immediately understanding letters by Mozart; indeed, the letters contain some passages that reveal their true sense only to the linguistically trained reader. Furthermore Mozart's German draws material from different dialectal sources. Probably taken from his father, the major constituent of his German was a number of Western Upper Germanic or Alemannic elements dominant in Bavarian Swabia, to which Augsburg belongs. Mozart's mother, who hailed from St Gilgen in the Salzkammergut, spoke a Southern Central Bavarian dialect; its sounds seem to have aroused little pleasure in Mozart, as one may deduce from his occasional sallies against Salzburgian. In contrast, Viennese, which is often linked thoughtlessly with the composer's manner of speaking and writing because he spent the last ten years of his life in this royal town of residence, would probably have been a less significant influence. In order to understand properly the linguistic form and content of Mozart's letters a double transcription is needed; namely, from dialectal into High German and from the historical status of the language into the present. In this process, close attention should be paid in particular to the development of semantics and the change in the relationship of linguistic utterances to the living environment. That these transcriptive processes cannot lead to complete congruence between what was and what is, comprises an experience as well known as the even greater blurring that occurs when texts are translated into foreign languages. A perusal of Mozart's letters thus leads only to partial understanding for both native and non-native speakers alike, even if the qualitative difference has a different magnitude in each case.

An approach to the 284 letters of Mozart – the number currently available – can be chronological, or related either to people or themes. While approaches orientated chronologically or towards people are self-explanatory, those relating to themes can be carried out very differently, whether with regard to Mozart's handling of, and play with, language, in relation to his worldview and religious persuasion, or by looking at his statements about himself. For our cursory examination, we will initially study Mozart's linguistic usage, moving on to explore other areas.

II

Hints about the variety of language in Mozart's letters have already been given, but it would be remiss not to note his use of a number of foreign languages. Even the first preserved letter, from 1769, ends with a Latin quotation. Mixing languages and dialects is one of Mozart's favourite writing practices, especially in closing flourishes, such as that of 12 August 1773: 'hodie nous avons encountered per strada Dominum Edlbach who passed on to us di voi compliments, et qui commends himself tibi et ta mere. Adio. W. M. Mainroad the 12 Aug.'[8] He also makes virtuosic use of different stylistic levels, the elevated style often being used as the object of ironic imitation:

> I hope, my queen, you will be enjoying the highest degree of health and yet, now and again or, rather, occasionally or, better, from time to time or, even better, qualche volta, as they say south of the Alps, from your important and pressing thoughts |: which emerge constantly from the most beautiful and surest reason, which you possess besides your beauty; although in such tender years and in a woman almost nothing of that just mentioned is demanded, you, oh queen, possess these in such a manner that you shame the male persons, yes, even the aged woman :| you will sacrifice to me a number. Farewell.[9]

Placing himself at an ironic distance from a situation described or even from an entire letter shows that Mozart also looked over his own shoulder in the role of letter writer. His cousin, for example, is instructed on one occasion on the high import of an epistle:

> Now there is too little space to present yet more cleverness, and cleverness all the time leads to a headache; my letter is, after all, full of clever and learned things anyway; if you have already read it, you will have to admit this, and if you have not read it, then please read it soon, you will derive much profit from it, you will shed bitter tears at some of the lines.[10]

Other addressees, such as his sister, fall victim to closing nonsense:

> What fault is it of mine that it has just now sounded quarter past 7? – – – Nor does my Papa carry any blame in this – – Mama will hear more about this from my sister. But now things have not been going well, because the Archbishop will not stay here long – – they are even saying he will stay until he departs again. – – My only regret is that he will not see the first evening concert. I commend myself to Baron Zemen, and to all good friends of both sexes. I send hand-kisses to Mama. Farewell. I will collect you at once. Your faithful Francis von Noseblood. Milan. 5th May 1756[11]

The broad range of play on words opens up in front of us. From Mozart's inexhaustible stock, let us concentrate only on play with proper names and individual words. In Augsburg, the arrogant 'Mister von Longcoat' (Langenmantel) becomes 'the young ass von Shortcoat',[12] and the composer Seydelmann (= 'Pint-man'), not very capable in Mozart's eyes, would be better called 'Quart-man', more aptly 'if not *Drum-Bowl*man, then at

[8] MBA, vol. I, p. 487.
[9] MBA, vol. I, p. 488 (14 August 1773). And a comparable passage: 'If Your Grace, [regarding] my most reasonable, gracious Lady von Robinig and her Gracious Journey To Munich . . . [. . .]', MBA, vol. III, p. 54 (13 December 1780).
[10] MBA, vol. II, p. 95 (31 October 1777).
[11] MBA, vol. I, p. 518 (18 January 1775).
[12] MBA, vol. II, p. 63 (16/17 October 1777).

least *Gill*man';[13] his assistant Süßmayr (= 'Sweet-dairyman') has to accept apostrophization as 'Sauermayer' (= 'Sour-dairyman').[14] Occasionally, the correct name is dispensed with altogether: 'There was a plethora of nobility there, the Duchess Bohemian-Bum, Countess Fond-Pisser, Princess Smell-Like-Dirt, with her 2 daughters, who are already married, however, to the 2 Princes Mash-Belly of Pig-Prick.'[15] Acoustic similarity in the words allows the (literal) 'physiognomy' of a merchant from Meiningen to slip into 'symphony';[16] for a verb like 'affirm' a synonym 'assolid' is created;[17] and the crab treatment of a fugue theme receives the less refined designation 'arse-ling'.[18] Associative ambiguities occur frequently:

> It seemed to me the whole time as if I still had something to say – [. . .] – only no idea came down on me, as is usually the case with me; – I also often regret that I did not, instead of music, learn the art of architecture, for I have often heard that the best masterbuilders are those whose ideas do not fall from heaven.[19]

The linguistically creative fantasy of Mozart at the level of the word finds a continuation in freely invented stories. The wit in such stories usually lies in the way that a rising curve of suspense, constructed with much verbal elaboration, is finally left hanging in the air, and the point turns out to be trivial or even completely non-existent. Mozart, for example, announces to his cousin – who is the most important addressee for such fables – that he must 'tell her a sad story', yet the unfathomable, cumbersomely told events with their references to the senses of hearing and smell, although seemingly originating from the street, turn out finally to come from a fart.[20] The apparently rational report of a midday meal in the house of the Mannheim musician Johann Baptist Wendling finally loses its way completely and fizzles out.[21] Nothing less than a model of early nonsense literature in German is provided by the fairytale of the 11,000 sheep:

> It is no great time ago that this took place; it happened in this country. It has furthermore attracted much attention here, for it seems impossible; nor does anyone yet know, strictly between ourselves, the outcome of the matter. Thus, to keep it brief, it was about 4 hours from here, the place I can no longer say – – it was simply a village or the like; now, that is a thing after all, whether it was Tribsterill, where the dirt flows into the sea, or Burmesquick, where they turn the twisted arses; in a word, it was simply a place. There was a herdsman or shepherd, who was fairly old, but nonetheless still looked robust and sturdy for all that; he was a bachelor, and of substantial means, and lived in great contentment. Yes, I must say this to you before I finish telling the story, he had a terrible tone when he spoke; all had to feel fear

[13] MBA, vol. IV, p. 87 (16 May 1789).
[14] MBA, vol. IV, p. 150 (7 July 1791).
[15] MBA, vol. II, pp. 66–7 (16/17 October 1777).
[16] MBA, vol. II, p. 6 (23 September 1777).
[17] MBA, vol. II, p. 547 (10 May 1779).
[18] MBA, vol. II, p. 82 (23–5 October 1777).
[19] MBA, vol. III, pp. 233–4 (2 October 1782).
[20] MBA, vol. II, p. 106 (5 November 1777).
[21] MBA, vol. II, p. 165 (3 December 1777).

when they heard him talk. Now, to treat of the matter briefly, you must know – he also had a dog, which he called Barker, a very fine, large dog, white with black patches. Now, one day, he was underway with his sheep, of which he had 11 thousand altogether; he had a stick there in his hand, with a fine, rose-coloured stick band. For he went nowhere without a stick. That was indeed one of his customs; now, onward. As he had gone on this way for fully an hour, he was of course tired, and sat himself down by a river. At last, he fell asleep, and he had a dream that he had lost his sheep, and in this terror he awoke, and saw however, to his greatest joy, all his sheep again. At last, he rose, and went on again, but not for long; for there will be hardly half-an-hour gone past when they came to a bridge, which was very long, but well secured on both sides, so that one could not fall off; now, there he contemplated his herd; and, because he had to cross, he started to drive his 11 thousand sheep across. Now just have the equanimity to wait until the 11 thousand sheep are across, then I will tell you the whole history to its end. I have already told you that no-one knows the outcome. But I hope that, by the time I write to you, they will surely be across; if not, then it is all the same to me; as far as I am concerned, they could have remained up there. In the meantime, you must indeed be content with things so far; what I knew about it I have written. And it is better that I stop now than that I should make up lies. In the latter case, you would perhaps not have believed the whole shistory [schistori], but this way – – please believe me – not half of it.[22]

Sometimes, however, mere signs suffice instead of words in order to conjure up meaning out of nothing, as when the following important message for 'As Yet Nameless' – Franz Xaver Süßmayer – is to be passed on by Constanze:

```
= = = = = = = = =
= = = = = = = = =
= = = = = = = = =
= = = = = = = = =
```

Mozart then maintains that this message will hit his pupil and assistant where it is going to hurt most: 'What does he say to that? Is he pleased? I don't really think so, these are harsh expressions! and difficult to grasp.'[23] Through two examples, we can illustrate Mozart's joy at experimenting with syntax and word order. The postscript to the letter of 16 January 1773 appears in the autograph as follows (the original alignment is reproduced here):

1   [a]I to have write for primo ~~homo~~ the homo a to motet be performed
2   the at Theatines tomorrow. [b]Remain health in I you beg. Fare well. Addio.
3   [c]I regret I nothing, my   to good and   [d]fare [e]my to Mama. [f]I you
4   feel that know new, greetings all friends women-friends. well. handkiss our kiss
5   in and as your brother thousandfold remain ever faithful Milan[24]

---

[22] MBA, vol. II, pp. 308–9 (28 February 1778).
[23] MBA, vol. IV, p. 152 (9 July 1791).

[24] MBA, vol. I, pp. 475–6. Autograph in Salzburg, Internationale Stiftung

Mozart subjects each of the six sentences (a; b; c–f) to its own constructional model:

Sentence a (lines 1/2): groups of four words in the order 1 – 3 – 2 – 4

I to have write	I have to write
for primo ~~homo~~ the uomo	for the *primo uomo* ~~uomo~~
a to motet be	a motet to be
performed the at Theatines	performed at the Theatines
tomorrow.	tomorrow.

Sentence b (line 2): groups of three words in the order 1 – 3 – 2

Remain health in	Remain in health
I you beg	I beg you.

Sentences c–f, beginning (lines 3/4): word order distributed alternately over both lines:

^cI feel regret that I know nothing new, my greetings to all good friends and women-friends. ^dFare well. ^eMy handkiss to our Mama. ^fI kiss you

Sentence f, continuation and end (line 5):

The first and last words frame the phrase and form its ending (= 'in Milan').
The word 'thousandfold' forms the central axis, from which the words have
to be read leaping to right and left: 'thousandfold and remain as ever your
faithful brother'. Together with the beginning in line 4, the complete
sentence reads:
^fI kiss you thousandfold and remain as ever your faithful brother in Milan.

If the formation of word-groups and numerical combinations served in the previous examples as models for encoded sentence construction, purely internal linguistic principles dominate the end of the letter of 3 October 1777. My transcription once again follows the autograph precisely:

1	Tomorrow we
2	will give a slagademy together on the
3	miserable piano Nota bene. The pain! The pain! The pain. I wish
4	simply a restsome night and improve a good
5	wish in hearing, soon to hope, that our healthy completely
6	is Papa. I forgive to beg because of my abominable handwriting,
7	but ink, haste, sleep, dream, and simply everything – – –
8	I Papa to you, my most assorted kisses, 1000 times the most dear,
9	and my embrace, the hearts, sister I with my whole
10	guttersnipe, and am from now on until eternity, amen

Mozarteum, Bibliotheca Mozartiana. For the facsimile and transcription see *Briefe und Aufzeichnungen zu W. A. Mozart und seiner Familie aus den Beständen der Stiftung Mozarteum Salzburg* (http://dme.mozarteum.at/DME/briefe/, accessed 5 December 2013).

11   <u>Munich</u> the 3:^d octob: 1777

12   Wolfgang most obedient your, sir

13   Amadé Mozart son.[25]

The passage begins in line 2 with plays on words: from 'academy', the contemporary word for a concert, comes a 'slagademy', for which the decisive impulse may have been the association with slag, inspired by the subsequently mentioned 'miserable piano'. The following, nonsensical remark 'Nota bene' (= take good note!) spins the idea out further with three exclamations of 'Auweh' ('The pain!'), whose final vowel sound and emphasis harmonize well with 'bene'. A regularly formed sentence then starts with 'goodnight' wishes – although the word 'ruhsam' ('restsome') has an admittedly strange effect here – which immediately develops into what is initially a completely unintelligible succession of words. The principle used by Mozart works by having the words give up and interchange their correct places in the sentence, at the same time becoming different parts of speech and changing their syntactic function. In the section 'and recover a good wish', 'recover' and 'wish' are changed in the following way: from the verb 'wish' ('wünsch'), which should be placed earlier, the substantive 'wish' ('Wunsch') is formed, and from the correct substantive 'recovery' ('Besserung') the verb 'recover' ('bessern'). The right formulation would be 'and wish a good recovery'. To enable the construction of correct sentences from such distorted words, they must first of all be placed in the presumed right place in the sentence; a determination of their grammatical function must then follow. A translation of the passage would then read as follows, with normalization of orthography and punctuation:

> I wish a good recovery, in the hope of hearing soon that Papa is completely well. I beg forgiveness for my abhorrent handwriting, but ink, haste, sleep, dream and simply everything – – I kiss your hands 1000 times, my dearest father, and my sister, the guttersnipe, I embrace with my whole heart, and am, from now on into eternity, amen,
> Sir, your most obedient son Wolfgang Amadé Mozart.

Supplementing such linguistically creative transformations, the repeatedly encountered passages in secret codes in the correspondence between father, son and family deserve attention.[26] The Mozarts used this procedure in order to protect their communications from the inquisitiveness of the

---

[25] MBA, vol. II, p. 33. Autograph in Salzburg, Internationale Stiftung Mozarteum, Bibliotheca Mozartiana. For the facsimile and transcription see *Briefe und Aufzeichnungen zu W. A. Mozart und seiner Familie* (http://dme. mozarteum.at/DME/briefe/, accessed 5 December 2013).

[26] In MBA all these passages have been resolved, easily identifiable for the reader by words set in angle brackets. (On this issue, see the Foreword to MBA, vol. I, p. xii).

censorship purportedly exercised in Salzburg and Vienna. The code used, presumably developed by Leopold, is relatively easy to decipher; the Mozarts simply exchanged ten letters of the alphabet with each other (code=intended text):

a=m b=b c=c d=d e=l f=i/j g=g h=u i (j)=f k=k l=e m=a/ä
n=n o=s p=p q=q r=r s=o/ö t=t u=h v=v w=w x=x y=y
z=z

The following example of an encoded text, reproduced here true to the original line breaks in the autograph, comes from Mozart's letter of 24 November 1780 to his father. The encoded words and sentence elements are typographically accentuated; in each case, the intended text appears immediately afterwards in angle brackets:

> What you write to me concerning Count olnoulfa ‹se[i]nsheim› already happened long ago –
> [. . .] I have already dined at his house once
> at midday; twice with Bmhagmrtln ‹Baumgarten› and once with
> Elrculniled ‹Lerchenfeld› – of whom Mistress BmhaEtc. ‹Baum[garten]› is a daughter. – There is no day on which at least someone of these people does not come to Cannabich;
> – concerning alfnlr splrm ‹meiner opera/my opera› rest unworried, my dearest father –
> I hope all of this will go quite well. – lfnl kelfnl Cmbmel ‹eine kleine Cabale/a little cabal›
> will no doubt have it taken off – [. . .]
> – for – I have amongst the Nsbelool ‹Noblesse/nobility› the mnolunefcuotln ‹ansehnlichsten/most respected›
> and vlrasgefcuotln umholr ‹vermöglichsten häuser/wealthiest houses› – and the lrotln Bly dlr ahofck ‹ersten Bey der musick/first in music›
> are all for me. – I cannot tell you how much Cannmbfcu alfn irlhnd fot. ‹Cannabich mein freund ist/Cannabich is my friend.› – how *tumtfg* – wfrkoma ‹thätig – wirksam/active – effective› – in
> a word, he is a Emhlrlr ‹Lauerer/on the lookout› – when it comes down to doing flamndln ghtlo
> zh ‹jemanden gutes zu/someone a good turn›.[27]

III

Mozart's linguistic ability is in no way exhausted in amusing games of this kind or in code as a precautionary measure. Nowhere is this more evident than in descriptions of recent interactions with influential personalities, that

[27] MBA, vol. III, p. 29.

is, of events that usually show Mozart in the position of a subordinate. Conversations with rulers, superiors and persons of rank concerning the development of his career, possible posts at court and his attitude in service become, in the composer's narratives in the letters, lively protocols, even dramulets. The meeting with Elector Max III Joseph in the Residenz in Munich on 30 September 1777 left such a deep impression on Mozart that he could play it back, so to speak, in the letter to his father written immediately after the conversation in question. This section of the letter, with little changes to the original line alignment and the addition of role names, can be printed like a theatrical scene:

As the Elector came up to me, I spoke thus.

[MOZART]	May Your Electoral Highness permit that I lay myself most humbly at his feet, and that I might offer my services:
[ELECTOR]	Yes, entirely away from Salzburg?
[MOZART]	Entirely away. Yes, Your Elect. Highness.
[ELECTOR]	But why then, have you got into a tight spot? – –
[MOZART]	Ah, indeed, Your Highn., I requested merely to make a journey, he refused me it, so that I was forced to take this step; although I had long been thinking about going away. For Salzburg is no place for me. Yes, most certainly.
[ELECTOR]	My God, a young person! But your father is of course still in Salzburg? –
[MOZART]	Yes, Your Elect. Highn., he lays himself most humbly etc. I have also been in Italy three times, have written 3 operas, with [recte: am] member of the academy in Bologna, have had to pass an examination, in which many maestri worked 4 to 5 hours and sweated, I finished it in one hour: that may serve as testimony that I am capable of serving at any court. My only wish is, however, to serve Your Elect. Highn., who is himself a great = =
[ELECTOR]	Yes, my dear child, there is no vacancy there. I am sorry. If only there were a vacancy.
[MOZART]	I assure Your Highness: I would certainly bring honour to Munich.
[ELECTOR]	Yes, all of that does not help. There is no vacancy there.

This he said in going. I commended myself to His Most Serene Grace.[28]

Renderings of dialogue are provided quite often in Mozart's letters, and not unusually concern key moments (retrospectively considered) in his biography. The composer always exercises diligence regarding the correct tracing of the course of the dialogue, although always, self-evidently, from the perspective of his own subjective experience and with a tendency to emerge from the conversational situation with integrity and as the moral

[28] MBA, vol. II, pp. 23–4 (29/30 September 1777).

victor at least. But, precisely because these accounts are conveyed so honestly and thus credibly, they sometimes provide the present-day reader with pointers towards historical reality that remained concealed from Mozart himself. Let us consider only the Munich example. It may indeed have been the case that there was 'no vacancy' in the Hofkapelle in 1777, namely no regular post that Mozart could have occupied: surely this would have been known to both men even before the conversation began. Had the Elector wanted to employ Mozart, there would have been no difficulty for him in doing so, within the governmental mechanisms of the time and in this electoral residence. Yet, obviously, this was not the Elector's wish, and for a good reason from his point of view, as his almost shocked reaction to Mozart's request demonstrates: Mozart must have appeared an unreliable subject who was prepared simply to leave his noble lord just because his wish to travel had not been granted. Of other background information, of course, Mozart knew nothing. To run the risk of friction with the Prince-Archbishop of Salzburg for the sake of such a 'young person' must have been more than the matter was worth to him (and the fact that he enquired as to Leopold's position indicates that he feared disadvantages for the father in the event of a move on the part of the son). In this case, it is revealing to interpret Mozart's account of the conversation not solely from Mozart's standpoint, as usually happens, but rather by placing the dialogue partners in relation to each other. The same is especially applicable to Mozart's hefty disputes with Prince-Archbishop Colloredo and Count Arco in Vienna.[29] But less dramatic dialogues are also worthy of consideration in this respect, such as the exchange with Count Seeau after the conversation with the Elector in Munich quoted above,[30] the discordant battles of words over the 'Order of the Golden Spur' with the previously mentioned Mister von Langenmantel of Augsburg,[31] and the interlocution with Elector Karl Theodor regarding a temporary position of teacher to the children from the liaison with his favourite, the Countess von Heydeck.[32]

A precise analysis of the letters, which seeks to penetrate deep into the semantic and syntactic structure of the language, is especially *de rigeur* if exceptional source value has to be assigned to a letter as the only information source relating to a particular matter of biography or work history. Mozart's letter of 4 January 1783 to his father serves as an example: it represents the only authentic extra-musical document on the issue of the occasion for the genesis and performance history of the C minor Mass K. 427, on events in

[29] MBA, vol. III, pp. 110–12 (9 May 1781); MBA, vol. III, p. 124 (2 June 1781).
[30] MBA, vol. II, pp. 31–2 (2/3 October 1777).
[31] MBA, vol. II, pp. 62–6 (16/17 October 1777).
[32] MBA, vol. II, pp. 160–1 (3 December 1777).

part still unclarified today and essentially taking place in 1782. The relevant sentences are as follows (preserving the original line alignment):

> *– for the*
> *New Year wishes we both send thanks, and freely confess*
> *like asses that we have completely forgotten our duty – we*
> *are thus belated with the fulfilment, and express no New Year's wishes, but*
> *wish our general everyday wishes – and there*
> *we leave the matter; – concerning the morals, everything has its full pro-*
> *priety; – it did not flow from my pen unintentionally – I*
> *promised it truly in my heart, and also hope to keep it*
> *truly. – My wife was still single when I made the promise – but, as I*
> *was firmly resolved to marry her shortly after her recovery,*
> *it was easy for me to make the promise – time and circumstances,*
>   *however, thwarted*
> *our journey, as you yourself know; – but as a proof of the verac-*
> *ity of my promise the score of half of a Mass can be of service to you,*
> *which still lies there in the best of hopes. –*[33]

Mozart is responding to the New Year letter from his father at the beginning of 1783. That particular piece of correspondence itself has not come down to us. Besides the usual good wishes, it must have contained at least two accusations, for Mozart is obviously responding to something of that order. The first reproach referred to the failure on the part of Mozart and his wife to fulfil or comply with the usual duty, or at least custom, of New Year wishes. Mozart forthrightly admits the lapse and attempts to put the matter to rest with rather jocose words. His father's second accusation was graver, and the son reacts to it correspondingly more volubly and with more differentiated argumentation. The statements include references to ultimately unspecified occurrences from the summer of 1782, treated in preceding and now lost letters.

> *– concerning the morals, everything has its full propriety;*

Leopold had censured his son for threatening to break, in a certain matter, the precepts or principles that regulate interpersonal conduct and are generally regarded as binding – which is what the word 'morals' means. Mozart appears to disregard the requirements of good usage and decency by neglecting to fulfil a certain commitment, as the content of that letter must have conveyed. This, in his view, did not have 'its propriety'.

> *– it did not flow from my pen unintentionally – I have promised it truly in my heart, and also hope to keep it truly.*

---

[33] MBA, vol. III, pp. 247–8. Transcribed from the autograph in Staatsbibliothek zu Berlin – Preußischer Kulturbesitz (Berlin State Library – Prussian Cultural Heritage).

Mozart contradicts this. His promise was apparently communicated previously and very deliberately to his father in writing; he made a firm resolution at that time and now hopes to see it honoured as well.

> – *My wife was still single when I made the promise – but, as I was firmly resolved to marry her shortly after her recovery, it was easy for me to make the promise*

Mozart mentions circumstances that were important at the time the promise was made, but which did not stand in a causal relationship with it. Initially, he recalls the moment at which the promise was made, namely before the marriage to Constanze on 4 August 1782. The promise in question, however, was directed towards an action in which Constanze would have to be involved ('my wife was [...] still single'): he promised something that he wanted to fulfil with Constanze once she was his wife. The wedding, a precise precondition for the fulfilment of the promise, could not be conducted at that time because of Constanze's illness. As it was to be fulfilled after her recovery, however, there was at that juncture no perceptible risk attached to making the relevant promise. In turn, the promise appears to have been given in the expectation of its early discharge, for Constanze's imminent recovery and their immediate wedding thereafter were amongst the conditions under which Mozart believed that he was in a position to pronounce his binding commitment.

> – *time and circumstances, however, thwarted our journey, as you yourself know;*

The promise was therefore linked to a journey, most probably to Salzburg, even if no place name is mentioned. It had apparently not been possible to discharge it, as the Mozarts' circumstances and, ultimately, the prompt commencement of Constanze's first pregnancy purportedly or genuinely prevented the departure from Vienna.

> – *but as proof of the veracity of my promise the score of half of a Mass can be of service to you, which still lies there in the best of hopes. –*

Finally, Mozart counters a further possible accusation by his father that the promise given was simply spoken thoughtlessly, despite the protestation to the contrary at the beginning of this paragraph in the letter: he mentions the already started and substantially drafted score of a mass (the comment that 'half' of the score is complete will not have been meant literally, but as a reflection of its advanced stage of preparation). The mass itself was not the primary subject of the promise – Leopold heard of it here for the first time, otherwise Mozart would have written more definitely of 'the' not 'a' mass – but rather offers secondary evidence of him taking the promise seriously; Mozart had not yet given up his plan of finishing the mass.

If one reads this excerpt from the letter with the appropriate sobriety, taking the form of the language seriously, the leeway available for interpretations is considerably narrower than is often assumed. The supposition that Mozart composed the C minor Mass with Constanze's recovery in mind or with his eye on the longed-for marriage as the fulfilment of a vow of some kind – conveyed even in recent literature – is certainly not stated unambiguously in the text cited here. And there is no other authentic source available.

IV

Mozart enjoyed a Catholic upbringing and remained true to Catholic principles throughout his life. For some time now, it has been rare to express oneself in this lapidary form about the deeply Christian moulding and the faith of the composer, as if it were embarrassing to call to mind such self-evident historical facts in an age largely disillusioned by religion at the end of a long process of secularization. None of the critical utterances in the correspondence between father and son regarding (high-ranking) clerics, suspected laxness in observing ecclesiastical stipulations – reports that Mozart did not comply with contemporary Catholic conventions remain unsubstantiated – and Mozart's membership of a Masonic lodge provide sound criteria for doubts about Mozart's devoutness. No one has yet provided answers to questions about the individual nature of Mozart's faith, how he felt supported by it, and his views on dogmatic statements. Sanctimoniousness and bigotry were foreign to him: 'An obvious vice is preferable to me than an ambiguous virtue; at least I know what course I should take.'[34] Regardless of whether a present-day reader confesses to a religious belief, he or she will only with difficulty be able to deny the presence of the Christian view of the world and of mankind: it is encountered everywhere in Mozart's letters, and with it comes a specifically religious linguistic tone. The motif of surrender to the governance of the divine will alone permeates his correspondence from the early 1770s onwards, as can be illustrated by a selection of supporting passages:

> I grieve in my heart because of the illness, of such long duration, which the poor spinster Martha has to suffer and bear with patience. I hope, with the help of God, she will again become well; if not, one should not be too dejected, for God's will is the best at all times, and God will certainly know better whether it is better to be in this

---

[34] Before 19 February 1786; MBA, vol. III, p. 506.

world or in the next, but she should take comfort in the fact that she can now come from the rain into the fine weather[35]

May Papa remain at ease in his mind. I have God constantly before my eyes. I acknowledge his omnipotence, I fear his wrath: but I also acknowledge his compassion and mercy towards his creatures. He will never leave his servants – – If things go according to his will they also go – – according to mine; therefore nothing can go wrong – –[36]

Now let us leave the question of how it is and how it will be; what use, then, are the superfluous speculations; we do not know, after all, what will happen, yet – – we do know! – – what God wills.[37]

Just be patient. Let us hope in God, who will not leave us. It shall not fail on my account.[38]

I hope in God. I ask him for what I believe to be useful to me and to us all, but always add: Lord, thy will be done, on earth as it is in heaven. We mortals often think, 'that is evil', and in the end – it is in fact good. God always knows best how it must be.[39]

After the death of his mother in July 1778 – an experience that tested the son to his limits and which he had to bear largely alone – Mozart sought to impart comfort to his father by quoting the article of faith concerning the resurrection of the dead. The impressive and touching correspondence of this period derives its effect from the disciplined attempt to overcome the grief for the deceased by keeping in mind, in a most composed way, widely accepted assurances of faith. (Incidentally, the graphical form of the original letter shows, contrary to what might be expected from Mozart in view of his highly agitated state, a striking regularity in handwriting: he was in command of himself in this regard too.)

> Out of this wish [to die with his mother], and out of this desire, my third consolation at last developed, namely that she is not lost to us for ever – that we shall see her again – we will be together more contented and happier than in this world; only the time is unknown to us – but that does not make me anxious at all – when God wishes it, then I wish it too – Now, the divine, most holy will has been fulfilled – let us then pray a devout Our Father for her soul – and stride onwards to other things; for everything there is a time.[40]

Although it is taken from a completely different context, a statement from the early Viennese period should be read alongside this affirmation: 'I am meant to think that I have an immortal soul – not only do I think this, but I believe it; – in what otherwise would the difference between man and beast consist?'[41] And the famous communication with which Mozart reacts to the news of his father's severe illness that would ultimately lead to his death in

[35] MBA, vol. I, p. 393 (29 September 1770).   [39] MBA, vol. II, pp. 320–1 (7 March 1778).

[36] MBA, vol. II, p. 85 (23–25 October 1777).   [40] MBA, vol. II, p. 394 (9 July 1778).

[37] MBA, vol. II, p. 146 (26 November 1777).   [41] MBA, vol. III, p. 179 (5 December 1781).

[38] MBA, vol. II, p. 306 (28 February 1778).

1787 exudes the same firm, practised attitude, leading to man's 'blessedness', of surrender to God (which, in this particular case, is something other than the supposed response to Moses Mendelssohn's successful work, *Phädon oder über die Unsterblichkeit der Seele* [*Phaedon or On the Immortality of the Soul*] posited by authors copying from each other over many years):

> As death |: to take it precisely :| is the true ultimate purpose of our life, I have therefore, over the past few years, made myself so familiar with this true, best friend of man that its image not only no longer holds anything terrifying for me, but a great deal that calms and comforts! And I thank my God that he has granted me the good fortune to create the opportunity |: you understand me :| to come to know it as the *key* to our true blessedness – I never lay myself down in bed without recollecting that I perhaps |: so young as I may be :| may no longer exist the following day – and surely none of all those who know me will be able to say that I am sullen or sad in my comportment – and for this blessedness I thank my creator every day and wish the same to all my fellow men. –[42]

If meaningful sources revealing Mozart's Masonic thoughts and sentiments existed – we have no direct knowledge of his internal ties with the world of the lodges – insight into further aspects of his faith might have been forthcoming. But the totality of his letters provides inadequate evidence, which one may very much regret but cannot change, and which should perhaps have led many earlier, enthusiastic interpreters to adopt more circumspect positions.

V

Throughout his life, Mozart's understanding of himself centred (unsurprisingly) on his existence as 'a person of superior talent'.[43] He knew exactly who he was, at least in regard to his artistic profession:

> I am a composer and born to be a Kapellmeister. I should not and cannot thus bury my talent for composition, which our benevolent God has given me so richly, | I may without arrogance speak thus, for I feel it now more than ever | and that is what I would be doing with the many pupils, for it is a very untranquil occupation. I would prefer, *so to speak*, to neglect the keyboard rather than composition. For the keyboard is only a sideline, but, thanks be to God, a very strong sideline.[44]

He felt composing to be his 'only joy and passion'.[45] He attempted to keep at a distance whatever ran 'completely contrary to [his] genius – inclination – knowledge and joy',[46] for he apparently required 'at such times a serene

---

[42] MBA, vol. IV, p. 41 (4 April 1787).
[43] MBA, vol. II, p. 473 (11 September 1778).
[44] MBA, vol. II, p. 264 (7 February 1778).

[45] MBA, vol. II, p. 46 (10/11 October 1777).
[46] MBA, vol. II, p. 409 (18 July 1778).

spirit – light head – and zest for work – and one does not have that when one is sad':[47] he repeatedly expressed himself in this way or a similar fashion. He regarded teaching especially less as a satisfying task than a necessary evil (although the preserved materials from his theory lessons for Thomas Attwood, Barbara Ployer and Franz Jakob Freystädtler are evidence of the thoroughness with which he attended to his pupils):

> I will now do everything possible to keep myself going here with pupils, and to make as much money as possible – I do it now in the sweet hope that a change may soon occur, for, this I cannot deny before you, rather I must admit it, that I will be glad when I am released from here; for giving lessons is no fun – one must pretty well exhaust oneself for it, and, if one does not take *many*, one does not make money; you should not believe that this is laziness – No! – but, because it is completely contrary to my genius, to my way of living – you know that I am immersed, so to speak, in music – that I walk around with it all day – that I like to speculate – study – consider – Now, I am hindered from this by my way of life here – I will of course have some hours free, only – the few hours will be more necessary for me to rest and recover than to work.[48]

Mozart's enormous output, even taking his genius into account, had iron discipline as a prerequisite. Little time remained for things outside creative activity. Recipients of his letters often had to read how extremely busy he was and how he could write only a few lines; indeed, many of the letters are relatively short, occasionally very disconnected in lines of thought, the handwriting reflecting the fleeting haste with which words were committed to paper. While in Leopold's writing a systematic layout, circumspect narration and also careful accounts of events usually dominate – he might be described as a mnemonic technician in correspondence – in the letters of his son, particularly those from the Viennese period, the persistent presence of work holds sway. Disrupting influences often make themselves felt: illnesses, financial worries, burdensome obligations that must in some way be managed or at least thrust aside. These are the subject matter of many letters and sometimes of upsetting correspondence such as the urgent pleas to the merchant Johann Michael Puchberg between 1788 and 1791. The travel correspondence of 1789 and 1790 and the late letters to Constanze from the year of his death have, in contrast, a somewhat calmer tone. The effect of confessions bursting immediately from Mozart's breast are all the more striking then – words that come from a lonely man. In 1777, he responded to the pre-eminence of 'blessedness', as solemnly adjured by his father, with the lapidary comment that it exists 'only in the imagination',[49] voicing this opinion again when writing from Frankfurt in 1790:

---

[47] MBA, vol. III, p. 31 (24 November 1780).   [49] MBA, vol. II, p. 153 (29 November 1777).
[48] MBA, vol. II, p. 427 (31 July 1778).

If people could see into my heart, I would almost have to be ashamed. – Everything is cold to me – ice-cold – Yes, if you were with me, I would perhaps take more pleasure in the complimentary behaviour of the people towards me, – but, as it is, it is empty.[50]

And from Vienna in 1791:

Now I wish for nothing else than that my affairs were already in order, only so that I could be with you again, you cannot believe how the whole time dragged here for me because of you! – I cannot explain my feelings to you, there is a certain emptiness – which is simply pain to me, – a certain longing which is never satisfied, consequently never ceases – continues constantly, yes, grows from day to day; – When I think how good-humoured and childish we were together in Baden – and what sad, boring hours I go through here – nor does my work bring me joy, because, accustomed to pausing occasionally and exchanging a few words with you, this pleasure is now unfortunately an impossibility – I go to the keyboard and sing something from the opera, then I have to break off immediately – it stirs up too many feelings in me – Enough! – if my business ends this hour, then certainly the next hour I will no longer be here.[51]

A contrast to such radically sobering moments is provided by those of effortless high-spiritedness in which a little normal happiness in everyday things is conveyed. Mozart is sitting at ease with a tankard of beer, puffing at his pipe, or he is delighting in roast meat offered by a street trader: 'and took my favourite walk over the glacis to the theatre – what do I see? – what do I smell? – – It is Don Primus with the pork chops! – che gusto! – now I am eating to your health – it is just striking 11 o'clock'.[52] This is the context in which his lifelong joy in elegant, fashionable clothing and finely appointed apartments belongs: after Mozart's death, it was not the physicians and pharmacists (for example) who had the highest outstanding debts to collect, but the tailors and wallpaperers. He could occasionally pine for smart shoe-buckles or exquisite mother-of-pearl buttons. The longing for beauty and order in all circumstances of life also resulted in distraught reactions to the misery of his fellow man. After a visit in Munich to his older composer colleague Joseph Mysliveček, whose nose had had to be burned away as a result of advanced venereal disease, he was dejected for days by the thought of his suffering:

Why is that that I have written nothing about Misliwececk until now? – – because I was glad when I was able not to think about him [...] I therefore resolved to go to him. But I went to the administrator of the Duke's Hospital the day before and asked him whether he could not arrange for me to speak with Misliwececk in the garden, for, although everyone and also the physicians said that there was nothing left to be passed on, I nevertheless did not want to go into his room, because it is very small,

---

[50] MBA, vol. IV, p. 114 (30 September 1790).   [52] MBA, vol. IV, p. 158 (7/8 October 1791).
[51] MBA, vol. IV, p. 150 (7 July 1791).

and smells pretty strongly. [...] We therefore had them call him. I saw him coming towards me from the side, and recognised him immediately from his gait. [...] There you see, said he, how unhappy I am! For me, these words, and his shape, which Papa already knows from the description, went so straight to my heart that, half-weeping, I could not say anything other than, 'I pity you from the depths of my heart, my dear friend!' He noticed that I was moved and immediately started in quite high spirits. [...] |: I was so confused and trembled so in my whole body that I could hardly speak :| [...] But I could not possibly resolve to go to him in his room and, if I wanted to write, I had to, in the garden I could not write. So I promised him I would certainly come. But I wrote a letter to him in Italian the following day, *completely naturally*: 'I could not possibly come to him; I have been able to eat absolutely nothing, and to sleep only 3 hours. By day I was like someone who has lost his reason. That he is constantly before my eyes etc.' A lot of things which are as true as the sun is clear. He gave me the following answer: lei é troppo sensibile al mio male. io la ringrazio del suo buon Cuore. [...] When his illness was most intense, he composed an opera for Padua. There is no remedy in this case; they even say themselves here that the physicians and surgeons have ruined him. It is simply nothing less than bone cancer. The surgeon Caco, the ass, burned away his nose; just imagine the pain now.[53]

The way Mozart perceived events on the world stage can be at best surmised from his letters. The greatest political event of the late 1780s and early 1790s, the outbreak of the French Revolution, receives no mention. His earlier terse utterance, however, that he was 'an Arch-Englishman'[54] can perhaps be considered an expression of a tendentially liberal disposition. He always saw himself as belonging to the Holy Roman Empire of the German Nation. Particularly in an effort to distance himself from the French and Italian lifestyles as well as to espouse a critical attitude towards the Italian-dominated opera business, he emphasized that he was an 'honest German',[55] and also 'that in almost all the arts the Germans were always the ones who excelled': 'If Germany, my beloved Fatherland, of which I |: as you know :| am proud, will not receive me, then, in God's name, either France or England must become richer by yet one more skilled German; – and that to the shame of the German Nation.'[56]

All the utterances collected here, which of course could be considerably augmented and expanded to include other thematic issues, yield in their totality no more than a mosaic with many missing pieces. They give no satisfactory answer to the question of who Mozart really was. But they can serve as bits of evidence for ever-new portraits of the composer's personality. And the sum of these portraits has provided a fascinating panorama of silhouettes and colourful mosaics for over 200 years. This may seem

---

[53] MBA, vol. II, pp. 43–6 (10/11 October 1777).

[54] MBA, vol. III, p. 239 (19 October 1782).

[55] MBA, vol. II, p. 368 (29 May 1778).

[56] MBA, vol. III, p. 220 (17 August 1782).

unsatisfactory, but it is considerably more than we know about most out-standing persons of the late eighteenth century. Mozart once said about himself:

> I cannot write poetically; I am no poet. I cannot arrange the figures of speech with such artistry that they yield shadow and light; I am no painter. I cannot even express my mind and thoughts by signs and pantomime; I am no dancer. But I can do it with tones; I am a musicus.[57]

This fine rhetoric will not be subjected to contradiction here. But perhaps it is permissible to augment it. Poesy, shadow and light, gestures and pantomime, sound: all are to be found in Mozart's letters and in their language, as the reflection and echo of a fascinating life.

[57] MBA, vol. II, pp. 110–11 (8 November 1777).

2   Mozart 'stuck in music' in Paris (1778): towards a new biographical paradigm

Simon P. Keefe

Biographers of Mozart from Otto Jahn (1856) onwards have consistently explored links between Mozart's life and music, varying the emphasis on each according to biographical orientations, predilections and interpretations of available evidence. Ever since *Biographie W. A. Mozart* (1828) by Georg Nikolaus von Nissen, Constanze's second husband, biographers have drawn on the remarkable body of family correspondence as their primary aid. The period of Mozart's life covered most fully is September 1777 to January 1779, when Mozart journeyed with his mother Maria Anna through Munich, Augsburg and Mannheim to Paris (where she died on 3 July 1778), returning to Salzburg via Strasbourg, Mannheim, Kaisheim and Munich. Correspondence comprises around 200 letters in total, primarily between Mozart and his father Leopold, and occupies almost an entire 550-page volume of the complete edition.[1] Reliance on the letters has inevitably led writers to focus on the pronounced problems Mozart encountered on his trip, including disagreements with Leopold inter alia over money, work and travel plans, the turmoil associated with Maria Anna's death and with Aloysia Weber's rejection, and the inability to secure an appointment. In general, and judged by Mozart's high standards, the sixteen-month trip was not an especially fertile period for him as a composer. Implicit or explicit links made by biographers between problems experienced and limited compositional productivity reinforce the sense of failure.[2] According to

I would like to thank Cliff Eisen for his comments on an earlier draft of this chapter.
[1] See MBA, vol. II. The eight-volume complete edition comprises four volumes of letters followed by two of commentaries, one as an index, and a final short volume (published 2005) of additional materials not contained in the main body of correspondence. All translations from Mozart's letters and contemporary documents are my own unless otherwise indicated; references to MDB and LMF are given in spite of differing from my translations.

[2] On the trip as a failure, see (among biographies of the last thirty years or so) John Rosselli, *The Life of Mozart* (Cambridge, 1997), p. 26; Georg Knepler, *Wolfgang Amadé Mozart*, trans. J. Bradford Robinson (Cambridge, 1994), p. 54; Wolfgang Hildesheimer, *Mozart*, trans. Marion Faber (New York, 1983), p. 121. On the failure in Paris specifically, see Hermann Abert, *W. A. Mozart* (1923–4), trans. Stewart Spencer, ed. Cliff Eisen (New Haven and London, 2007), p. 497.

Leopold's own objectives for the trip, obtaining an appointment or making money, Mozart was unsuccessful.[3] The trip has even been described recently by a rational, even-keeled writer on Mozart's life as 'one of the most famous disasters in musical biography'.[4]

If the trip as a whole is considered a failure, then the six-month stay in Paris (24 March to 26 September 1778) is its inevitable lowpoint. In addition to experiencing personal tragedy, Mozart hated the French capital and much of what it represented, fell out spectacularly with his host and advisor Melchior Grimm, failed to secure an acceptable appointment, earned insufficient income, and was unsuccessful in procuring an operatic commission.[5] Unsurprisingly, when faced with such well-documented emotions and events and relatively few major works from the period, biographical accounts have orientated themselves more towards Mozart's life than his music. Perhaps influenced by the spectre of failure, biographers and critics have given a mixed reception to Mozart's unambiguous triumph, the 'Paris' Symphony, K. 297, performed at the *Concert spirituel* on 18 June. In the first half of the twentieth century, it was described by distinguished Mozartians as 'quite superficial', uninventive and 'somewhat ordinary', 'on the whole ... [falling] flat' and '[lacking] something of the charm, the amiability, and the unconscious depths of many a shorter and less pretentious Salzburg symphony'.[6] More recently, it has been regarded as stylistically unadventurous, containing 'grandiose gestures ... strangely empty compared with his symphonic best'; it 'disquiets ... [becoming] uncomfortably unclear just where the mock-heroic and the mock-pathetic delimit themselves'.[7]

In this chapter I shall attempt to move beyond relatively unnuanced polemics of musical–biographical success and failure in the context of exploring the kind of organic connections between Mozart's life and works

---

[3] See MBA, vol. II, p. 148; LMF, p. 393 (27 November 1777). Before Mozart travelled to Paris, Leopold instructed him to make 'great strides, [achieve] fame, honour and a great name ... and thereby also make money': MBA, vol. II, p. 233; LMF, p. 450 (19 January 1778).

[4] Ruth Halliwell, *The Mozart Family: Four Lives in a Social Context* (Oxford and New York, 1998), p. 231.

[5] The flautist Johann Baptist Wendling, resident orchestral performer in Mannheim and one of the stars at the *Concert spirituel* in spring 1778, also set a criterion for success in Paris that Mozart did not match. Mozart reported Wendling as saying that he (Mozart) would acquire a settled yearly income in Paris once he had written two operas. See MBA, vol. II, p. 162; LMF, p. 401 (3 December 1777).

[6] Georges de Saint-Foix, as given in Louis Biancolli (ed.), *The Mozart Handbook* (New York, 1954), p. 335; Eric Blom, *Mozart* (New York, 1935), p. 174; Alfred Einstein, *Mozart: His Character, His Work*, trans. Arthur Mendel and Nathan Broder (New York, 1945), p. 228.

[7] Konrad Küster, *Mozart: a Musical Biography*, trans. Mary Whittall (Oxford and New York, 1998), p. 98; Daniel Heartz, *Haydn, Mozart and the Viennese School, 1740–1780* (New York, 1995), p. 635; Robert Gutman, *Mozart: a Cultural Biography* (New York, 1999), p. 446.

in 1778 that point biographical discussion in new, musically orientated directions. I shall therefore revisit his correspondence as a catalyst for re-examining his Parisian works. The letters from 1777 to 1779 provide fascinating material for charting the evolving relationship between Mozart and Leopold, leading many writers to explore Mozart's strategies and tactics for dealing with his father, who attempted to direct proceedings from afar.[8] Clearly, the trip gave Mozart a degree of independence and freedom that he had not as yet experienced.[9] But independence cannot be measured exclusively in the relationship between father and son. For, as will be shown, it also emerged in Mozart's own individual reactions to the (musical and non-musical) world, reactions that transcended issues of filial loyalty, rebellion and motivations in between. I shall begin on the night of 3–4 July 1778 with Mozart's biggest personal challenge of his life so far, namely processing the death of his mother and relating it to his father back home in Salzburg. On account of its significance as a momentous life event, it could be construed as a potential obstacle for a musically orientated biographical account of this period. As will be explained, though, Mozart's discussion of musical matters in the initial letter to Leopold after Maria Anna's death has far-reaching biographical implications.

Mozart, Maria Anna Mozart's death and music

By any criteria, the circumstances under which Mozart wrote to Leopold on the night of 3–4 July 1778 were extraordinary. His mother had died far from home and away from her husband, who at that stage had no idea she was seriously ill; Mozart therefore needed to communicate the news to Leopold, against the backdrop of a relationship already strained by disagreements that had arisen since his departure from Salzburg ten months earlier. He wrote to

[8] In this regard, see in particular Maynard Solomon, *Mozart: a Life* (New York, 1995), especially pp. 137–60; David Schroeder, *Mozart in Revolt: Strategies of Resistance, Mischief and Deception* (New Haven and London, 1999), *passim*; and Gutman, *Mozart*, pp. 369–474. For a sensitive account, inter alia identifying tactical lies from Leopold (as well as from Mozart) in an attempt to expedite Mozart's return to Salzburg, see Halliwell, *The Mozart Family*, pp. 231–333. Peter Gay's remark that '[the] duel now shifted [from Colloredo – Leopold, over Mozart's resignation from the Salzburg Court] to father and son as principal antagonists' and John Rosselli's observation

that the trip was a 'disaster' in the context of the 'crisis in his relationship with his father' are representative of many implicit and explicit assumptions made in the biographical literature. See Gay, *Mozart* (New York, 1999), p. 54; Rosselli, *Life of Mozart*, p. 26.

[9] On Mozart's new sense of independence, freedom and liberation on the 1777–9 trip including his desire to grow up, see for example: Otto Jahn, *Life of Mozart* (1856), trans. Pauline D. Townsend, 3 vols. (London, 1882), vol. II, pp. 350, 351; Abert, *W. A. Mozart*, p. 517; Michael Levey, *The Life and Death of Mozart* (London, 1971), p. 110; Hildesheimer, *Mozart*, p. 88; Knepler, *Wolfgang Amadé Mozart*, p. 35.

Leopold between 10:21pm (Maria Anna's death) and 2am, at which time a further letter was written to his Salzburg friend Abbé Bullinger.[10]

The beginning of Mozart's letter to Leopold concerns Maria Anna's serious condition, describing her symptoms, the visit from Grimm's doctor, the slim chances of recovery, and the faith Mozart and Leopold must put in God deciding her fate (a subject to which he also returns briefly at the end). But it does not reveal that she had actually already died. The subsequent letter to Bullinger gives the full truth, imploring Bullinger to prepare Leopold gently for it. Almost all biographers praise Mozart's considerateness, sensitivity and circumspection in employing this strategy.[11] But biographical consensus on the remainder of Mozart's letter is not forthcoming. After describing the situation for his mother, Mozart writes 'now something else; let us leave these sad thoughts' and turns to other issues. He describes at length the rehearsal and performance of the 'Paris' Symphony, relates in blunt terms the death of the 'godless' Voltaire (who 'so to speak snuffed it like a dog, like a beast, that's his reward!'), gives the possible subjects for his planned opera, asks whether Leopold would like copies of Johann Schröter and Nikolaus Hüllmandel's sonatas sent to Salzburg, and explains why he turned down the Versailles organist post, before mentioning his mother's condition again at the end in signing off.[12] Some biographers express astonishment at the confluence of topics in the letter as a whole, at Mozart's ability to move on so quickly to matters unrelated to his mother's illness, and at the letter's apparent normality in many respects.[13] Other writers see Mozart

---

[10] The timings come from Mozart's letters: see MBA, vol. II, pp. 390–1, 393; LMF, pp. 559–60 (letter to Bullinger, 4 July 1778), 561 (letter to Leopold, 9 July 1778). A third letter was also written to Fridolin Weber, Aloysia's father, on the night of 3–4 July, but is now lost. See the listing in MBA, vol. II, p. 392.
[11] See, for example, Edward Holmes, *The Life of Mozart, including his Correspondence* (1845), ed. Christopher Hogwood (London, 1991), p. 126; Jahn, *Mozart*, vol. II, pp. 53–4; Abert, *W. A. Mozart*, pp. 509–10; W. J. Turner, *Mozart: the Man and his Works* (London, 1938), p. 219; Marcia Davenport, *Mozart* (New York, 1979), p. 120; Heartz, *Viennese School*, p. 635; Knepler, *Wolfgang Amadé Mozart*, p. 39; Solomon, *Mozart*, pp. 182–3; Halliwell, *The Mozart Family*, p. 305; Jane Glover, *Mozart's Women: His Family, His Friends, His Music* (London, 2005), p. 86; Julian Rushton, *The Master Musicians: Mozart* (Oxford and New York, 2006), p. 62; Stanley Sadie, *Mozart: the Early Years, 1756–1781* (Oxford and New York, 2006), p. 460. Hildesheimer is a rare dissenting voice. He

considered Mozart removed from 'superficial necessities of life' (p. 80), further explaining: 'Nowhere is the lack of human insight revealed more clearly than during the great journey [1777–9], in those letters from Mannheim and Paris' (*Mozart*, p. 129).
[12] MBA, vol. II, pp. 388–90 (with the Voltaire quote on 389); LMF, pp. 557–9. Mozart's cryptic request in his letter for ultimate approval from Leopold on a matter upon which he does not yet wish to elaborate, has been interpreted among others by Gutman (*Mozart*, pp. 431–32) and more cautiously the MBA (vol. V, p. 534) as approval to marry Aloysia. But there is no evidence to confirm this hypothesis.
[13] Einstein, *Mozart*, p. 57; Pierre-Petit, *Mozart ou la musique instantanée* (Paris, 1991), pp. 188–9; Knepler, *Wolfgang Amadé Mozart*, p. 42; Schroeder, *Mozart in Revolt*, pp. 104, 119, 120; Glover, *Mozart's Women*, p. 84. For Gutman (*Mozart*, p. 429), the shift away from the topic of Maria Anna's illness would have 'astounded a prostrate Leopold'.

controlling his grief when writing about issues not concerning his mother, or '[diverting] attention from this distressing subject', and answer charges of insensitivity.[14] The crude description of Voltaire's death, in the context of the main subject of the letter, elicits particular attention: it is evidence of the chasm that had opened up between Mozart and Grimm, of the strain that life in Paris had placed on Mozart, of Mozart writing exactly what Leopold wanted to hear, and even of admiration for Voltaire.[15]

Much of the content of the letter after the description of Maria Anna's illness can be explained at least in part by themes and issues Leopold raised in preceding correspondence. Mozart's description of accommodating the Parisian audience in all three movements of the 'Paris' Symphony reflects Leopold's advice about writing for the French taste.[16] Leopold recommends the discussions about the Versailles post with Grimm and others that Mozart reported.[17] And Mozart's offer to send sonatas to Leopold picks up on a request in an earlier letter.[18] Mozart's repeated references to his religious devotion – saying the Rosary after the successful performance of the 'Paris' Symphony, living life as a good Christian and submitting to God's will[19] – and his desire to engage dutifully with issues raised in previous correspondence are no doubt further markers of the sensitivity shown towards Leopold in delaying news of Maria Anna's death. Juxtaposed descriptions of Voltaire's death and Maria Anna's illness may have startled some twentieth- and twenty-first-century ears, but probably not Leopold's. We witness very varied reporting of deaths in the family correspondence, from the serious and impassioned to the perfunctory, blunt and humorous, according to the individuals concerned and their relationship (or lack of relationship) with the Mozarts.[20]

---

[14] Levey, *Life and Death of Mozart*, pp. 119–20; Holmes, *Mozart*, p. 128; Sadie, *Mozart: Early Years*, p. 462.

[15] See, respectively, Abert, *W. A. Mozart*, p. 510; Davenport, *Mozart*, p. 120; Hildesheimer, *Mozart*, p. 76; Gutman, *Mozart*, p. 427; and Schroeder, *Mozart in Revolt*, pp. 104–5.

[16] See Leopold's letters in MBA, vol. II, pp. 325, 341, 354; LMF, pp. 515–16 (16 March 1778), 529 (12–20 April 1778), 536 (29 April–6 May 1778). For more on Mozart's appeal to his Parisian audiences in K. 297, amateurs and connoisseurs alike, see Simon P. Keefe, 'The Aesthetics of Wind Writing in Mozart's "Paris" Symphony in D, K. 297', in *Mozart-Jahrbuch 2006*, pp. 329–45.

[17] See Leopold's letter in MBA, vol. II, p. 365; LMF, pp. 541–2 (28 May 1778).

[18] See Leopold in MBA, vol. II, p. 374; LMF, p. 548 (11 June 1778).

[19] On Leopold and Mozart's different interpretations of God's will, see Halliwell, *The Mozart Family*, p. 268. Mozart's passivity, relative to Leopold's, emerges clearly in Leopold's letter from 4 December 1777: MBA, vol. II, p. 166; LMF, p. 405.

[20] For a representative sample, see LMF, pp. 38, 39 (Leopold on Countess von Eyck), 59 (Leopold on Emperor Francis I), 74 (Leopold on Princess Josepha), 110 (Mozart on Gellert), 113 (Leopold on Marchese Litta), 180 (Leopold on Kapellmeister Francesco di Majo), 196 (Leopold on deaths from dysentery), 207–8 (Mozart on hangings in Lyon and Milan), 245 (Mozart on Dr Niderl), 436, 438 (Maria Anna on Adlgasser), 439 (Mozart on the Elector of Bavaria), 686 (Mozart on Maria Theresia), 798 (Mozart on Herr Auernhammer), 906 (Leopold on Mozart's son Johann Thomas Leopold). Even in the letter relating Maria Anna's death to

Moreover, in describing Voltaire as having 'snuffed it', Mozart may simply have processed atheist Voltaire's death as 'bad', or 'unhappy' in contrast to the 'happy' one witnessed for his God-fearing mother.[21]

But Mozart's lengthy description of the premiere of the 'Paris' Symphony at the *Concert spirituel*, occupying almost half of the material unrelated to Maria Anna's illness and nearly a third of the letter overall, merits further consideration, in relation to both content and motivation for inclusion. Mozart is more impassioned here, when recalling a recent, live musical experience, than later in the letter: he relates his nervousness and dejection at the quality of the rehearsal, his desire to jump into the orchestra to snatch the violin from Pierre Lahoussaye and lead the concert performance himself if poorly played, and his eventual delight at the end result and the excellent audience reactions. To be sure, his references to accommodating the audience's expectations play to Leopold's earlier advice. But could he really have expected Leopold, reeling at the immediately preceding news of Maria Anna, to have been able properly to process and appreciate his own emotional swings at the rehearsal and premiere of a symphony? Could his account have been a product only of epistolary skill, then, 'perhaps with a touch of overkill',[22] or are other motivations at play? For whom, in short, is the passage on the 'Paris' Symphony actually written? To answer these questions, we need to delve deeper into Mozart's letters from Paris and, indeed, the 1777–9 trip as a whole.

On several occasions during the sixteen-month journey in addition to the 'Paris' Symphony premiere, Mozart relates the positive emotional impact on him of his own performances and compositions. In fact, the effects were sometimes palliative. Playing at the Duchesse de Chabot's home, freezing cold, with a headache and only a poor clavier and unreceptive audience as company, he explains he would prefer to return on another day when a better instrument was available: 'But she did not give up; I had to wait another half hour, until her husband came. He sat with me and listened with all his attention, and in the meantime I – I forgot all the cold and headache and despite the awful clavier, I played – as I play when I am in a good mood.'[23] In Strasbourg, on route back to Salzburg, keyboard playing again warmed him up: '[the concert hall] was so cold! – but I soon warmed

---

Leopold (9 July 1778), Mozart remarked jovially on the Abbot of Baumberg dying 'the usual [namely drink induced] abbot's death', immediately following it with a more sensitive reaction to the Abbot of the Holy Cross Monastery's death. See MBA, vol. II, p. 396; LMF, p. 563.
[21] Mozart mentions Maria Anna's 'happy' (*glücklich*) death both to Bullinger and to

Leopold. See MBA, vol. II, pp. 391, 394; LMF, p. 560, 561 (4 and 9 July 1778).
[22] As suggested by Schroeder, in *Mozart in Revolt*, p. 120. Gutman (*Mozart*, pp. 531–2) also reads Mozart's letter almost entirely in tactical terms relating to its recipient, Leopold.
[23] MBA, vol. II, p. 344; LMF, pp. 531–2 (1 May 1778).

myself ... for I played quite a lot for my own amusement, gave one more concerto than I promised – and at the end improvised [*aus den Kopf*] for a long time.'[24] Recently recovered from a headache in Mannheim, Mozart excuses himself from writing a long letter to Leopold anxious that it would bring back the malady, but obviously had no such fear where composition was concerned as he felt much more inclined towards that activity: 'I ask for your forgiveness if I don't write much this time; I fear it would bring back my headache ... I am not in the mood for letter writing today, but more for composing.'[25] And listless in Paris, 'neither hot nor cold ... [finding] much pleasure in nothing', he apparently picked up when recalling eight hours of solid music with Count von Sickingen:

> Yesterday I was sent for by Count von Sickingen for the second time ... [He] is a charming man, a passionate lover and true connoisseur of music. There I spent eight hours completely alone with him. We were at the clavier morning, afternoon and until ten o'clock in the evening; we went through all sorts of music, playing, praising, admiring, reviewing, discussing and criticizing.[26]

Mozart was not the only one to report the soothing effects of music in 1778. On Wednesday 15 April, the *Journal de Paris* carried a story about Mozart's close friend, the then Paris-based singer Anton Raaff, visiting the Princess of Belmonté-Pignatelli of Naples in 1776:

> During all the time that the arietta lasted [sung by Raaff], the fever with which the Princess was consumed totally stopped. Surprised by such a prompt change, the doctors did not find any remedy as appropriate to the recovery from the illness as the singing of Mr (Anton) Raaff. There you are, Madame, one of the physicians said to her, there is your true medicine.[27]

Concurrent performance-compositional activities and high spirits for Mozart, including abundant organ playing in Mannheim that came 'right from the heart',[28] relate to his total absorption in music. 'You know that

[24] MBA, vol. II, p. 502; LMF, p. 627 (26 October 1778).
[25] MBA, vol. II, pp. 290–1; LMF, pp. 487–8 (22 February 1778).
[26] MBA, vol. II, p. 368; LMF, p. 544 (29 May 1778). On Count von Sickingen's collection, see Paul Corneilson and Eugene K. Wolf, 'Newly Identified Manuscripts of Operas and Related Works from Mannheim', *Journal of the American Musicological Society*, 47 (1994), pp. 244–74; and Corneilson, 'Count Sickingen's Music Collection', *Society of Eighteenth-Century Music Newsletter*, 19/1 (April 2012), pp. 1, 9–12.
[27] As given (in French), in Rudolph Angermüller, *W. A. Mozarts musikalische Umwelt in Paris (1778): Eine Dokumentation* (Munich and Salzburg, 1982), p. 50: 'Pendant tout le tems que dura l'Ariette [the arietta Raaff was singing], la fièvre dont la Principesse étoit devorée, cessa totalement. Étonnee d'un changement aussi prompt, la Faculté ne trouva point de remède aussi propre à la guérison de la malade que le chant du Chr. (Anton) Raaff. Voilà, Madame, lui dit un des Esculapes, voilà votre véritable Médecin.'
[28] See MBA, vol. II, p. 206; LMF, p. 435 (27 December 1777). For a similar remark at this time about Mozart's high spirits playing the organ, see MBA, vol. II, p. 120; LMF, p. 370 (13 November 1777).

I am, so to speak, stuck in music [*sie wissen dass ich so zu sagen in der Musique stecke*], that I am involved with it the whole day and that I like to plan, study, think [it] over', he wrote to Leopold on 31 July 1778.[29] Leopold knew full well that the all-consuming allure of music for his son could detract from other responsibilities: 'Do you think that Wolfgang will now take care of his affairs?' he wrote to Maria Anna on 18 December 1777. 'I hope he is becoming used to it and does not always have a head full of notes.'[30] Mozart often appeared to process life events through music and musical experiences on his trip. He famously depicted Rosa Cannabich in the middle movement of one of his piano sonatas, probably K. 309 (1777), thinking of her as he wrote.[31] After it emerged that the Elector would not offer him a post in Mannheim, making eventual departure from the city inevitable, heightened emotions were rendered poignant for Mozart (and others) in a performance of the sonata by Rosa: 'She played my sonata entirely seriously ... I tell you, I could not contain my weeping. In the end, the mother, the daughter and the treasurer also had tears in their eyes. For she played my sonata, and it is the favourite of the whole house.'[32] He attended High Mass in Mannheim in order to hear the music, according to Maria Anna,[33] rather than (apparently) for reasons of religious devotion. And, as implied by Jahn and Abert, it is possible (if ultimately undeterminable) that Mozart fell in love with Aloysia Weber more for her musical talent than anything else.[34] Her musical qualities above all are promoted to Leopold, from the first mention of her in the family correspondence onwards.[35] Moreover, half of the one extant letter from Mozart to Aloysia comprises musical advice for singing his arias.[36] Whatever the reasons for Mozart's love, it is clear that he focuses on prospective musical experiences for Aloysia and him in the presence of one intense emotion (love) just as he turns to a positive musical experience on the night of 3–4 July in the wake of another (grief).

Mozart's high spirits when performing and composing and penchant for processing life through music come together in a report of Mannheim musical activities that leads on to good wishes for Leopold's name-day and birthday:

[29] MBA, vol. II, p. 427; LMF, p. 587 (31 July 1778).

[30] MBA, vol. II, p. 194; LMF, p. 425 (18 December 1777).

[31] MBA, vol. II, pp. 170–1; LMF, p. 408 (6 December 1777).

[32] MBA, vol. II, p. 178; LMF, p. 414 (10 December 1777).

[33] MBA, vol. II, p. 198; LMF, p. 428 (20 December 1777).

[34] See Jahn, *Mozart*, vol. I, pp. 416–17, and Abert, *W.A. Mozart*, p. 423.

[35] See, for example, MBA, vol. II, pp. 226–7, 253, 286–7; LMF, pp. 447–8 (17 January 1778), 462 (4 February 1778), 485–6 (19 February 1778).

[36] See MBA, vol. II, pp. 420–1; LMF, pp. 581–3 (30 July 1778).

Today, after lunch right at two o'clock, I went with Cannabich to the flautist Wendling . . . I then played. I was in such an excellent mood today that I cannot describe it. I played only off the top of my head, and three duets with violin that I had never seen in my life and whose composer I have never heard of. They were so content on all sides that I had to kiss the ladies . . . Afterwards we went back [to the Elector and his children]. I played again there with my whole heart. I played three times. The Elector himself continually made requests of me. He sat down next to me every time and remained motionless. I also had a certain Professor give me a theme for a fugue and developed it. Now come my congratulations.

Dearest Papa!

I cannot write in verse; I am no poet. I cannot arrange idioms [*Redensarten*] so artistically that they provide light and shade; I am no painter. I cannot even express my views and thoughts through signs and through mime; I am no dancer. But I can do it through sounds; I am a musician. So tomorrow at Cannabich's I will play a whole congratulations for your name-day and your birthday.[37]

So, improvised performance-composition was Mozart's chosen method of communication on this occasion. Similarly, when processing his mother's death on 3–4 July, he turned to the best substitute for a live musical experience, namely a recollection of one. Remembering such experiences, capturing the presentness of the recent past, was high on Mozart's priority list when writing letters on his trip. While reluctant to give a lengthy account of his mother's death in a letter on 31 July, for example, as it was all over and could not be undone, he was happy four months earlier to relate in very considerable detail musical activities in Mannheim once in Paris, in spite of those events now also being confined to history.[38] After an exhausting journey of nine-and-a-half days that had ended on 23 March, and now at the heart of one of Europe's most exciting musical cities in which he was to seek fame and fortune, Mozart chose to recollect with great precision a concert at the Cannabich's 325 miles away and twelve days earlier. On Aloysia's performance of his concert aria K. 294, for example: 'Here I heard it for the first time with instruments. I wish you also could have heard it, but exactly as it was produced and sung there, with that accuracy in taste, piano and forte . . . The orchestra has not stopped praising the aria and talking about it.'[39] He then went into minute detail on Rosa Cannabich's playing, including her trills, timing and fingering. Perhaps he wanted to prove his worth as a teacher to Leopold or to express continued resentment at having to leave Mannheim without an appointment. But he surely knew that an account of Mannheim musical activities would hardly have distracted Leopold from practical issues of the present, most notably the

[37] MBA, vol. II, pp. 110–11; LMF, pp. 362–3 (8 November 1777).
[38] See, respectively, MBA, vol. II, p. 423 and pp. 326–8; LMF, p. 584 (31 July 1778) and pp. 516–18 (24 March 1778).
[39] MBA, vol. II, p. 327; LMF, p. 517 (24 March 1778).

immediate prospects in Paris. Mozart did mention looking up various individuals in Paris in his letter; the discrepancy in the number of non-musical details about the present and the number and nature of musical details about the past is revealing nevertheless. It is difficult to avoid the impression that Mozart wrote primarily for himself in relaying this musical information – out of an inner need to write about and process musical experiences – rather than for his interlocutor.

The same can be said, then, for his account of the 'Paris' Symphony on 3–4 July. With performance and composition often absorbing Mozart in beneficial ways, his cry to banish 'sad thoughts' of Maria Anna was aimed more at himself than at Leopold, ultimately resulting in the ebullient prose about the rehearsal and premiere of the work.

A comparison of subsequent letters from Mozart and Leopold in the aftermath of Maria Anna's death suggests that Mozart continued to use music as a means either of coping with the tragic events or of moving on from them. There is little in the family correspondence more heart breaking than Leopold's three-stage letter to Mozart dated 13 July.[40] He began on 12 July by wishing Maria Anna well for her name day, expressing sadness at their continued separation, and describing the tense military and political situation in Prussia, Bohemia and beyond. By the next morning he had received Mozart's letter of 3 July and was inconsolable. He briefly paused to congratulate Mozart on the success of the 'Paris' Symphony at the *Concert spirituel*, principally admonishing him for the outrageous thought of jumping into the orchestra to take over the performance, which, if carried out, could have cost him his life, and to relate news of musical appointments and salaries in Mannheim and Munich. But he quickly returned to Maria Anna, expressing his and Nannerl's desperation at the situation. Later, at 3:30pm, he finished the letter, with tears in his eyes, Bullinger now having told him of Maria Anna's death; no thought of music entered the equation for Leopold after the news hit, as it had for Mozart. Seven days after learning of his wife's death, Leopold was a broken man: the brevity and content of his next letter, almost entirely involving Maria Anna and responses to her death in Salzburg, concerns for Mozart's health and a reprimanding of his son for not providing more detail on the illness and death, reveal his state of mind.[41] But at a corresponding point after Maria Anna's death for Mozart, six days later on 9 July, the tone and content of his own letter was very different.[42] He told Leopold of Maria Anna's death, apologizing for the necessary deception in the letter of 3 July, was consoled by her 'very happy death', by the

[40] See MBA, vol. II, pp. 400–4; LMF, pp. 566–9, which cuts some material, including on the political situation in central Europe and on appointments in Mannheim and Munich.

[41] MBA, vol. II, pp. 412–13; LMF, pp. 575–76 (20 July 1778), which again makes cuts.

[42] MBA, vol. II, pp. 393–9; LMF, pp. 361–6.

submission to the will of God and by the thought of seeing her again in heaven. As on 3–4 July he signalled a desire to 'proceed to other matters, as everything has its time', implored Leopold and Nannerl to remain strong, and reassured them of his loyalty. The vast majority of the letter (about 75 percent) was then devoted almost entirely to musical matters, often related in considerable detail, inter alia the poor state of music in Salzburg in comparison to Mannheim, Raaff's imminent departure from Paris, the successful reception of his pieces for Noverre's *Les petits riens*, the dreadful state of native French music, disappointment at the non-performance of the sinfonia concertante, and the commissioning of the 'Paris' Symphony and subsequent composition of a second Andante movement at *Concert spirituel* director Joseph Le Gros's request. When Mozart finally gave Leopold the detailed account of Maria Anna's illness and death that had been requested, he integrated it into the letter that also affirmed his immersion in music and the strong impact a (envisioned) musical experience could have on him in communicating with others: 'when I often imagine that I have really got the [opera] commission, I feel a fire in my whole body and tremble from head to toe with eagerness to teach the French still more to know, value and fear the Germans'.[43] It is perhaps no surprise that writing and receiving letters invariably cured Mozart's 'attacks of melancholy' at that time;[44] writing them (at least) principally involved engaging with musical issues.

Even if Mozart's turn to music in his letters of July 1778 is interpreted as consoling Leopold or as indicating self-absorption and lack of consideration for others,[45] I would contend that the message it sends about Mozart's own psychology is more significant, revealing a willingness and ability to engage in detailed, impassioned musical discussion in the wake of one of the most traumatic (non-musical) events in his life. As we have already seen, his complete commitment to, and absorption in, music was not solipsistic, and involved engaging players and listeners. After describing his performance for the Duc de Chabot, where rapt attention was received, Mozart continued: 'Give me the best clavier in Europe but an audience who understand nothing, or do not want to understand and who do not feel with me what I play, and I will lose all pleasure.'[46] His improvisations, unifying performance and compositional activities, were an overwhelming experience for many listeners, in part because of Mozart's own special commitment to them in informal and formal concert

[43] MBA, vol. II, p. 427; LMF, pp. 587–8 (31 July 1778).
[44] MBA, p. 422; LMF, p. 583 (31 July 1778).
[45] See Halliwell on the latter point (*Mozart Family*, pp. 305–6), concerning Mozart's behaviour in general after Maria Anna's death.
[46] MBA, vol. II, p. 344; LMF, p. 532 (1 May 1778).

settings.[47] Improvisations were even used to demonstrate to others how to compose, implicitly dealing with their problematic music in the process. On hearing Friedrich Hartmann Graf play a double flute concerto soon after arriving in Augsburg and remarking on the overly brusque and charmless modulations, Mozart took charge:

> At last a clavichord – one of Stein's – was brought out of the closet, a really good one, only covered in dust and dirt. Herr Graf, who is Director here, stood there like someone who has always thought that his journeys through sounds are quite special and now finds that one can be even more special without causing earache. In a word, they were all astonished.[48]

Mozart's passionate commitment as a performer–composer was complemented by an intense desire both to hear his works performed effectively by others and to exert control over instrumental effects and sound worlds as best he could – hence the detailed vocal instructions to Aloysia Weber; the delight at experiencing the aria K. 294 with full orchestral accompaniment; the pleasure of immediate sound decay and evenness in tone quality without jangling and vibration on Stein's fortepianos; and the desire for 'all notes, appoggiaturas etc.' to be played 'as written, with the necessary expression and gusto, so that we believe that the one who plays had composed [the piece] themselves'.[49] It is no surprise, then, that Mozart's proposed solution to a poor performance of the 'Paris' Symphony was to have been to find his way into the orchestra, grab a violin and direct the work himself, re-asserting authorial control in a performance setting.

   Thus, the principal biographical challenge in examining Mozart's stay in Paris is not to try to determine (for example) whether Mozart suffered 'creative shock' after Maria Anna's death,[50] or whether works reflect troubled circumstances[51] or were compromised in number on account of personal difficulties. Rather we should assess how Mozart's steadfast commitment to performance and composition, manifesting immersion in music even at the most troubled of times, emerges in works written during this period. Continuities between performance and composition were a practical reality for Mozart, in his formative years, in his dealings with the great and the good, in his improvisations and piano concertos, in his career

[47] See Simon P. Keefe, '"We hardly knew what to pay attention to first": Mozart the Performer–composer at Work on the Viennese Piano Concertos', *Journal of the Royal Musical Association*, 134/2 (2009), pp. 185–242, at 187–9.
[48] MBA, vol. II, p. 56; LMF, p. 317 (14 October 1777).

[49] On the last two points, see MBA, vol. II, pp. 68–9, 228; LMF, pp. 327–8 (17 October 1777), 449 (17 January 1778).
[50] As claimed by Daniel Heartz in 'Mozart, his Father and *Idomeneo*', *The Musical Times*, 119 (1978), pp. 228–31, at 229.
[51] See Hildesheimer (*Mozart*, p. 83) on the biographical propensity to process Mozart's Parisian works K. 304 and K. 310 in this way.

aspirations, and in critical acclaim he received.[52] In short, we need to explain how Mozart encourages in renditions of his music by others the kind of vibrant, vital continuities between performance- and composition-related activities and thought that he clearly experienced and valued himself.

Works for public performance: the 'Paris' Symphony, K. 297, and *Les petits riens*, K. 299b

Mozart's commitment to a successful premiere of the 'Paris' Symphony at the *Concert spirituel* did not manifest itself only in a drastic proposal for taking control of the performance and in a series of popular orchestral effects such as the *premier coup d'archet* at the opening, the appealing passage in the first movement brought back towards the end, and the *piano* followed by *forte* opening to the finale.[53] It also comprised an array of timbral effects to engage connoisseurs of French musical-aesthetic discussion from the preceding fifteen years.[54] Notwithstanding Mozart's experience at the rehearsal of K. 297, performers at the *Concert spirituel* – orchestral and virtuosi alike – were repeatedly praised in the Parisian press in 1778.[55] Its director, Le Gros, had also been commended a year earlier for reducing the number of orchestral musicians, with greater orchestral effects possible in performances as a result.[56] Mozart had the opportunity to attend a glut of concerts around Easter at the *Concert spirituel* – nine in the two-week period 12–26 April[57] – and thus fully to gauge the skills and capabilities of the orchestra in advance of his own symphonic venture.

Meticulous markings in K. 297, especially dynamics, appear to anticipate a high quality of orchestral performance by requiring carefully shaded

---

[52] See, for example, Simon P. Keefe, 'Mozart the Child Performer–composer: New Musical-Biographical Perspectives on the Early Years to 1766', in Gary McPherson (ed.), *Musical Prodigies: Interpretations from Psychology, Musicology and Ethnomusicology* (Oxford and New York, forthcoming); and Keefe, 'Mozart the Performer–composer at Work on the Viennese Piano Concertos'. For advice from Leopold pertaining to continuities between performance and composition, see MBA, vol. II, pp. 18–19, 74–5, 112, 182, 295–6; LMF, pp. 281–2 (29 September 1777), 333 (18 October 1777), 364 (10 November 1777), 417 (11 December 1777), 492 (23 February 1778). For Mozart's letter claiming he was 'born to be a Kapellmeister', with composition as his primary activity and keyboard performance as a sideline, see

MBA, vol. II, p. 264; LMF, p. 468 (7 February 1778). For Leopold's frustrated response, see MBA, vol. II, pp. 295–6; LMF, p. 492 (23 February 1778).

[53] See MBA, vol. II, pp. 378–9, 388–9; LMF, p. 553 (12 June 1778), 558 (3 July 1778).

[54] Keefe, 'Aesthetics of Wind Writing in Mozart's "Paris" Symphony'.

[55] See, for example, Angermüller, *W. A. Mozarts musikalische Umwelt in Paris*, pp. 51, 53, 68.

[56] See Constant Pierre, *Histoire du Concert spirituel 1725–1790* (Paris, 1975), pp. 164–5.

[57] For concert listings for this period, culminating in high praise from the *Mercure de France* for works and performances in the *Concert spirituel* 1778 season thus far, see Angermüller, *W. A. Mozarts musikalische Umwelt in Paris*, pp. 48–68.

orchestral playing ultimately to support (and perhaps reciprocate) Mozart's own commitment to the successful rendition of the work. Mozart no doubt envisaged dynamically orientated effects as important expressive components of his finished compositions, alongside – and often in tandem with – harmonic, rhythmic, melodic and textural effects. But for their appropriate realization he required more proactive input and interpretation from performers than in these other areas on account of the discretion and variation in application that dynamics invited.[58] For example, the secondary theme in the first-movement reprise (bar 206ff.), including *fps* for violins but not the accompanying viola, a *pp* for trumpets with concomitant *ps* for oboes and horns and a *pp* timpani roll against the prevailing *p* (and coinciding with a turn to the tonic minor), necessitates close attention from players to the different simultaneous nuances required in individual parts.[59] The main theme of the 6/8 Andante (bars 1–16, see Example 2.1), with a dynamic instruction for every segment of every wind part, asks for delicate surges and releases in its *p, mf, f* and crescendo markings. With the preponderance of *mf*s and *p*s, Mozart invites his players to maintain a modest overall volume level but also consequently to exploit the isolated *forte* moments (bars 1, 4, 9, 12). The outer extremes of the 3/4 Andante, including an opening *sotto voce* that requires an emotional quality, and a succession of *p–pp*–crescendo–*f–p* at the end, also invite distinctive interpretations.[60]

We know from Mozart that he wrote the overture and eleven or so dances for the revival of choreographer Jean-Georges Noverre's ballet *Les petits riens* at the Opéra on 11 June; audiences received the four performances enthusiastically.[61] In the absence of an autograph, it cannot be conclusively determined which dances are by Mozart as opposed to other composers, although the overture (definitely by Mozart) is similar to the first movement of the 'Paris' Symphony in combining grand gestures and dynamic nuance. A bold opening, with the orchestra at collective *forte* and *piano* levels, is followed by a second theme (still in the tonic, C) in which dynamic levels for

[58] On the latter point, see in particular Eva and Paul Badura-Skoda, *Interpreting Mozart: the Performance of his Piano Pieces and Other Compositions*, 2nd edition (New York, 2008), 'Dynamics', pp. 43–69.

[59] Mozart produced two versions of the first movement, lightly revising the original in the month following the premiere, according to the NMA. The later version adds 'Solo' markings to the viola and clarinet parts (bars 206, 210) and a *pp* in the timpani (bar 218); otherwise all dynamic markings are the same. See NMA, IV/11/5, pp. 57–78, 106–27.

[60] On *sotto voce*, see Badura-Skoda, *Interpreting Mozart*, p. 48. Mozart wrote a second Andante at the request of Le Gros (MBA, vol. II, p. 398; LMF, p. 565 [9 July 1778]). Whether the 6/8 movement came before or after the 3/4 movement is not known, and remains a matter of scholarly debate. For representative proponents of the 'traditional' view that the 6/8 Andante came first and the alternative opinion that the 3/4 movement was first, see, respectively, Sadie, *Mozart: Early Years*, p. 476, and Alan Tyson, *Mozart: Studies of the Autograph Scores* (Cambridge, MA, 1987), pp. 106–13.

[61] MBA, vol. II, p. 397; LMF, pp. 563–4 (9 July 1778).

Example 2.1 Mozart, Symphony in D ('Paris'), K. 297, 2nd movement, bars 1–12.

individual parts need to be distinguished in performance: *p*–crescendo–*p* strings and wind melodic instruments are set against *f*–*p* crotchets in the lower voices (bars 28–9); and isolated *f*–*p* and *sf*–*p* markings are given to the violins (bars 35–45). Just as Mozart disparaged his prospective Parisian audience for the 'Paris' Symphony before the premiere, so he wrote scathingly about *Les petits riens*, condemning the 'old lousy French airs' that made their way into the score in addition to his numbers.[62] But negativity compromised neither Mozart's commitment to the finished products nor his expectation of committed renditions from players in public performances.

A private commission: the Concerto for Flute and Harp, K. 299

The Concerto for Flute and Harp K. 299 was written not for a specific public performance, but for a Paris-based ex-military man and amateur flautist, Comte de Guines, and his harpist daughter. De Guines was no stranger to having works dedicated to him. Johann Baptist Wendling, the Mannheim-based flautist who encouraged Mozart's trip to Paris and starred at the *Concert spirituel* during Mozart's stay having performed there periodically from 1750 onwards, wrote six flute-based trio sonatas for De Guines in 1769, as did Philippe Prouver; Pierre Vachon also dedicated six string quartets to him in 1773.[63] It is possible, then, that Wendling introduced Mozart to De Guines and was indirectly responsible for the commissioning of K. 299. The sinfonia concertante was a well-established genre in Paris at that time. Also (and surely not escaping Mozart's notice), the harp was a popular instrument in the city in 1778: the *Journal de Paris* in the spring carried advertisements for 'divertissemens' by Mr Luigy (harp and keyboard), for two sinfonia concertantes by Johann Ludwig Adam (keyboard and harp), for harp sonatas with violin accompaniment by Jean-Baptiste Cardon, and for a *Journal de harpe* available from the offices of the *Journal de musique*; the *Mercure de France* in September advertised a quartet by Saint-Georges from the Parisian publisher Sieber arranged for harp, violin, alto and bass by Mr Deleplanque; and Sieber's edition of Mozart's accompanied sonatas K. 301–6, giving previously published works on the front page under different headings, listed solo works for harp and only two other single instruments.[64] Thus, having

[62] See MBA, vol. II, pp. 378–9, 397; LMF, pp. 552–3 (12 June 1778, on K. 297), 563–4 (9 July 1778, on *Les petits riens*).

[63] See *Bibliographie Parisienne ou catalogue des ouvrages de sciences, de littérature et de tout ce qui concerne les Beaux-Arts: Année 1769* (Paris, 1774), pp. 252, 253. The composer for the first is identified as 'Mr. Windlino', but is clearly Wendling, as his post as first flute of the Palatinate orchestra is also mentioned. On Wendling's performances at the *Concert spirituel* between 1750

and 1780, see Ardal Powell, *The Flute* (New Haven, CT, 2002), p. 109. For the Vachon dedication, see MBA, vol. V, p. 507.

[64] See Angermüller, *W. A. Mozarts musikalische Umwelt in Paris*, pp. 42, 107, 75 (for the *Journal de Paris* listings); *Mercure de France* (5 September 1778), p. 70; and *Six sonates pour Clavecin ou Forte Piano avec accompagnement d'un violon par Wolfgang Amadeo Mozart fils* (Paris, 1778). On the harp's popularity at the *Concert spirituel* from 1778 onwards, see Pierre, *Histoire du Concert spirituel*, p. 168.

written K. 299 early in his Parisian sojourn, Mozart might have hoped for future (possibly public) performances, in spite of it originating as a private commission.[65]

Mozart considered De Guines and his daughter excellent performers; others before and after also commended De Guines.[66] Little else is known about De Guines's playing, aside from that his instrument apparently had an extension to c' as K. 299 is one of only two Mozart works to feature a flute part below d'.[67] Mozart did not rate the daughter (one of his students) as a composer, but praised her skills on the harp: 'She has a great deal of talent, and genius, and especially an incomparable memory, so that she plays all her pieces, of which she actually has about two hundred, by heart.'[68]

Mozart entrusted De Guines and his daughter with crucial interpretative decisions, thereby empowering solo performers to creative ends. The famous entry of the soloists in the second movement, for example, seamlessly interleaves composition and performance, inviting proactive interpretation from the players (see Example 2.2). The opening orchestral statement of the main theme hints at a broadening of the melody – the *p–f–p* of bars 1–4 followed by an unbroken line and extended *f* in bars 5–8 – but does not fully realize it in an unchanging texture. When the soloists participate in the main theme (Example 2.2), all is transformed: textures, dynamics and instrumentation create a special sound world into which the flute and harp are drawn. Mozart's three different, closely related harp figures in the first five bars – broken chords, grace notes in a broken chord formation and demisemiquaver arpeggiated chords – immediately challenge the harpist to produce three slightly different renditions. The harpist is asked an interpretative question straight away and needs imaginatively to answer it. Bar 17 will make an impact not only on account of its compositional qualities, including a texture and sound new to the movement (harp and flute soloists with strings), but also by coming alive in performance; Mozart requires active input from his solo players. By interpreting Mozart's different notations the harpist assumes responsibility for determining how exactly broken chords and a grace-note chord broaden out into protracted demisemiquaver arpeggios; flute and harp must then decide together how much their *f*s at bar 17 are to contrast with the *p*s in the orchestra. In the Coda (see Example 2.3), the harp's

---

[65] Mozart reports Duc de Guines as having had K. 299 for four months on 31 July, which does not quite align with Maria Anna's statement that Mozart was working on it on 5 April, and is probably a slight exaggeration. See MBA, vol. II, pp. 426, 329; LMF, pp. 587, 519.

[66] See MBA, vol. II, p. 356; LMF, p. 538 (14 May 1778); Barthélémy Tort, *Mémoire pour*

le Sieur Royer, ci-devant secretaire du Comte de Guines (Paris, 1775), p. 4; *Correspondance secrète, politique & littéraire* (London, 1789), vol. XXVI, p. 369.

[67] Neal Zaslaw, 'Mozart's Orchestral Flutes and Oboes', in Cliff Eisen (ed.), *Mozart Studies* (Oxford, 1991), p. 204.

[68] MBA, vol. II, p. 356; LMF, p. 538 (14 May 1778).

Example 2.2 Mozart, Flute and Harp Concerto in C, K. 299, 2nd movement, bars 12–18.

variously arpeggiated material is re-ordered and interrupted by the first plain, uninflected harp chords of the movement; another new effect follows in the last two bars, namely *pp* chords recapturing the mood of the original flute/harp entry and now including orchestral strings. Mozart again throws down the gauntlet to his players, asking them to navigate a path to the end of

Example 2.3 Mozart, Flute and Harp Concerto in C, K. 299, 2nd movement, bars 104–18.

the movement in the light of past and present events and relationships between these events. By demanding astute interpretative attention, then, Mozart requires from De Guines and his daughter an analogous commitment in performing K. 299 to the kind of commitment to performance and composition he regularly demonstrated himself. Mozart thereby recognized the creative role of performers in communicating the full effect of his music.

As in the Andantino, Mozart invites his soloists to take interpretative stands on fundamental issues (now primarily involving dynamics) in the first movement. The oscillation of *p* and *f* at the opening of the orchestral ritornello, alongside a single crescendo marking, is replicated for the soloists at the beginning of the solo exposition (Example 2.4). The existence of crescendo indications in bars 6 and 49 perhaps implies that immediately

Example 2.4 Mozart, Flute and Harp Concerto in C, K. 299, 1st movement, bars 44–50.

preceding moves from *p* to *f* in the main theme are to produce sudden onset *forte*s, rather than *forte*s achieved through (unnotated) crescendi. At any rate, the degree of emphasis placed on the single-crotchet *forte*s is a matter for the flautist and harpist. If forcefully emphasized, the *forte*s will promote

Example 2.5 Mozart, Flute and Harp Concerto in C, K. 299, 1st movement, bars 67–74.

musical discontinuity ultimately to contrast with the smooth continuity arising from the crescendo to *forte* in bars 49–50 and the concomitant flowering of the octave semiquavers into a steady stream of arpeggiated semiquavers. Thus Mozart foregrounds surface-level discontinuity and continuity as issues to which the solo performers' interpretative acumen needs to be directed.

Discontinuity and continuity are also a matter for performers in the transition (bar 68ff.), where the flute is heard by itself for the first time in the concerto and the flute and harp then play an extended unaccompanied passage (Example 2.5). The harp is marked *sotto voce–forte–sotto voce* necessitating a different interpretation from the opening of the solo exposition (*p–f–p*). But how the harp semiquaver arpeggios are conveyed relative to earlier material is for the performer to decide, especially in the context of projecting discontinuity or continuity. Similarly, the dynamic level at which the flute begins in bar 68 in the absence of a marking from Mozart is not insignificant. For the decision taken may affect how the relationship between flute and harp is perceived in this passage – from seamlessly collaborative, blended soloists, to contrasting, individualistically inclined ones – and how the response to the immediately preceding strident orchestra is processed.

By inviting Duc de Guines and his daughter to take decisions and fashion interpretations that carry ontological significance, Mozart gave them a fundamentally creative role in realizing their own commission. As a result of Mozart's tuition, De Guines wanted his daughter to be able above all to compose works for flute and harp.[69] While Mozart made clear that she lacked the necessary imagination and flair for composition, he nurtured a type of creative engagement with his music in K. 299 that promoted fluid boundaries between composition and performance and provided a model of a flute–harp relationship at least partially determined and communicated to audiences by decisions taken by imaginative performers of these instruments.

Published accompanied sonatas: K. 304 and K. 306

Mozart wrote two accompanied sonatas in Paris in 1778, K. 304 in E minor and K. 306 in D, and published them with Sieber alongside K. 301–3 and K. 305 (written earlier in the trip). His inability to see and correct proofs before being ushered quickly from Paris by Grimm in late September 1778 was a matter of considerable irritation; he only received a copy of the edition in late December shortly before presenting it to the dedicatee, the Electress, in Munich on 7 January 1779.[70] It is unclear whether Mozart performed any of the sonatas for the Electress when handing them over; he went to visit her with Cannabich, who could have played the violin part, and stayed for over half an hour.[71] A desire so to do would have been natural, replicating experiences of youthful accompanied sonatas presented to European royalty on the Grand Tour of 1763–6. At any rate, as the composer of sonatas to be played by a musical public beyond his immediate control, Mozart will have wanted to find ways to accommodate, encourage and guide prospective players.

With the mindset of a performer–composer, Mozart directs attention to moments where distinctive interpretations are desired while also making

[69] MBA, vol. II, p. 357; LMF, p. 538 (14 May 1778).
[70] MBA, vol. II, p. 529; LMF, p. 645 (29 December 1778).
[71] MBA, vol. II, pp. 536–7; LMF, p. 649 (8 January 1779). An angry Leopold believed that Mozart was using the delayed receipt of his sonata edition and its presentation to the Electress as an excuse for holding up his return to Salzburg: MBA, vol. II, p. 528; LMF, p. 645 (29 December 1778).

Example 2.6 Mozart, Sonata for Keyboard and Violin in E minor, K. 304, 1st movement, bars 112–21.

some music come alive in performance even in the absence of markings, thus requiring interpretative commitment and action from his players. Statements of K. 304/i's main theme, for example, capture both types of passage. The demonstrative opening to the recapitulation (Example 2.6) comprises heavy keyboard chords concentrated in the lower register, and harmonies that gravitate to B^7 (via ostentatious diminished harmony) and A minor (via a I^7–iv inflection) as well as the tonic, thus in effect summarizing the modest tonal events of the development section.[72] *Fps* in the violin and keyboard at bar 114 – heard simultaneously in both instruments for the first time in the movement – encourage performers actively to contribute to the impact of the passage (even if *fps* are nuances rather than accents as such[73]). In the Coda, too, the movement's first and only *mf* invites a distinctive dynamic rendition of the main theme.

Elsewhere in K. 304/i, though, creative engagement with Mozart's music is required in order for effects to be fully realized in performance. The austere atmosphere of the opening twelve-bar unison (Example 2.7) is transformed in the violin's repeat of the main theme (bar 13ff.) by a harmonized accompaniment in the keyboard and independent registral territory for the keyboard right hand and the violin. The violinist is surely expected to accentuate

---

[72] The development section moves from B minor (bar 85) to E minor (bar 96), to A minor (bar 100) to V/e (bar 104).

[73] Badura-Skoda, *Interpreting Mozart at the Keyboard*, pp. 53–8.

Example 2.7   Mozart, Sonata for Keyboard and Violin in E minor, K. 304, 1st movement, bars 1–21.

the theme's richness and breadth here relative to what comes before, even if the notes themselves and the single *p* marking are identical in both statements. Bar 13ff., a passage energized in performance, does not achieve its full effect through contemplation on the page. It brings to mind Carl Friedrich Cramer's claim that Mozart's accompanied sonatas K. 296 (written in Mannheim in March 1778 shortly before the Paris trip) and K. 376–80 had to be played in order to be properly appreciated:

> These sonatas are quite unique ... [The] violin accompaniment is so craftily combined with the clavier part that both instruments will constantly remain prominent; so that these sonatas demand as accomplished a violinist as clavier player. But it is not possible to give a full description of this original work. Amateurs and connoisseurs must play them through themselves, and then they will find out that we have exaggerated nothing.[74]

[74] MDL, p. 190; MDB, p. 214 (Cramer, *Magazin der Musik*, 4 April 1783). For a comparable moment to the beginning of K. 304/i in Mozart's later accompanied sonatas, see the twofold opening statement to K. 377/i as described in my work-in-progress, *Mozart in Vienna: the Final Decade* (Cambridge University Press).

Mozart's first impulse was apparently not to include the material between bars 8 and 19 inclusive: he crossed out a four-bar draft of bars 8–11 for the violin,[75] identical to the violin part in bars 20–3, presumably originally envisaging a statement analogous to those at the beginning of the reprise and in the coda. The finalized opening not only solidifies initial austerity (bars 8–12) but also invites the violinist to accentuate different qualities of the theme on its repeat (bar 13ff.).

In K. 304/ii, comprising two minuets, the variety of performance indications invite players actively to contemplate effects at transitions between sections and at onsets of sections. Mozart's different, if closely related, markings at key junctures necessitate different renditions: the *sotto voce* for the main theme; the *pp* at the transition to tonic-major Minuet 2 (bar 90); and the *p dolce* in the second minuet. In addition, both the keyboard acceleration into the Minuet 1 reprise via a chromatic scale in ever shortening note values attached to a pause implying flexible performance and the four-crotchet silence preceding the Minuet 2 *dolce* reprise demand interpretation. Of course Mozart will have expected performers to make important contributions to the movement's expression. But the frequency of his markings is less an indicator of interpretative prescription than licence to his performers to create a musical narrative for the movement as a whole informed by interpretations of individual markings and relationships among them. Above all, Mozart demonstrates complete compositional commitment to the expressive dimension of his movement, in the process asking for comparable commitment from his players.

K. 306/i brings together passages containing a number of performance indications (including the quick succession of *fp, mf, p, cresc* and *f* dynamics in cadential figures towards the end of the exposition) and those with very few (such as the development section). It is no small matter for performers to decide whether to remain at a consistent dynamic level between the *f* at bar 83 – the second of only two marked dynamics in the development – and the *p* at bar 111. On the surface, the section primarily promotes harmonic development, especially during the extended sequences (bars 83–105). But choices about dynamic levels where no markings are given – whether violin and keyboard dynamics are aligned, opposed, or similarly or differently graded – will affect how the relationship between the instruments is perceived. It is ultimately for the two performers to decide, against the backdrop of individual and collective identities forged elsewhere, whether Mozart's dynamic synchronization of violin and keyboard from the opening of the development is to continue, or is to be contravened later in the section.

---

[75] See Eduard Reeser's *Kritische Berichte* for
NMA, VIII/23/1–2 (Kassel, 1977), pp. 57, 121.

Example 2.8 Mozart, Sonata for Keyboard and Violin in D, K. 306, 2nd movement, bars 1–13.

Mozart does not dictate to performers the extent to which similarities and differences are rendered significant, then, but leaves it to their discretion. Thus, he remains committed in K. 306/i both to indicating expressive nuances *and* to empowering players to take creative decisions that assume ontological significance (as in the Concerto for Flute and Harp) by influencing the listener's perception of instrumental interaction, engagement and relationships.

While more thoroughly notated with dynamic and character markings than the first movement, K. 306/ii also combines written compositional nuances with creative empowerment of performers. Following the keyboard statement at the opening, the character of the main theme is transformed by the violin's participation in the restatement (Example 2.8). The trill-like semiquavers in bars 8 and 9 fill gaps left by the keyboard, the violin and keyboard weaving seamlessly together to project forwards to the *forte* in bar 10 (via a crescendo in bar 9), which as an unambiguous melody-accompaniment texture is heard as a genuine moment of arrival. Following

Cramer again, it is a moment to be experienced in performance. Furthermore, by setting the scene for a kind of instinctive collaboration in the remainder of the exposition, it promotes to the performers the evolving relationship between violin and keyboard; they are therefore encouraged to decide the extent to which dynamics assigned to only one of the two instruments in the development section will contribute to a sense of individual rather than collective identities. And decisions are ontologically significant once more, ultimately determining whether the recapitulation is heard as a 'resolution' of 'tensions' from the development, as a continuation of collaboration from the development, or as something in between. The creative input required from players is not simply cosmetic, then, but an organic component of the movement. The same can be said of the sonata-rondo finale: a lengthy, forty-seven-bar cadenza (one-fifth of the movement), shortly before the final reprise of the main theme, sounds improvised even though written down, with fermatas and a tempo change encouraging liberties to be taken in performance. A subsequent one-bar insert into the concluding A section, marked Adagio and including a further fermata, shows a cadenza-related mindset infiltrating the main theme as well.

Published keyboard works: variations K. 354 and sonata K. 310

Mozart left two works composed in Paris with his friend François-Joseph Heina, perhaps for a payment to help fund the return trip to Salzburg: the keyboard variations on the French song 'Je suis Lindor', K. 354, and the sonata in A minor, K. 310.[76] Heina began a publishing business in 1773 and brought out K. 354 in 1778, alongside Mozart's previously composed keyboard variations K. 179 and K. 180.[77] In 1781 he published six string quartets by Josef Fiala, a pupil of Johann Baptist Vanhal, and six duos for violin and viola by Joseph Antoine Lorenziti; one accompanied sonata by Antonio Rosetti and two by Martin Schmit followed in 1782, the year that K. 309, 310 and 311 also appeared.[78]

Mozart's keyboard variations exist at the nexus of performance and composition, many sets (probably including K. 354) beginning life as

[76] Heina also received from Mozart the keyboard sonatas K. 309 and K. 311, composed in Mannheim in late 1777.

[77] For an advertisement, see *Almanach Musical*, 5 (1779), p. 80. (This volume also carries an advertisement on p. 82 for Mozart's six accompanied sonatas published by Sieber.)

[78] See advertisements in *Almanach Musical*, 6 (1781), pp. 183, 178 and *Journal Encyclopédique*, 5/1 (July 1782), pp. 149–50.

improvised performances and building on his high stock as a keyboard player.[79] The ebb and flow of K. 354 no doubt mirrors Mozart's own spontaneous improvisations: figurative patterns are passed from one hand to the other across several adjacent variations (1–2, 5–6, 10–11); imitation between hands in no. 4 reappears in nos. 7 and 9; intricate ornaments characterize nos. 3 and 9; and tempo changes in variations 8 and 12 coincide with peaks of improvisatory and embellishment activity (including the capricious Presto at the end of no. 8 and the hemidemisemiquaver roulades in no. 12).

The keyboard sonata in A minor, K. 310, foregrounds issues similar to those raised by the Parisian accompanied sonatas and by K. 354. It is not an easy sonata immediately attractive to amateur players. Judging by an advertisement for Lorenziti's string duos published by Heina that contains a description equally applicable to K. 310, Heina would not have been put off by the difficulty of Mozart's sonata: 'This musical work can only suit people who have acquired a very great understanding of the instruments for which it was composed.'[80]

As in K. 306, Mozart's dynamic markings across the first movement of K. 310 vary considerably in number.[81] After an opening twenty-three bars that feature *f* and *p* markings, plus a *calando* (bar 14), dynamics disappear for the remainder of the exposition (which ends at bar 49). It is unlikely that Mozart intended dynamic uniformity from bar 23 onwards, which coincides with the arrival of the secondary key area (C) and the onset of a stream of melodic semiquavers continuing almost uninterrupted until the end of the exposition: the lack of dynamics in the corresponding passage of the recapitulation (where the secondary theme is in A minor) shows that Mozart does not simply equate minor-mode passages in the movement with dynamic changeability and major-mode material with dynamic consistency; and running semiquavers without dynamics in the exposition are followed by figurative semiquavers with dynamics in the development. Thus, Mozart was probably expecting his player to assume responsibility for putting dynamic nuances into effect. Mozart's *ff–pp–ff* early in the development section

[79] On origins in improvised performances, see Katalin Komlos, '"Ich praeludirte und spielte Variazionen": Mozart the Fortepianist', in Peter Williams and R. Larry Todd (eds.), *Perspectives on Mozart Performance* (Cambridge, 1991), p. 40. For praise of Mozart's keyboard playing during the 1777–9 trip, see MBA, vol. II, pp. 45, 83, 90, 208; LMF, p. 305 (11 October 1777), 340 (23 October 1777), 345 (29 October 1777), 436 (28 December 1777); MDL, p. 150; MDB, p. 168.

[80] *Almanach Musical*, 6 (1781), p. 178: 'Cette oeuvre musicale ne peut convenir qu'aux personnes qui ont acquis une très-grande connoissance de l'instrumens pour lequel elle a été composée.'
[81] The NMA Preface (IX/25/1, p. xvi) draws attention to this fact; Wolfgang Plath and Wolfgang Rehm rightly resist the temptation to add more to their edition (except the implicit *forte* at the opening).

Example 2.9 Mozart, Sonata for Keyboard in A minor, K. 310, 2nd movement, bars 1–12.

(bars 58–66) – *ff* being a very rare dynamic in his keyboard oeuvre – indicates that dynamic contrasts are to be increased a notch relative to those at the opening of the exposition.[82] But whether contrasts are to feature later in the section (and if so, how) is a matter for the performer.

K. 310/ii sits midway between the model performance conveyed in the K. 354 variations – where embellishments and elaborations are given in the notated text – and the creative performances encouraged in the accompanied sonatas and K. 310/i. The *con espressione* and plethora of dynamic indications in the exposition capture Mozart's desire for attentive, expressive playing; in effect, the message to the keyboard player is that Mozart's compositional commitment has to be matched by interpretative commitment. The notated embellishments in bars 1–7 and 8–12 (see Example 2.9)

---

[82] As Derek Carew points out, the *ff* passages represent 'the "development" of actual keyboard technique within a movement', in this case 'an intensification of elements from the Codetta'. See Carew, *The Mechanical Muse:* *The Piano, Pianism and Piano Music, c. 1760–1850* (Aldershot, 2007), p. 278. The *ff*s here are two of only a handful in Mozart's keyboard works; see Badura-Skoda, *Interpreting Mozart*, p. 47.

are also supported by dynamic 'embellishments': *fps* and crescendos are exchanged at corresponding points of thematic statements (bars 2 and 6, 9 and 11). Even performers with access only to a harpsichord in Paris could perhaps have conveyed the expression Mozart required: the *Mercure de France* in spring 1778 reported the arrival of an instrument from a Flemish maker that could do crescendi 'marvellously', allowing the player to augment and diminish the sound at will by using a knee-operated button.[83] The development section contains fewer dynamic nuances than the exposition. Having been provided with a model of expression in the exposition, Mozart's players were equipped with the necessary tools and knowledge to determine whether – and if so how – comparable sensitivity could be introduced into the development.

Conclusion

Mozart's Parisian works are by no means unique among those composed on the 1777–9 trip in exhibiting continuities and close relationships between composition and performance. K. 309/ii models the spontaneity of elaboration that Mozart would have put into effect in his own performances; the melody-accompaniment texture at bar 8 of K. 311/ii is a moment transformed in performance – the semiquavers in the left-hand arpeggiated bass growing out of the right-hand semiquavers in the preceding bar – even though no new markings are present; the dynamic nuances supporting notated variation procedures in K. 305/ii encourage the construction of dynamic-related narratives; and (as already explained) the concert aria K. 294, written to suit Aloysia, requires a full orchestral rendition in order for its effects to be properly appreciated, not simply contemplation in score. But the Parisian works discussed above carry special musical-biographical significance, on account of the extraordinary upheaval of the six-month stay. In spite of utter disillusionment with French music, musicians and audiences and weighed down by personal tragedy, Mozart established an implicit contract with all those who performed his works: his intense compositional commitment had to be complemented by their commitment to his music. Mozart would have been prepared to enforce the contract at the premiere of the 'Paris' Symphony, by jumping into the orchestra and taking control as performer–composer, but had to employ less ostentatious means when writing a private commission or for

[83] As given (in French) in Angermüller,
W. A. Mozarts musikalische Umwelt in Paris,
p. 72.

publication. At times he provided detailed performance markings, thereby encouraging players to decide whether to apply them at unmarked moments as well; elsewhere he asked for proactive and creative interpretation of his notated texts as a matter of ontological significance, or modelled his own performance style. It is testimony to the musical immersion Mozart experienced that he was willing and able to fulfil his side of the bargain even as his world fell apart around him.

Standard biographical narratives of Mozart's musical failure in Paris are no doubt in need of revision: the number of works from this period looks considerably better once several that are documented in letters but no longer extant are factored into the final equation, including the Sinfonia concertante K. A9, the eight movements for Holzbauer's *Miserere* K. A1 and the *scena* for the castrato Giusto Ferdinando Tenducci K. A3; the eight known performances of Mozart's new Parisian music between mid-June and mid-July 1778,[84] plus repeat renditions of K. 297 at the *Concert spirituel* on 15 August and 8 September, was an impressive tally for a composer who only arrived in the city in late March; and criticisms of the 'Paris' Symphony, including those cited at the beginning of this chapter, are unreasonably harsh. But a musically based biographical account of Paris 1778 ultimately points in more important, far-reaching directions. Free of a Salzburg court appointment on his travels in 1777–9, Mozart focused his attention not only on procuring another appointment but also on the kind of musician he wanted to become, namely a composer first and foremost. Thus, simultaneously demonstrating compositional attentiveness and facilitating and empowering attentiveness in performers was a practical, not theoretical, strategy for engaging, nurturing and sustaining the interests of players (and listeners) over time. A move to Vienna was mooted in the correspondence with Leopold in January 1778, albeit in the context of an appointment either at the German opera or elsewhere.[85] Once relocated to Vienna without an appointment three years later in spring 1781, Mozart drew directly on his experiences from 1777–9 both of writing specifically for esteemed musicians (including himself) and the performing musical public and of cultivating audiences inter alia through noteworthy effects.[86] Mozart had to use musical guile in large part acquired on his 1777–9 tour to help him navigate ways forward, now without Leopold to bankroll time away from Salzburg. And, as he also learned from the Paris

[84] MDL, pp. 157–8; MDB, pp. 175–6.
[85] MBA, vol. II, pp. 222, 243–4; LMF, pp. 444–5 (10/11 January 1778), 454–5 (29 January 1778).
[86] See Mozart's early Viennese works such as the Rondo for Violin and Orchestra K. 373,

the concert aria K. 374, the Rondo for Piano and Orchestra K. 382, the Sonata for Two Pianos K. 448, and the accompanied sonatas K. 376, 377, 379, 380, as discussed in my work in progress, *Mozart in Vienna: the Final Decade*.

sojourn, he had to work productively, efficiently and effectively at a time of personal crisis, on this later occasion acrimonious disputes with both his employer Archbishop Colloredo and his father.

We can only imagine Mozart's depressed state of mind on the eve of his return to Salzburg, the hometown he had come to detest, given everything that had gone wrong since his departure, especially in Paris. But experiences that had not killed Mozart ultimately would make him (musically) stronger. The title of Pierre-Jean-Baptiste Nougaret's comedy staged in Paris on the night of Maria Anna's death, *Il n'y a plus d'enfants* (There are no more children),[87] has bitterly ironic undertones for someone facing the most adult of situations head-on at that very moment. But the title also captures a crucial stage in the progression of Mozart's musical career towards an independent existence. On his 1777–9 trip, with Paris at its apogee on account of the unremitting challenges he faced and through which he continued to work with steadfast commitment to his musical causes, Mozart had laid a firm musical foundation for an extraordinary career as a freelance performer–composer in Vienna.

[87] See the listing in Angermüller, W. A. *Mozarts musikalische Umwelt in Paris*, pp. 155–6.

3   Mozart's association with the Tonkünstler-Societät

David Black

For a musician of Mozart's reputation in Vienna, surprisingly little is known of the circumstances surrounding his public concert appearances. While he is known to have organized numerous concerts for his own benefit and participated in the concerts of others, the details of venue hire, recruitment and payment of musicians, selection of repertoire, audience size and box office takings at these concerts are generally unknown.[1] It is only when Mozart was working with larger institutions that produced and retained extensive records of their transactions that we have a more accurate sense of this contextual information. The most obvious example of major musical institutions in Vienna is the court opera, where the commercial business of contracting singers and mounting productions required that extensive records were produced.[2] Another institution with a need for meticulous recordkeeping was the 'Musicalische Societät der freyen Tonkunst für Wittwen und Waisen' or Tonkünstler-Societät (hereafter TKS), the charitable body founded in 1771 to provide a basic social safety net to the widows and children of deceased musicians. Although the Society's charitable objects were of course at the forefront of its members' concerns, today the TKS is better remembered for the fundraising academies it mounted during Advent and Lent each year. These academies provided an opportunity for leading musicians to display their talents in both performance and composition, albeit on an unpaid basis.

Mozart and his music made appearances at the Society's academies on six known occasions during the composer's lifetime, spanning almost the entire

I am grateful to Dexter Edge, Michael Lorenz and Neal Zaslaw for clarifying a number of details about the sources discussed in this chapter.

[1] For a list of known Viennese concerts featuring Mozart, see Mary Sue Morrow, *Concert Life in Haydn's Vienna: Aspects of a Developing Musical and Social Institution* (New York, 1989) and Dexter Edge, 'Review Article: Mary Sue Morrow, Concert Life in Haydn's Vienna', *Haydn Yearbook*, 17 (1992), pp. 108–66. A further concert on 28 February 1787 is discussed in David Black,

'Mozart Benefit Concert in the Kärntnertortheater', in Dexter Edge and Black (eds.), *Mozart: New Documents*, http://dx.doi.org/10.7302/Z20P0WXJ. For an overview of Viennese concert life at this time, see Otto Biba, 'Grundzüge des Konzertwesens in Wien zu Mozarts Zeit', in *Mozart-Jahrbuch 1978/79*, pp. 132–43.

[2] Many relevant documents are transcribed in Dorothea Link, *The National Court Theatre in Mozart's Vienna: Sources and Documents, 1783–1792* (Oxford, 1998).

length of his residence in Vienna.[3] The basic details of Mozart's association have long been known through their citation in Carl Ferdinand Pohl's history of the Society, and Mozart's letters record a number of additional details about the preparation and reception of the TKS academies.[4] Yet the Society's archives preserve a wealth of information about late eighteenth- and nineteenth-century music in Vienna, much of which remains unstudied. Documents relating to Mozart are no exception, for the standard documentary collections (MDB, MDL and NMD) do not provide a complete survey of TKS references to the composer.[5] Together with the surviving parts of the Society's music collection, which also remains generally unknown, the TKS archive provides contextual insight into the works that Mozart performed and composed for the Society and the history of his unsuccessful efforts to become a member. In view of the general unfamiliarity of the TKS collections, this chapter will provide a short evaluation of the available documentary and musical sources from the eighteenth century before considering the background to each occasion that featured Mozart's music during the composer's lifetime.

The history of the Society's documentary and musical archives is a typically convoluted example of transmission in Austrian sources, but may be summarized briefly. The Tonkünstler-Societät, which in 1862 renamed itself in honour of Haydn, was forced to disband by the Nazis in 1939. The Society's documentary archive was then given to the Wiener Stadt- und Landesarchiv, where it remains today.[6] The TKS musical archive had already been mostly given to the Hofoper in 1882 and transferred in 1927 to the Österreichische National-bibliothek; the exception was the Haydn sources, which were retained by the Society and ultimately given to the Stadt- und Landesbibliothek in 1939.[7] The

---

[3] I define an 'occasion' to mean one or both of the academies held within a few days of each other during Advent and Lent. There were a total of nine academies featuring Mozart's music, but where that music appeared identically on both evenings I regard it as a single 'occasion' for the purposes of this chapter. Much of the TKS repertoire remains unidentified, and it is possible that works by Mozart appeared on further occasions. In December 1788, for example, Josepha Auernhammer performed an unidentified piano concerto at the Society's Advent academies. Given her previous association with Mozart, it is possible that Auernhammer performed a concerto by him; Dexter Edge, 'Mozart's Viennese Orchestras', *Early Music*, 20 (1992), pp. 64–8, at 87 n58.

[4] Carl Ferdinand Pohl, *Denkschrift aus Anlaß des hundertjährigen Bestehens der Tonkünstler-Societät* (Vienna, 1871). No satisfactory modern history of the TKS exists; Claudia Pete,

'Geschichte der Wiener Tonkünstler-Societät' (PhD diss., Universität Wien, 1996) takes the story to 1939 but adds little to Pohl.

[5] For a recent use of the TKS documentary archive, see Rita Steblin, 'Beethoven Mentions in Documents of the Viennese Tonkünstler-Societät, 1795 to 1824', *Bonner Beethoven-Studien*, 10 (2012), pp. 139–88.

[6] Steblin, 'Beethoven Mentions', p. 140. The TKS concert posters are now in Vienna, Gesellschaft der Musikfreunde (A-Wgm).

[7] The first surviving detailed inventory of the TKS music holdings is a 'Musicalien Catalog' begun in 1839 by the secretary, Stephan Franz; Vienna, Wiener Stadt- und Landesarchiv (A-Wsa), Haydn-Verein, B 1/11 (all subsequent citations of TKS documents in this article refer to A-Wsa). The collection as inherited by the Hofoper is listed in Vienna, Österreichische Nationalbibliothek, Musiksammlung (A-Wn), Inv. I/Opernarchiv I (olim Mus. Hs. 2473), 124ff. Unfortunately, when the ÖNB inherited

Table 3.1 Surviving performance material used by the Tonkünstler-Societät to *c.* 1810

Work	Signature (most in A-Wn)	Type; date of first use
Cherubini: *Medea*	olim HV 10 (lost)[8]	Parts; 7 April 1805
Cherubini: Mit Blumen lasset uns bekränzen (*Anacreon*)	Mus. Hs. 2008, HV 9	Parts; 7 April 1805
Eybler: *Die Hirten bei der Krippe zu Bethlehem*	Mus. Hs. 3231	Score; 22 December 1794
Handel: Fermo sul Trono adamantin (*Samson*)	HV 24	Score and Parts; 20 December 1778
Handel: Il Sacro Trono (*Samson*)	HV 23	Score and Parts; ?20 December 1778
Handel arr. Starzer: *Judas Maccabeus*	Mus. Hs. 3239, HV 16	Score and Parts; 21 March 1779
Handel: Four Choruses (*Israel in Egypt*; see discussion)	HV 26	Parts; 22 December 1782
Haydn: *Gott erhalte Franz den Kaiser*	A-Wst, MH 13551–2	Score and Parts
Haydn: *Il Ritorno di Tobia*	A-Wst, MH 13566–72	Parts; 2 April 1775
Haydn: *Der Sturm*	A-Wst, MH 13554	Score and Parts; 22 December 1793
Haydn: *Die sieben letzten Worte*	A-Wst, MH 13573–4	Score and Parts; 1 April 1798
Haydn: *Die Schöpfung*	A-Wst, MH 13555–9	Score and Parts; 17 March 1799
Haydn: *Die Jahreszeiten*	A-Wst, MH 13560–5	Score and Parts; 22 December 1801
Righini: *Il natale di Apollo*	OA 456	Score; 22 December 1789
Salieri: Concerto in C for Flute and Oboe	Mus. Hs. 3723	Parts; ?22 December 1784[9]

surviving eighteenth-century documentary sources are extensive, and include annual account books, records of board meetings, correspondence to and from members, lists of performers and summaries of box office receipts. Musical sources have fared far less well; Table 3.1 gives a provisional summary of all surviving TKS performance material that appears to date from before 1810 on the basis of papertype and handwriting evidence.[10]

the TKS music collection it did not catalogue the collection under a single class. Generally, manuscript scores were catalogued under the class S.m. (now Mus. Hs.), manuscript parts under HA (Hofoper Archiv, recatalogued in the 1980s as Fonds 89 Haydn-Verein), and prints under M.S. 8223–7.

[8] HV = Fonds 89 Haydn-Verein.

[9] On the Salieri concerto parts, see Dexter Edge, 'Manuscript Parts as Evidence of Orchestral Size in the Eighteenth-Century Viennese Concerto', in Neal Zaslaw (ed.), *Mozart's Piano Concertos: Text, Context, Interpretation* (Ann Arbor, 1996), pp. 427–60, at 438. These parts were once part of the secular holdings of the *Hofkapelle*, but were probably used by the TKS on this occasion.

[10] The TKS Haydn sources are the only part of the collection to have received any substantial attention, and they are taken into account in the relevant volumes of *Joseph Haydn: Werke*. On the score of *Judas Maccabeus*, see Andreas Holschneider, 'Die "Judas Maccabäus" Bearbeitung der Österreichischen Nationalbibliothek', in *Mozart-Jahrbuch 1960/61*, pp. 173–81. There are a number of manuscript scores in A-Wgm, some discussed below, which appear to have served as source material for the TKS concerts. It is possible that some or all of these derive from the estate of Salieri, who joined the Society in 1780, directed its concerts from the early 1780s and served as its president from 1788.

These sources, particularly the parts, are useful in identifying the precise works scheduled at the TKS academies, with implications for our knowledge of Mozart's musical influences. For example, because the academies often featured many short items, the participating musicians understandably numbered each of their parts in order to keep them in the correct sequence, and these numbers can be matched with the known schedules to link the parts with a particular academy. A large set of parts for four Handel choruses from *Israel in Egypt* has many parts marked '3' on the first two choruses and '9' on the second two.[11] These numbers correspond to the position of the otherwise unidentified Handel 'choruses' in the running order for the academies of Advent 1782, and other annotations on the parts confirm that they were used on these occasions.[12] That the Society performed 'The people shall hear' from *Israel in Egypt* in December 1782 is of considerable interest, as this chorus has been identified as a potential inspiration for the 'Qui tollis' of the C minor Mass, K. 427, on which Mozart was working at this time.[13] Although we do not know if Mozart regularly attended the TKS academies when he was not performing in them, these performances could have given him a unique opportunity to hear a full-scale rendition of 'The people shall hear'.[14]

Despite the seemingly chance survival of these sources, the vast bulk of the performance material that once existed for the Society's academies is now lost, including all the material for Mozart's music. Some insight into its

[11] The choruses are 'Gl'Israeliti oppressi' (And the children of Israel sighed), 'Non pioggia loro' (He gave them hailstones), 'Il popolo vedrà' (The people shall hear) and 'Vuo cantare al mio signor' (I will sing unto the Lord).

[12] The programme is given in Pohl, *Denkschrift*, p. 60. The cover page of the Trombone Primo part bears the annotation 'N° 1. von Gluck Tacet. / N° 2. Aria Tacet'. As it happens, the opening items in the concerts of Advent 1782 were the overture and two choruses from an unidentified French tragedy by Gluck, and an aria by Naumann sung by Johann Valentin Adamberger. Many of the performers signed their parts.

[13] Silke Leopold, 'Händels Geist in Mozarts Handen. Zum "Qui Tollis" aus der c-Moll-Messe KV 427', in *Mozart Jahrbuch 1994*, pp. 89–112; Ulrich Konrad, 'On Ancient Languages: The Historical Idiom of Wolfgang Amadé Mozart', in Sean Gallagher and Thomas F. Kelly (eds.), *The Century of Bach and Mozart: Perspectives on Historiography, Composition, Theory & Performance* (Cambridge, MA, 2008), pp. 253–78.

[14] In an illuminating article, Bernd Edelmann has discussed the Society's early Handel performances and drawn attention to a number of manuscript scores in A-Wgm and A-Wn that are likely related to these performances; see Bernd Edelmann, 'Händel-Aufführungen in den Akademien der Wiener Tonkünstlersozietät,' *Göttinger Händel-Beiträge*, 1 (1984), pp. 172–99. Edelmann was able to identify many plausible candidates for the Handel 'choruses' performed by the TKS, but did not consider the Society's own parts. Although the score A-Wgm, Q 21002 contains all the Handel choruses performed in 1782 and has an underlaid Italian text in the hand of Salieri (who directed the performances), it does not contain the additional woodwind and brass instrumentation found in the parts. The Society's parts confirm the enormous size of the choir and orchestra, with ten copies each of Violin I and II and up to seven copies of each of the eight choral parts. Other early Handel sources, such as A-Wn, Mus. Hs. 1958 and 4039–43 are also possibly related to the performances.

extent can still be gained from the records of payment to the Society's music copyist Joseph Arthofer (1742–1807), who worked for the TKS from 1772 until his death and who also worked for Mozart personally.[15] In addition to the total payments recorded for his work in the annual account books, an inventory prepared in 1795 gives more detail about payments for music that still existed in the Society's archives at that time.[16] The preparation of the performance material for a TKS academy must have been challenging for Arthofer and his assistants: the scheduled music often changed, composers (including Mozart) delivered works at the last minute, and the huge forces at the academies required more than the usual copies of each part. To give some sense of the effort involved, Arthofer was paid an initial sum of 93fl 55kr for his work on the academies of Lent 1785, which included the premiere of Mozart's *Davide penitente*. As we know that Arthofer charged 5kr per bifolium (*Bogen*), he and his assistants appear to have delivered more than 1,100 bifolia, most of them presumably covered with music, within a matter of weeks.[17] These manuscripts would have required a large amount of storage space, which may explain why so many were eventually discarded when there was no further practical use for them. The Appendix gives a summary of the known appearances of Mozart's music at the TKS academies during the composer's lifetime, including details of programmes, rehearsals, box office takings, and payments for music copying.

By the time of Mozart's arrival in Vienna in 1781, the TKS occupied an established place in the musical life of the city, usually mounting four academies a year: two in Advent and two in Lent. With few exceptions, the two academies in each season took place within a few days of each other and featured similar or identical repertoire. Due to the death of Empress Maria Theresia on 29 November 1780, there had been no academies during Advent 1780, so unusually the Society held two sets of academies in Lent 1781. Mozart's arrival in Vienna early on 16 March coincided with preparations for the second set, scheduled for 1 and 3 April. It appears that the composer

---

[15] On Arthofer, see Dexter Edge, 'Mozart's Viennese Copyists' (PhD thesis, University of Southern California, 2001), chapter 8, supplemented by Steblin, 'Beethoven Mentions', pp. 166–8. Some, but by no means all of the surviving material from the TKS is in Arthofer's hand; given the scale of the task he understandably employed assistants.

[16] The inventory is in A 3/1, and is based on copyist invoices that are no longer extant. It has two lists, with the items distinguished more or less according to whether they are choral works on the one hand or solo vocal and instrumental works ('Konzerten und Arien') on the other. The choral items are

identified by name, but the solo and instrumental items are left unidentified. They can, however, be cross-referenced with the known programmes to infer their identity. For example, the inventory lists a payment of 6fl 15kr under 'Konzerten und Arien' for the academies of Advent 1789; this probably refers to the copying of performance material for Mozart's Clarinet Quintet K. 581 (22 December) and a concertino by Devienne (23 December; see Pohl, *Denkschrift*, p. 63 and the Appendix to this chapter).

[17] On the meaning of *Bogen* in this context, see Edge, 'Mozart's Viennese Copyists', pp. 132–7 and Edge, 'Manuscript Parts', p. 438.

was engaged almost immediately, for the minutes of the board meeting of 16 March already have him scheduled for the second night.[18] Unfortunately, like all the TKS minutes, these records only note the board's resolutions and not the preceding discussion, so it is not known who suggested that Mozart should be invited. However, Mozart later reported to Leopold that Joseph Starzer, an *Assessor* of the TKS, had requested his appearance.[19] With Archbishop Colloredo reluctantly granting permission by 28 March after an initial refusal, Mozart appeared on 3 April alongside the second performance of Albrechtsberger's new oratorio *Die Pilgrime auf Golgatha*. In addition to contributing a symphony before the oratorio, generally assumed on little evidence to have been K. 338, the composer played an unidentified solo work to conclude the academy.[20] On Mozart's account, both the symphony and the solo were a great success. Following the usual pattern, however, the second academy featuring Mozart's music had lower box office takings than the first, which had only the premiere of Albrechtsberger's oratorio. The 1781 account book records a large payment to Arthofer for copying the oratorio, and a further payment of 12fl 50kr that may have been for the Mozart symphony.[21]

It was two years before Mozart had another opportunity to appear at a TKS academy, but on 22 December 1783 for the first Advent academy the composer performed a concerto and Johann Valentin Adamberger sang a Mozart 'rondò', both unidentified. It seems that Mozart's appearance was not part of the original plan, for the minutes of the board meeting of 21 November show that the clarinet-playing Stadler brothers were intended to have a concerto, with no reference to the vocal rondò. Eventually, however, the Stadlers' concerto was replaced with Mozart's, and Adamberger's item was introduced.[22] The second academy on 23 December had a violin

---

[18] '*Concerten* . . . bey der zweyten *production*. Zum Anfange eine *Sinfonia* von Herrn *Mozart*, dann ließ sich Herr *Mozart* auf dem *Forte piano* hören, zum Beschluß das *Oratorium*'; A 2/1 and B 2/1, 11/1781. Because the minutes were often written up several days after the meeting, it is possible that the writer incorporated subsequent developments. At first the minutes were also written up in fair copy in the Society's *Haupt Sessions Prodocoll* (B 2/1), but this practice was abandoned after August 1785.
[19] Mozart's reports of the preparations and the academy are in MBA, vol. III, pp. 99–106.
[20] On the identification of the symphony heard at this academy, see Edge, 'Mozart's Viennese Copyists', p. 628 n102. The symphony was rehearsed at least twice; according to Mozart the second rehearsal was 'beym Bonno' (MBA, vol. III, p. 106), but it is

not clear if he was referring to one of the three known rehearsals.
[21] 'für *Copiatur* laut Beylag . . . 12[fl] 50[kr]'; B 5/11, Erstes Quartal, Extra Ausgaben.
[22] '*Concerto*. am 1. Tag. zwey Herrn Städler [*sic*]', with a remark later added, evidently after the poster had been printed: 'NB: Hr *Mozart* und das übrige nach dem *Avviso* Zetl.' The fair copy of the minutes follows the final order, with '*Concerto* am ersten Tag von Hr: *Mozart* auf dem *forte piano*' and '*Rondo* gesungen von Hr *Adamberger*'; A 2/1 and B 2/1, 62/1783. Adamberger's item has been traditionally identified as K. 431 but John Rice has suggested that it may have been K. 420; see John Rice, 'Problems of Genre and Gender in Mozart's Scena "Misero! o sogno, o son desto?" K. 431', in *Mozart-Jahrbuch 2000*, pp. 73–89.

concerto performed by Martin Schlesinger in place of Mozart. Writing to Leopold on Christmas Eve, Mozart reported that the theatre was full on the first night but empty on the second, which might imply he attended the second academy as an audience member.[23] The claim of a full theatre for his performance is not exactly borne out by the summary of the box office receipts, despite the fact that this academy had the highest receipts of any TKS academy featuring Mozart's music. Although it is not possible to arrive at a specific estimate of attendance from the box office figures, they imply that seated ticket holders occupied between half and two-thirds of the capacity of the theatre. Whether or not Mozart was misrepresenting the success of the academy to his father, the report of the empty theatre the following night is consistent with the box office takings, which were less than half of those on 22 December.[24] Arthofer seems to have received additional compensation for these academies on account of onerous last-minute copying.

Mozart's next appearance for the TKS featured the only work he is known to have written specifically for its academies, the cantata *Davide penitente* K. 469. The composer had harboured thoughts about writing an oratorio-like work for Vienna ever since his arrival in the city,[25] but it appears that the original intention was not to set *Davide* for the TKS but another libretto entirely. In a letter to his sister of 21 July 1784, Mozart wrote: 'I beg Papa not to forget to send me by the next mail coach what I asked him for. I should be delighted if he could send me my old oratorio *La Betulia liberata* too. I have to compose the same oratorio for the Society in Vienna and possibly I might use bits of it here and there.'[26] Just what lay behind this statement is unclear, for there is no reference in the minutes of the TKS to any request for an oratorio from Mozart. From the composer's perspective, his 1771 oratorio for Padua might have been especially suitable for reworking as it had apparently never received a performance. Perhaps Mozart also thought that his setting of Metastasio's libretto might rival Gassmann's setting, which featured at the very first TKS academy in 1772. Mozart may have heard a chorus from Gassmann's

---

[23] MBA, vol. III, p. 299.

[24] The box office summaries are in A 1/4. The total takings on 22 December 1783 were 540fl 7kr, from 493 individual seats and forty-five boxes. It is not possible to calculate an exact attendance from these figures, as the number of attendees in each box could vary. The attendance estimate does not include potential additional numbers from free admission, standing room or subscribed boxes; it is not entirely clear whether boxes subscribed for the theatrical season were released for charitable events. On the interpretation of such evidence, see Dexter Edge, 'Mozart's Reception in Vienna, 1787–91', in Stanley Sadie (ed.), *Wolfgang Amadè Mozart: Essays on his Life and his Music* (Oxford, 1996), pp. 66–117 at 73–6.

[25] MBA, vol. III, p. 99 (letter of 24 March 1781).

[26] MBA, vol. III, p. 319; translation from LMF, p. 881.

La Betulia liberata during his appearance for the Society on 22 December 1783 (see Appendix).[27]

There are no further references to *Betulia* in Mozart's letters, and one might otherwise be tempted to dismiss the rather vague intention to rework it without further comment. Yet there is some evidence to suggest that Mozart's planning for a setting of *Betulia* reached an advanced stage. A surviving copy of the libretto for Gassmann's setting of *Betulia*, printed for the TKS's revival of that work on 18 December 1776, contains extensive handwritten additions and pasteovers in ink and *Rötel* (red chalk). This copy was likely in Mozart's possession, and was almost certainly one of the 'two libretti for *Betulia liberata*' that Constanze Mozart sold to Johann André in 1800 along with the rest of the composer's 'estate'.[28] On the title page of the libretto, the date of Advent 1776 has been crossed out and replaced with 'nella quadragesima del' 1785'. Another hand has deleted this in turn and replaced it with 'nell' advento', which was itself crossed out and replaced it with 'nella quaresima dell' Anno 1786' (see Figure 3.1). On the cast list on the next page, the statement giving Gassmann as the composer has been deleted. Thus there is good evidence that a new setting of the oratorio based on a revised version of Metastasio's libretto was planned for 1785–86, and circumstantial evidence that Mozart and the TKS were involved, perhaps even after the premiere of *Davide penitente*.

The libretto has been subject to extensive curtailment in recitative passages, in some cases by crossing out the text in ink or chalk, in others by pasting a piece of paper over the deleted passages and adding bridging words in ink as necessary. The arias 'Del pari infeconda' (No. 5) and 'Quel nocchier' (No. 11) have been cut entirely. The intention appears to have been to tighten the action, removing more reflective moments such as the extended discussion on the nature of God at the beginning of Part Two. But not all

---

[27] The posters for the Advent 1783 academies list choruses by Hasse, Sacchini and Dittersdorf (Pohl, *Denkschrift*, p. 61), but the 1795 inventory lists an associated payment for the copying of 'vorfindige Stuke, als *L'Ester* von Hr *Dittersdorf. La Bettulia liberata* von Herrn *Gasmann* Partituren betragen zusammen ... 3[fl] 37[xr] 2[pf]'. The inclusion of an amount in *Pfennig* is unusual, as copyist rates did not usually employ this denomination.

[28] MBA, vol. IV, p. 305. The libretto today is in A-Wn, Mus. Hs. 4837. It is now bound out of order, and f. 5 (in the library's pencil foliation) belongs between f. 8 and 9. According to notes on the flyleaf by Robert Haas, the libretto was inherited by André's son Carl August André, who bequeathed it along with other manuscripts to his student and assistant Heinrich Henkel in 1886/7. It then passed to Henkel's daughter Dorothy, who sold it on the advice of the Frankfurt music critic Karl Holl to the ÖNB in 1930. The libretto is noted in Wolfgang Plath, 'Mozartiana in Fulda und Frankfurt', reprinted in Marianne Danckwardt (ed.), *Mozart-Schriften: Ausgewählte Aufsätze* (Kassel, 1991), pp. 126–78, at 134. On Mozart's 'estate', see Edge, 'Mozart's Viennese Copyists', chapter 8 and Jürgen Eichenauer (ed.), *Johann Anton André und der Mozart-Nachlass: Ein Notenschatz in Offenbach am Main* (Weimar, 2006).

Figure 3.1 Libretto of Gassmann: *La Betulia liberata* from Mozart's 'estate', showing numerous changes. A-Wn, Mus. Hs. 4837, f. 2r, 4r.

instructions were to delete passages: the beginning of the libretto, which lacked an opening chorus, and the aria and chorus 'Pietà, se irato sei' (No. 6) are both marked 'coro nuovo'. Above the aria 'Te solo adoro' (No. 13) is marked 'Quintett.'[29]

The obvious question, of course, is who was responsible for these revisions. A note on the flyleaf by Heinrich Henkel (1822–99), who once owned the libretto, attributes the revisions to Metastasio himself, but this was probably nothing more than a guess on Henkel's part and is almost certainly incorrect.[30] In the mid-1780s, however, the Society's board was interested in procuring revised and shortened versions of 'old' oratorio libretti from the first half of the century that could be suitable for setting and performance at its own academies. In April 1786 the board commissioned Lorenzo da Ponte to revise and shorten eight old libretti, and when he failed to complete the

---

[29] The words for the chorus 'All'armi, all'armi!' in the recitative following No. 11 are marked with a mostly illegible note beginning 'Coro'.

[30] The flyleaf at the end of the libretto is covered in 'doodling' including a column of numbers and their total, similar to the mathematical calculations found on a number of Mozart's autographs.

task, the board hired da Ponte's rival Nunzio Porta, who managed to complete some.[31] Although the chronology of these revisions does not quite match the *Betulia* libretto and *Betulia* does not appear among the known list of titles revised by Porta, the TKS's interest in this kind of works shows that a similar intention probably lay behind the revisions to the libretto in Mozart's possession.[32]

Did Mozart ever set any of the revised *Betulia* to music? In the years following his acquisition of Mozart's musical 'estate', Johann André worked tenaciously to track down works that he did not yet possess. He came to believe that Mozart had indeed written two additional numbers for *La Betulia liberata*, and even wrote to Mendelssohn in Berlin enquiring unsuccessfully whether the Königliche Bibliothek might hold a copy of them.[33] If André were to be believed, Mozart had written an introductory chorus 'Qual fiero caso' and a quintet 'Te solo adoro' for a performance of the oratorio in Lent 1786. These details agree so well with the libretto once in André's possession that the libretto is probably the principal source for his belief in the 1786 revival and the two purported new numbers, although he seems to have overlooked the 'coro nuovo' against 'Pietà, se irato sei'.

One mystery, however, remains to be explained. Although the libretto indicates that there should be a new opening chorus, it does not give the text. Yet André believed that there had been an opening chorus beginning 'Qual fiero caso' – a phrase that appears nowhere in the libretto, suggesting that André had another source for his belief that Mozart had written new items in 1786. Although the sentiment of the phrase is generic, the source of the text may be the opening chorus of Giovanni de Gamerra's *Perseo*, 'compiled and curtailed' by Giovanni Gualberto Bottarelli and set by Sacchini for London in 1774.[34]

[31] Bernd Edelmann, 'Haydns *Il Ritorno di Tobia* und der Wandel des "Geschmacks" in Wien nach 1780', in Georg Feder (ed.), *Tradition und Rezeption: Bericht über die Jahrestagung der Gesellschaft für Musikforschung, Köln 1982* (Regensburg, 1985), pp. 184–214, at 196–97; Steblin, 'Beethoven Mentions', pp. 153–7.

[32] A setting of *La Betulia liberata* by the obscure Francesco Piticchio (fl. 1760–1800) dated 1786 survives in A-Wgm. Although Piticchio is said to have lived in Vienna from 1786 to 1791, and his setting also makes extensive cuts and changes to the original libretto, the text does not match the libretto owned by Mozart; see Elisabeth Birnbaum, *Das Juditbuch im Wien des 17. und 18. Jahrhunderts* (Frankfurt, 2009), pp. 224–5.

[33] André's notes on *La Betulia liberata* are found in his Mozart catalogue of 1833 (copy in GB-Lbl, Add. 32412); I am grateful to Neal Zaslaw for providing me with a copy of the relevant pages. For the Mendelssohn correspondence, see Helmut Loos and Wilhelm Seidel (eds.), *Felix Mendelssohn Bartholdy. Sämtliche Briefe* (Kassel, 2008–), vol. 8, pp. 260–1. See also Otto Jahn, *W. A. Mozart*, 4 vols. (Leipzig, 1856–9), vol. I, p. 328 n20.

[34] *Perseo: A Serious Opera. To be performed at the King's Theatre in the Haymarket* (London, 1774), pp. 4–5. For a partial edition of Sacchini's setting, see Ian Woodfield, *Opera and Drama in Eighteenth-Century London: The King's Theatre, Garrick and the Business of Performance* (Cambridge, 2001), pp. 62–5.

Qual fiero caso! Che strano evento!	Oh ill-omen'd day! What strange event is this!
Freddo spavento tremar ci fà.	A deadly terror has seized on our senses!
Vacilla il Tempio! Strepita il fulmine!	Behold the temple shakes! The thunder rolls!
Chi non sà piangere, chi non sà gemere,	Whoever is not now oppressed with grief;
Ha priva l'anima d'umanità!	Whoever does not lament and weep, has lost the tender feelings of humanity.

This text could conceivably be appropriate for the opening of *La Betulia liberata*, whose plot begins with the Assyrian army besieging the city of Bethulia. Although the TKS never mounted a complete production of a Sacchini opera, a number of Sacchini's choruses were heard at the Society's academies in the late eighteenth century, so the text was possibly available in Vienna. Perhaps the second of the two 'librettos to *Betulia liberata*' that Constanze sent André in 1800, and whose location is presently unknown, contained a direction that led André to believe Mozart had set this text. But whatever André may have surmised, it has long been recognized that the purported new numbers are unlikely to have ever existed: there is no reference to them in Mozart's own catalogue of his works, and no musical material extant in the composer's hand.

Whatever informal discussions the TKS had with Mozart, the earliest concrete evidence of its intention to request a new work from him is found in the minutes to the board meeting of 3 January 1785. On the matter of the academy for the coming Lent, the board resolved to schedule a chorus from Gassmann's opera *Amore e Psiche* (first performed in 1767) and the chorus 'Svanisce in un momento' from Haydn's *Il ritorno di Tobia*, the revised version of which had been performed by the TKS the previous year. Mozart and Righini were to be asked for unspecified choruses, arias and recitatives.[35] Those present at the meeting included Bonno, Salieri and Starzer, but as usual it is not known who in particular put forward the suggestion that Mozart and Righini should be asked to contribute. Presumably the general nature of the request, with no indication of the texts to be set or the required length of the music, was to allow for negotiations with the composers. Righini appears to have declined the TKS's request as no more is heard of his contribution, although he was soon invited again and ultimately contributed the large cantata *Il natale di Apollo* in 1789.

[35] '*Referenda.* 1. *Academie* Anstalten für die Fasten. *Conclusa.* Ist indessen von Seel: Gassmanns *Amore e Psiche* das beste samt einen Chor zu wahlen, wie auch der zweyte neue Chor das Hr: *Joseph Haydn* zu desselben *Oratorio*: ferner sind *Monsieur Mozart*, und *Signor Righini* wegen Verfertigung neuer Chör [sic], und allenfalls vorgehenden *Arien* mit Recitativen zu ersuchen: die Antwort hierüber ist bey nächster vorzunehmender *Session* zu überbringen, allwo das weitere beschlossen warden solle'; A 2/1 and B 2/1, 1/1785.

Mozart accepted, and judging from the detailed programme for the Lenten academies agreed on 11 February, he was to contribute a 'Psalm'.[36] This was probably not a Latin psalm as would be suitable for liturgical use but a work in Italian or German, in the same vein as Marianna Martines's Italian psalm settings.[37] Mozart was to direct the academies (apparently replacing Salieri), with Ignaz Umlauf at the piano.

Perhaps spurred on by a desire to demonstrate his financial responsibility to Leopold, who was about to arrive in Vienna, Mozart took the opportunity at this time to request membership of the TKS, which would have granted Constanze a modest pension on the death of her husband. As is well known, the request was ultimately unsuccessful, with the sticking point being Mozart's inability to produce his birth certificate. He tried again in August the same year, pointing out his services to the TKS and offering further contributions, but the Society continued its suspension of Mozart's application 'in part for the lack of the birth certificate, and further, until the Society's disputes are resolved'.[38] The 'disputes' were an ongoing saga initiated the previous year by the Society's secretary and *Rechnungs-Revisor* Joseph Scheidl, who had complained of irregularities in the TKS accounts; the matter eventually led to multiple petitions and appeals to the *Stadthauptmannschaft*.[39] Mozart could do nothing about this dispute, but neither is he known to have written to the parish of Salzburg Cathedral for an extract of his birth certificate. There the matter appears to have rested, and Constanze was eventually to obtain a declaration that her husband was never a member of the TKS in support of her case for a pension from the court.[40] All these requests are known only from the minutes of the Society, as no written correspondence from Mozart survives in the TKS archives.[41]

Mozart was busy with concert appearances and composition in the early months of 1785, to which was added the obligation of hosting his father and Leopold's student Heinrich Marchand. These conditions were not conducive to the creation of a new major choral work, and fewer than ten days after the TKS had agreed that Mozart should provide it with a 'Psalm', the composer

---

[36] NMD, pp. 34–5.

[37] See Irving Godt, *Marianna Martines: A Woman Composer in the Vienna of Mozart and Haydn*, ed. John Rice (Rochester, 2010), pp. 79–132.

[38] '*Referenda*. 13 (22) Herr Wolfgang Amadeus *Mozart* bittet um Aufnahme in die Societæt, weil er schon mehrmallen ersprießliche Dienste geleistet hat, und noch ferner zu leisten erbietig ist; der zur Aufnahme nothwendigen Taufschein wird er, so bald er ihn überkommet, nachtragen.

Conclusa. Wenn der Taufschein wird beygelegt seyn, folgt ferner Bescheid'; A 2/1 and B 2/1, 13 (22)/1785.

[39] The documents dealing with the dispute are in A 3/1, beginning in June 1784.

[40] MDL, p. 385; MDB, p. 439.

[41] An inventory of the TKS prepared in 1795 (in A 3/1, Inventarium Nr. 1, 20) includes an entry for 'Briefe an die Societät. 18 Stücke'. It is possible that correspondence from Mozart was found in these eighteen letters.

informed the Society that he could not finish it in time. Instead, Mozart offered another 'Psalm' that was 'completely new to Vienna' – what was to become *Davide penitente*.[42] The board accepted this proposal and agreed to a revised programme that now additionally featured at least one symphony by Haydn (Hob. I:80), the aria 'Come in sogno' as well as the abovementioned chorus from *Il ritorno di Tobias*, a 'Coro von Sacchini in E♭',[43] an aria sung by Stefano Mandini, and items by the visiting oboist Ludwig Le Brun and his wife, Francesca (née Danzi).[44] A concerto to be played on the second night by the mysterious 'Monsieur Schenker' was ultimately replaced by a violin concerto performed by Heinrich Marchand.[45]

With less than three weeks before the 'Psalm' was due for rehearsal, Mozart made the natural choice in pressing into service the C minor Mass K. 427 as the main source for the work.[46] Not only did the mass possess the minor-key grandeur that seems to have been expected at the TKS academies, but also large choral forces from the city's churches were available to accommodate the five-part and double choir scoring. The text, previously speculated to be the work of Lorenzo da Ponte, is in fact derived from *I libri poetici della Bibbia*, a popular collection of free translations from the psalms by the Neopolitan poet Saverio Mattei (1742–95). Irene Brandenburg, who established the correct attribution, speculates that Metastasio, Marianna Martines, Salieri or other figures with Italian contacts were responsible for popularizing Mattei's translations in Vienna and ultimately leading to their use in K. 469. It may well be that Mozart's original 'Psalm' was to have a text from this source. Mattei's original has been somewhat adapted to fit the music in *Davide*, and Brandenburg

---

[42] NMD, pp. 35–6.

[43] According to the 1839 catalogue of the TKS's music collection (B 1/11, f. 21v), the Society once owned a copy of 'Sachini / Choro ital.: / Nel oror lo spavento'. The chorus 'Nell'orror lo spavento la morte' is from Sacchini's opera *Montezuma*, first produced in London in 1775. Given that this chorus is in E flat major, it is a plausible candidate for the 'Coro von Sacchini in E♭'. Sacchini's choruses had appeared at TKS academies at least five times by 1806, and, as we have seen, the text of one may have been planned for Mozart's projected revision of *La Betulia liberata*.

[44] During their stay in Vienna, the Le Bruns probably performed the aria 'Der glänzende Himmel war finstere Wüste' from Holzbauer's *Günther von Schwarzburg*, and it is possible that this was the aria heard on 13 March 1785; see Edge, 'Mozart's Viennese Copyists', pp. 1216–19.

[45] Although Leopold mentions Heinrich's forthcoming appearance (MBA, vol. III, p. 379), he gives no indication of what Marchand was to perform, and there are no further details on the poster.

[46] On the history of the C minor Mass, see David Black, 'Mozart and the Practice of Sacred Music, 1781–91' (PhD thesis, Harvard University, 2007), pp. 84–126; Ulrich Konrad, 'Die *Missa in c* KV 427 (417a) von Wolfgang Amadé Mozart: Überlegungen zum Entstehungsanlass', *Kirchenmusikalisches Jahrbuch*, 92 (2009), pp. 105–19; Petrus Eder, 'Die Umstände der Uraufführung der Missa in ç-Moll KV 427 (417a)', in Lars E. Laubhold und Gerhard Walterskirchen (eds.), *Klang-Quellen: Festschrift für Ernst Hintermaier zum 65. Geburtstag* (Munich, 2010), pp. 200–8.

suggests that it could have been da Ponte or even Mozart himself who was responsible for the final shape of the text.[47]

The process of compiling the cantata presumably began with Arthofer and his associates making a score copy of the individual movements from the Kyrie and Gloria of K. 427 without words, allowing Mozart and perhaps even others to enter the new text. To these numbers were added copies of the two new arias for Johann Valentin Adamberger and Caterina Cavalieri (Nos. 6 and 8) and the undated cadenza for the soloists in the closing movement (No. 10). The production of the scores and new performance material would have been a tall order for any copyist in the time available, and involved not only Mozart's cantata but probably also the Haydn symphony and the Lebrun and Marchand concertos. It is not surprising therefore that Arthofer submitted another petition to the TKS after the academies, requesting an additional payment on top of the 93fl 55kr he had already received. The TKS agreed to his request, and Arthofer was granted an honorarium of a further two ducats (8fl 36kr) on 9 April.[48] Arthofer's petition survives, but unfortunately the half page containing the substantive portion has been torn out of the bifolio and the contents are known only in summary. The petition may have related to last-minute work on Cavalieri's aria 'Fra l'oscure ombre funeste', which Mozart only finished on the day before the second rehearsal in the Burgtheater. Neither the performing score nor any other original material for *Davide penitente* survives today, despite the allegations of the NMA and Carus editions.[49]

The box office takings for the premiere of *Davide penitente* were comparable with those for the successful academy of 22 December

[47] Irene Brandenburg, 'Neues zum Text von Mozarts Davide penitente KV 469', in Laubhold und Walterskirchen (eds.), *Klangquellen*, pp. 209–29. There is no surviving source from Mozart's lifetime that gives the name of the cantata as *Davide penitente*, but an early score probably copied from the lost TKS performing score confirms that the title was contemporary and the spelling is not *Davidde* (see note 50).

[48] The petition is in A 3/1, 46/1785. At its next meeting, the TKS considered the petition: '*Referenda*. 5.(14) Arthofer Joseph *Copist*, bittet wegen so vieler ausserordentlicher Bemühung und Gänge bey lezter Fasten Musik, wodurch er in seinem Arbeit sehr gehindert worden, um eine *Remuneration. Conclusa*. Werden ihme 2 *ordinar: Ducaten*, das ist 8fl 36xr für seine Bemühung zur Schadens Vergütung *accordirt*'; A 2/1 and B 2/1, 5 (14)/1785.

[49] The NMA's source B (Fulda, Hochschul- und Landesbibliothek, M 291), described by Monika Holl as a score 'die Mozart offenbar noch vor dem Konzert von einer Kopistenwerkstatt anfertigen ließ' (NMA, I/4/3, p. xv) was in fact produced around 1800, probably on the order of Constanze to remedy the absence of K. 469 in Mozart's 'estate'. The NMA's source C (A-Wn, Mus. Hs. 19903), again supposedly contemporaneous with the premiere, actually dates from 1800 or later; see Edge, 'Mozart's Viennese Copyists', pp. 536, 1093 and Black, 'Mozart and the Practice of Sacred Music', p. 120 n173. Holl was however undoubtedly correct in selecting the Fulda score as the principal non-autograph source, as it was probably copied from the now lost performing score of 1785. The source evaluations of the Carus edition (ed. Wolfgang Gersthofer, 2006) appear entirely derived from the NMA. The words 'Davide penitente' appear on the autograph of the piano concerto fragment K. Anh. 58 (Fr 1785g); the significance of this is unknown.

1783. As usual, the second academy saw a substantial drop, this time to the lowest total for any Mozart appearance at a TKS event. It would be unwise, however, to assume a direct relationship between the level of ticket sales and the reception of the cantata, as there were numerous other works on both programmes and the conversion of box office revenue to attendance is problematic.[50] Leopold presumably attended the academies, but unfortunately his letter to Nannerl that would have contained a report of the occasion is almost entirely lost.[51] The TKS still possessed a copy of *Davide penitente* in 1795, but this later disappeared and the Society did not revive the cantata until December 1860.[52]

Mozart was called upon again the same year for the Advent academies of 1785. At the meeting of 26 October, the board in the absence of Salieri decided that the main work would be a revival in shortened form of Dittersdorf's *Ester*, originally commissioned for the TKS in 1773. Mozart would be invited to perform a piano concerto at the second academy on 23 December.[53] According to Pohl, the concerto was to be 'new', and it has been traditionally identified as K. 482 on somewhat problematic grounds.[54] Interestingly, the accounts for this academy include a payment of 1fl for transporting a piano and a further 1fl for tuning a piano; perhaps this was Mozart's own instrument.[55] As usual for second academies, the box office receipts were rather low.

It was to be four years before Mozart's music was heard again at a TKS academy, but on 5 November 1789 the board scheduled Mozart's Clarinet Quintet K. 581 between the two parts of Righini's new cantata *Il natale di Apollo* for the first Advent academy on 22 December.[56] Although this is often said to be the occasion on which the Quintet had its premiere, the lead time

---

[50] Holl estimates an attendance of 660 at the first academy and 225 at the second (NMA, I/4/3, p. xiii) on the basis of four people per box. However, as noted above about these kinds of estimates, they do not take into account the potential for free admissions, standing room or possible subscribed boxes that were not recorded in the receipts.

[51] MBA, vol. III, p. 380.

[52] According to the inventory of music manuscripts held by the Society in 1795 and their copying costs (A 3/1, first quoted in Edge, 'Mozart's Viennese Copyists', p. 540), the Society possessed the 'Original' of *Davide penitente* (probably the conducting score), as well as a chorus and sinfonia (probably the Haydn symphony and one of the choruses from the Lent 1785 academies). It is not clear whether the TKS still possessed the parts for *Davide* at this stage; the surviving TKS parts for the cantata (A-Wn, Fonds 89 Haydn-

Verein 40) date from the nineteenth century and were used for the Society's performance in 1860.

[53] 'Bey der zweiten Production. Ist Herr Mozart zum *Concert* auf dem *fortepiano* einzuladen'; A 2/1, 38/1785. See also NMD, pp. 40–1.

[54] Pohl, *Denkschrift*, p. 61, apparently quoting a lost poster. On the identification of the piano concerto, see Edge, 'Manuscript Parts', p. 448 n9.

[55] '*fortepiano* tragen ... 1[fl]' and 'den *fortepiano* stimmen ... 1[fl]'; B5/15, Viertes Quartal, Extra Ausgaben. As often, there was also a payment of 1fl to transport a set of timpani.

[56] 'Concerten. Bey der ersten *Production*. Ein *Quintett* von Hr Mozart wobey Hr Stadler und Hr Zistler die Hauptstimmen aufführen werden'; A 2/1, 16/1789.

between the work's completion on 29 September 1789 and the Society's scheduling and performance of it suggests that it was not intended primarily for the TKS academy. The clarinettist was of course Anton Stadler, who unlike his brother Johann Nepomuk seems never to have joined the TKS, although he regularly appears in the lists of performers.[57] While the performance material for the Quintet is lost, the Society's conducting score of *Il natale di Apollo* unusually still survives. The score is in two volumes, and includes occasional corrections and continuo figuring in pencil, which might suggest it was used at the keyboard. It also features written out vocal cadenzas and ornamentation entered in pencil, giving a useful insight into contemporary performance practice. At least some of the annotations are in the hand of Salieri, who directed the performance. Although this was a first evening, the box office takings were relatively poor and halved again the second evening.

The final appearance of Mozart's music at the TKS academies during the composer's lifetime was agreed by the board on 1 April 1791, just two weeks before that year's Lenten academies. Both academies were to include 'Eine grosse Sinfonia von Hr Mozart' as the opening item, and extracts from Paisiello's *Fedra* with Mozart's bravura aria 'No, che non sei capace' K. 419 as an insertion.[58] The minutes in fact make no mention of Mozart's aria, and it may be that its presence was due to the suggestion of Aloysia Lange, who was the soloist at both the premiere of K. 419 in 1783 and this academy. A libretto of the extracts was printed for the performance, which is not known to have occurred for *Davide penitente* or any other TKS academy featuring Mozart's vocal music.[59]

As is well known, a contemporary manuscript score of the extracts from *Fedra* survives today in the Gesellschaft der Musikfreunde. This score includes both Mozart's aria and an otherwise unknown accompanied recitative preceding it, leading to speculation about whether Mozart was

[57] Johann Nepomuk Stadler was a member of the TKS from 1783 to 1798; Pohl, *Denkschrift*, p. 106. On the performer lists (in A 1/3), see Otto Biba, 'Beispiele fur die Besetzungsverhältnisse bei Aufführungen von Haydns Oratorien in Wien zwischen 1784 und 1808', *Haydn-Studien*, 4 (1976/80), pp. 94–104. Performer lists for the Mozart academies survive only for Lent 1781, Advent 1785 and Lent 1791.
[58] 'Academie Anstalten für die Fasten . . . 1. Eine grosse Sinfonia von Hr Mozart. 2. Ein auszug aus der Oper Phaedra. Von Hr Paisello [*sic*]'; A 2/1, 8/1791. On the background to the use of *Fedra* at these academies, see Walther Brauneis, 'Mozarts

Anstellung am kaiserlichen Hof in Wien. Fakten und Fragen', in Herbert Lachmayer (ed.), *Mozart: Experiment Aufklärung im Wien des ausgehenden 18. Jahrhunderts* (Ostfildern, 2006), pp. 559–71, at 568–9 and John Rice, 'The Operatic Culture at the Court of Emperor Leopold II and Its Connection to Mozart's La Clemenza di Tito', https://sites.google.com/site/johnaricecv/.
[59] *Diverse scene estratte dalla Fedra* (Vienna, 1791). The 1791 account book (B5/21, Erstes Quartal, Extra Ausgaben) has separate payments of 10fl 1kr and 22fl 30kr to the *Buchdrucker*; these payments were at least partially for the printing of posters, but it is possible that they were for the libretto as well.

responsible for the recitative as well.[60] Although the score lies outside the usual transmission of the TKS sources, it gives every impression of being the ultimate source for the performances.[61] Unfortunately, there seems no way to identify which of Mozart's symphonies were performed by the TKS, but all the symphonies written in Vienna are plausible candidates.[62] Unusually, the second academy had better box office receipts than the first, and the second evening's takings were comparable to the first evenings of Advent 1783 and Lent 1785. Mozart's own role in uncertain as he is not listed among the performers, but presumably he provided scores of the symphony and aria for copying and attended the academies.

With his six appearances in the academies of the Tonkünstler-Societät, Mozart made a sustained contribution to the concert life of the Society – more than one might expect for someone who was never a member of the TKS and apparently received no fee. It is not possible to tell whether Mozart's participation specifically improved the box office takings of each academy, as his contribution formed only one part of the evening's schedule. But it seems that a few of the academies were at least moderately successful, and in *Davide penitente* Mozart provided the TKS with an ambitious new work of equal stature to its previous major commissions. From the number of contemporary copies, prints and adaptations, it appears that *Davide penitente* enjoyed some popularity in the nineteenth century; presumably it filled the need for a religious but non-liturgical work by Mozart suitable for large choirs, which was otherwise satisfied only through the numerous contrafacta derived from the composer's masses and litanies.[63] Perhaps surprisingly, the TKS itself made little use of *Davide* and Mozart's other music after the composer's death,

[60] See Dexter Edge, 'Attributing Mozart. I: Three Accompanied Recitatives', *Cambridge Opera Journal*, 13 (2001), pp. 197–237, at 211–17.

[61] A-Wgm, IV 7751/Q 1812. The score includes added dynamic markings and tempo indications in *Rötel*, and changes to the parts of Aricia and Ippolito to accommodate the change of Ippolito's role from soprano castrato (as at the Naples premiere of *Fedra*) to tenor for the Viennese soloist Vincenzo Calvesi. As with many other manuscripts in A-Wgm, it is possible that the score derives from the estate of Salieri, who directed the performance. The 1795 TKS inventory lists '*Diverse Scene della Fedra del Sig. Paisiello* samt der Partitur del Sig. *Vogel*'; this may have been a conducting score copied from the Wgm source. The identity of the '*Partitur del Sig. Vogel*' is unclear.

[62] Landon seems to identify the symphony as the revised version of K. 550 on the basis of a supposed match between the work's scoring and the surviving personnel list for the academies (in A 1/3); H. C. Robbins Landon, *1791: Mozart's Last Year* (London, 1989), pp. 33–4. However, this overlooks the fact that the personnel list records the total attendance for all works on the programme, not specifically who performed in the Mozart symphony. Any of Mozart's symphonies could have been accommodated with the performers listed.

[63] Since the publication of the NMA critical report, a number of additional early scores of the cantata have come to light. These include A-Wn, Fonds 152 Zchetgruber 14 (allegedly c. 1800), and an early Viennese score offered by Ulrich Drüner in 2012 (Katalog 69, pp. 43–7).

but the Society's somewhat pedantic zeal in documenting its activities permits us a unique insight into the business of putting on a concert in eighteenth-century Vienna.[64] For Mozart, the motivation to take part was not only the opportunity to present his music before the public without the usual expenses, but perhaps also the ability to contribute to the altruistic objects of the Society in an environment where the financial stability of musicians' families was anything but certain.

[64] Later examples of Mozart's music in the TKS concerts include two piano concertos (30 March 1806 and 22 March 1807), a bass aria (1/2 April 1849), the revival of *Davide penitente* (22/23 December 1860), the piano concerto K. 466 and an aria from *Figaro* (9/10 April 1865), a piano concerto in C major (21/22 March 1869) and several performances of *Das Alexanderfest* and *Der Messias* in Mozart's arrangements.

Appendix: Known performances of Mozart's music at the Tonkünstler-Societät academies during the composer's lifetime

Theatre, Date[1]	Music[2]	Box office takings[3]	Total music copying costs[4]	Copying costs of choral works still held by the TKS in 1795	Copying costs for 'Konzerten und Arien'
Kth, Tues, 3.4.81 Rehearsals 27.3 (Rdt) 29.3 (Sw) 31.3 (KTh)	Mozart: symphony Albrechtsberger: *Die Pilgrime auf Golgatha* Mozart: piano solo	412fl 39kr (1.4: 663fl 45kr)	128fl 29kr	115fl 39kr (Albrechtsberger: *Die Pilgrime auf Golgatha*)	nil (but see p. 60)
Bth, Mon, 22.12.83 Rehearsal 19.12 (Rdt)	Haydn: symphony and chorus [from Hob. XXI:1] Sacchini: arias Mozart: piano concerto Kozeluch: symphony Mozart: rondo Sarti: trio Sacchini, Dittersdorf, [?Gassmann]: choruses [from *Ester* and *La Betulia liberata*]	540fl 7kr	50fl 10kr (incl. 'extra für seine [Arthofers] Bemühung')	3fl 37kr 2pf (items from Dittersdorf: *Ester* and Gassmann: *La Betulia liberata*)	24fl 15kr
Bth, Tues, 23.12.83	Haydn: symphony and chorus [from Hob. XXI:1] Sacchini: arias Violin concerto Kozeluch: symphony Mozart: rondo Sarti: trio Sacchini, Dittersdorf, [Gassmann]: choruses [from *Ester* and *La Betulia liberata*]	194fl 52kr	–	–	–

Appendix: (cont.)

Theatre, Date[1]	Music[2]	Box office takings[3]	Total music copying costs[4]	Copying costs of choral works still held by the TKS in 1795	Copying costs for 'Konzerten und Arien'
Bth, Sun, 13.3.85 Rehearsals 10.3 (Rdt) 12.3 (Bth)	Haydn: symphony [Hob. I:80] Arias Gassmann, Haydn: choruses Oboe concerto Mozart: *Davide penitente*	519fl 35kr	93fl 55kr, plus honorarium (8fl 36 kr)	26fl 10kr ('*Original* der *Cantate* von Herrn Mozart, nebst einem Kohr, und *Sinfonia*')	24fl 10kr
Bth, Tues, 15.3.85	Haydn: symphony [Hob. I:80] Arias Gassmann, Sacchini and Haydn: choruses Violin concerto Mozart: *Davide penitente*	168fl 44kr	–	–	–
Bth, Fri, 23.12.85 Rehearsal 20.12 (Rdt)	Dittersdorf: *Ester* Mozart: piano concerto	264fl 59kr (22.12: 508fl 4kr)	42fl 15kr	'fehlt alles'	11fl 35kr
Bth, Tues, 22.12.89	Righini: *Il natale di Apollo* Mozart: clarinet quintet [K. 581]	368fl 32kr (23.12: 163fl 25kr)	166fl 19kr	153fl 25kr (Righini: *Il natale di Apollo*)	6fl 15kr
Bth, Sat, 16.4.91 Rehearsal 14.4 (Rdt)	Paisiello: *Fedra* (excerpts), with Mozart aria [K. 419] Mozart: symphony Pleyel: cello concerto Albrechtsberger: chorus [Schröder H.1.15] Druschetsky: *Harmoniemusik* for 21 instruments	332fl 23kr	104fl 18kr	80fl 43kr (excerpts from Paisiello: *Fedra* 'samt der *Partitur* del Sigr. *Vogel*')	23fl 35kr

| Bth, Sun, 17.4.91 | Paisiello: *Fedra* (excerpts), with Mozart aria [K. 419] Mozart: symphony Dürand: violin concerto Albrechtsberger: chorus [Schröder H.1.15] Druschetsky: *Harmoniemusik* for 21 instruments | – | 524fl 40kr | – |

1 Bth = Burgtheater; Kth = Kärtnerthortheater; Rdt = Redoutensaal; Sw = Prince Schwarzenberg.
2 Only generic short titles are given and similar items are grouped together; secure identifications are given in brackets. The composer is not always identified in the sources.
3 The figures are from ticket sales only, and do not take into account donations by the imperial family and deductions for security (*Wache*). Where Mozart and his music were present on only one evening, the takings from the other evening are given in brackets for comparison.
4 Figures in this and the next two columns refer to the costs for both academies.

4   The hymn topic in Mozart's instrumental music

Stephen Rumph

'Ho i crini già grigi; ex cathedra parlo.' Don Alfonso's opening verses in *Così fan tutte*, which translate roughly as 'I'm old and grey and speak with divine authority', apply well to the conservative church style of Mozart's age. The venerable *stylus a cappella*, whose vestments trailed back into the sixteenth century, enjoyed unrivalled authority as musical emblem of ultramontane Catholicism and the Hapsburg dynasty. Beethoven confirmed the spiritual and temporal connotations of this style in an 1802 letter in which he declined a request for a 'revolutionary sonata':

> During the revolutionary fever, a thing of the kind might have been appropriate, but now, when everything is falling again into the beaten track, and Bonaparte has concluded a *Concordat* with the Pope—such a sonata as this? If it were a *missa pro Sancta Maria à tre voci*, or a *vesper*, etc., then I would at once take up my pen and write a *Credo in unum*, in gigantic semibreves.[1]

Such meanings did not trouble Mozart who drew liberally upon the old church style in his vocal and instrumental works. His lessons with Padre Martini stood him in good stead as he seasoned his works with *alla breve* fugues, fugatos, canons and passages in the Fuxian species.[2]

Don Alfonso embodies his claim musically in the Act 2 aria 'Tutti accusan le donne'. As the *éminence grise* delivers the moral 'Così fan tutte', unmistakable traces of the old church style emerge – *alla breve* rhythm, chordal texture, suspensions (see Example 4.1). The motto has already occurred twice in the overture, like an audible title page, framing the lightweight Allegro. Indeed, the Allegro itself contains a veiled statement of the title, quoting Don Basilio's teasing line 'Così fan tutte le belle' from the Act 1 trio of *Le nozze di Figaro*.[3] Don Alfonso's motto shares a closer affinity with

I am grateful to Simon P. Keefe and Danuta Mirka for their help and advice in the preparation of this chapter.

[1] Emily Anderson (ed.), *The Letters of Beethoven*, vol. I (New York, 1961), p. 73.

[2] See Warren Kirkendale, *Fugue and Fugato in Rococo and Classical Chamber Music*, trans. Margaret Bent and author (Durham, NC, 1979), pp. 152–81. For a general survey of Mozart's sacred works, see Karl Fellerer, *Die Kirchenmusik W. A. Mozarts* (Laaber, 1985); and David Black, 'Mozart and the Practice of Sacred Music, 1781–91' (PhD dissertation, Harvard University, 2007).

[3] See Bruce Alan Brown, *W. A. Mozart: Così fan tutte* (Cambridge, 1995), pp. 3–4.

Example 4.1 Mozart, 'Tutti accusan le donne', *Così fan tutte*, Act 2, bars 21–6.

Example 4.2 Mozart, Act 1 Trio 'Cosa sento', *Le nozze di Figaro*, bars 16–23.

Basilio's unctuous theme from earlier in the trio, another homophonic *alla breve* passage built over a bass line in descending thirds (see Example 4.2). Both operatic themes abstract the old church style from its accustomed place in musical life and play creatively with its cultural meanings. In short, both themes function as musical topics.

But what sort of topic is this? Leonard Ratner referred to the *alla breve* chordal writing exemplified by Alfonso's and Basilio's themes as the '*stile famigliare*', a sixteenth-century Italian term for note-against-note syllabic text-setting.[4] Ratner's term usefully distinguishes this Catholic style from the chorale harmonizations of the Lutheran tradition. An example of *alla breve* homophony occurs in Mozart's Mass in F, K. 192 (1774), composed long before he encountered Bach's vocal works and based upon a Gregorian melody (see Example 4.3). As Paul Laird noted, such passages were commonplace in the conservative church style:

> Homorhythmic textures had also been used for contrast by Renaissance composers as an antidote to continuous points of imitation, and eighteenth-century composers

[4] Leonard G. Ratner, *Classic Music: Expression, Form, and Style* (New York, 1980), p. 159.

Example 4.3 Mozart, Mass in F, K. 192, Credo, bars 1–2.

of Roman Catholic church music, with their hearts partly pledged to the *stile antico*, continued to use chordal passages in order to effect contrast.[5]

Another source of *alla breve* homophony lay in the Baroque polychoral tradition, which Mozart tapped in his twelve-voice canon 'V'amo di core', K. 348 (see Example 4.4). His late motet 'Ave verum corpus', for all its chromaticism, adheres to the same Catholic tradition.[6]

Eric McKee has located a particularly suggestive source of *alla breve* homophony in the priestly hymns and processions of French and Italian serious opera.[7] The Act 4 hymn from Gluck's *Iphigénie en Tauride*, 'Chaste fille de Latone', exemplifies this operatic convention (see Example 4.5). The characteristic features include *alla breve* metre, a primarily chordal texture, *piano* dynamics and suspensions. McKee has also identified a distinctive I–V[7]–vi progression as part of the prototype. In Gluck's hymn, this progression arises from the sequence of falling fourths in the bass, which generates a harmonic descent by thirds. The same I–V[7]–vi progression underlies Don Alfonso's motto, as well as Basilio's (with vii[7]/ vi substituting for V[7]); Basilio's theme also features the descending fourth sequence. Mozart's joined this operatic tradition with the procession of

[5] Paul Laird, 'Catholic Church Music in Italy, and the Spanish and Portuguese Empires', in Simon P. Keefe (ed.), *The Cambridge History of Eighteenth-Century Music* (Cambridge, 2009), p. 31.
[6] The two German hymns, K. 343 ('O Gotteslamm' and 'Als aus Ägypten') provide simpler examples of the *alla breve* homophonic style. For a survey of the *stylus a*

cappella during Mozart's formative years, see David Wyn Jones, 'Haydn's *Missa sunt bona mixta malis* and the A Cappella Tradition', in Jones (ed.), *Music in Eighteenth-Century Austria* (Cambridge, 1996), pp. 89–111.
[7] Eric McKee, 'The Topic of the Sacred Hymn in Beethoven's Instrumental Music', *College Music Symposium*, 47 (2007), pp. 23–52.

Example 4.4 Mozart, 'V'amo di core', K. 348, bars 1–3.

Example 4.5 Gluck, 'Chaste fille de Latone', *Iphigénie en Tauride*, bars 1–8.

the priests in Act 3 of *Idomeneo* and the march and chorus of the priests in Act 2 of *Die Zauberflöte*.

Similar passages occur sporadically throughout Mozart's instrumental music, most obviously in the opening theme of the Clarinet Quintet, K. 581. The Adagio in C major for Glass Harmonica, K. 356 provides a less familiar example (see Example 4.6). Adopting McKee's term with a nominalist grain of salt, we shall refer to such passages as tokens of a 'hymn' topic. While not every example resembles the operatic hymn, most reproduce its characteristic features. This chapter will trace the tokens of the hymn topic in Mozart's instrumental music (see Table 4.1), paying closest attention to the way in which its unusual texture interacts with the normative structures of late eighteenth-century style.

Table 4.1 Examples of the hymn topic in Mozart's instrumental works

Symphony in E flat, K. 16/i, bars 4–11, 15–22, 62–5, 73–80
Gallimathias musicum, K. 32/viii
Twenty Minuets, K. 103/xi, trio
Divertimento in E flat, K. 252/ii, trio, bars 1–8
Symphony in A, K. 201/i, bars 1–9, 107–16
Violin Sonata in E minor, K. 304/ii, trio
Piano Sonata in A, K. 331/i, theme
Adagio in C for Glass Harmonica, K. 356
Oboe Quartet in F, K. 370/i, bars 64–77
Horn Quintet, K. 407/i, bars 5–12, 77–84
Piano Concerto in B flat, K. 450/ii
Piano Concerto in B flat, K. 456/i, bars 54–60, 142–9, 299–306, 352–5
String Quartet in A, K. 464/iv, bars 62–3, 114–36, 206–13
Piano Quartet in G minor, K. 478/ii, bars 1–19, 75–93
String Quintet in G minor, K. 516/iii, bars 1–2, 38–9
Serenade in G (*Eine kleine Nachtmusik*), K. 525/i, bars 11–18, 86–93
Clarinet Quintet, K. 581/i, bars 9–15, 75–9
String Quintet in D, K. 593/i, bars 1–20, 233–51
Fantasy in F minor for Clock Organ, K. 608, Andante, bars 75–90

Example 4.6 Mozart, Adagio in C major for Glass Harmonica, K. 356, bars 1–8.

Topics and the limits of language

The term 'topic' has sown much confusion since Ratner popularized it in *Classic Music* (1980). Ratner applied the rhetorical term to the evocative styles and genres from which, as he demonstrated, late eighteenth-century composers mined their thematic material. His brilliant insight unveiled a wealth of semantic content lost in formalist accounts of Viennese classicism. Yet Ratner's 'topics' do not resemble the classical *topoi* (or *loci topici*) of Aristotle, Cicero and Quintilian, which were methods or strategies for deriving arguments.[8] He seems rather to have derived the term from Ernst Robert Curtius's monumental study *European Literature and the Latin Middle Ages* (*Europäische Literatur und lateinisches Mittelalter*, 1948).[9] Curtius's *topoi* were literary commonplaces, which he tracked across millennia of European literature. His sweeping narrative also inspired Raymond Monelle's masterful study of musical semantics, *The Musical Topic* (2006), which traces pastoral, military and hunting *topoi* from the Middle Ages to the late twentieth century.[10]

The rhetorical model, based on the metaphor of music as language, applies unevenly to musical topics. Topics do encode conventional meanings like a verbal lexicon; Wye Jamison Allanbrook could thus refer to 'an expressive vocabulary', while Monelle described the topic as 'a kind of musical term or word'.[11] Like words, topics also function as interchangeable paradigms within musical syntagms, whether periodic phrases or sonata rotations.[12] They also play an important role in musical narratives (characteristic symphonies, programmatic sonatas) and genres modelled on neoclassical rhetoric (serious opera arias, free fantasias).[13] In this sense, Ratner rightly referred to topics as 'subjects for musical discourse'.[14]

Yet the rhetorical model papers over the distinction between verbal and musical signs. Language uses symbols, in C. S. Peirce's sense, signs that represent their objects arbitrarily. The literary topic is thus defined by its signified, rather than its signifier. The *locus amoenus*, for instance, comprises a cluster of images and concepts – foliage, streams, Edenic purity – that poets could express in a limitless variety of words and languages.[15] Musical topics, however, are icons, signs that resemble their objects. A topic must imitate distinctive features of a musical style or genre, a constraint that limits the expressive means. The composer who wanted to imitate the pastoral style in a violin sonata had a mere handful of features with which to work – pedal

[8] See my *Mozart and Enlightenment Semiotics* (Berkeley, CA, 2011), pp. 78–84.
[9] Curtius, *Europäische Literatur und lateinisches Mittelalter* (Bern, 1948); translated by Willard R. Trask as *European Literature and the Latin Middle Ages* (Princeton, NJ, 1953). Wye Jamison Allanbrook, Ratner's student, has traced the derivation of his term to Curtius in *The Secular Commedia: Comis Mimesis in Late Eighteenth-Century Music*, ed. Mary Ann Smart and Richard Taruskin (Berkeley, CA, 2014), pp. 96–8.
[10] Monelle, *The Musical Topic: Hunt, Military and Pastoral* (Bloomington, IN, 2006).
[11] Wye Jamison Allanbrook, *Rhythmic Gesture in Mozart: 'Le nozze di Figaro' and*

'*Don Giovanni*' (Chicago, 1983), p. 2; Monelle, *The Musical Topic*, p. 3.
[12] See Kofi Agawu's structuralist analysis of topics in *Playing with Signs: A Semiotic Interpretation of Classic Music* (Princeton, NJ, 1991).
[13] See Melania Bucciarelli, *Italian Opera and European Theater, 1680–1720: Plots, Performers, Dramaturgies* (Turnhout, Belgium, 2000), pp. 1–31; and Elaine Sisman, 'After the Heroic Style: Fantasia and Beethoven's 'Characteristic' Sonatas of 1809', *Beethoven Forum*, 6 (1997), pp. 67–96.
[14] Ratner, *Classic Music*, p. 9.
[15] See Monelle, *The Musical Topic*, pp. 13–16.

points, compound or triple metre, triadic melody, simplified harmony. What topics lack in expressive means, however, they make up for in universality. Competent listeners across Europe could all identify the virile outdoor music imitated by Mozart's fourth 'Haydn' quartet, K. 458, although they might call it *Jagd, chasse, vadászat, lov*, or hunt.

The rhetorical model of topics thus transgresses the fundamental dichotomy of Enlightenment semiotics, the opposition between 'natural' and 'arbitrary' signs.[16] The Abbé Du Bos explained the distinction in his *Réflexions critiques sur la poésie et sur la peinture* (1719), the treatise that largely set the terms for eighteenth-century sign theory: 'Just as painting imitates the shapes and colours of nature, so the musician imitates the tones, accents, sighs, vocal inflections, indeed, all the sounds through which nature herself expresses the sentiments and passions … Words draw their meaning and value solely from human institution, and enjoy currency only within a particular country.'[17] Succeeding aesthetic theorists, including Rousseau, Noverre, Baumgarten, Lessing and Herder, all located music on the side of nature, alongside painting, sculpture and pantomime.[18] These imitative arts preserved a primitive sensibility that the growth of human language had dulled. As Thomas Reid wrote in his *Inquiry into the Human Mind on the Principle of Common Sense* (1764): 'Abolish the use of articulate sounds and writing among mankind for a century, and every man would be a painter, an actor, and an orator.'[19] Linguistic comparisons deny topics the signal virtue accorded music by Enlightenment aesthetics: the power to bypass the Babel of human tongues and communicate directly to the heart.

Curtius's longitudinal approach, finally, obscures the historicity of musical topics as a representational practice. It does not explain why composers began to abstract genres from their normal contexts, imitating sacred motets in string quartets or military fanfares in piano sonatas. Nor does it account for the stylistic fluidity of late eighteenth-century music, which moves indifferently between churchly, theatrical and popular styles, often with bewildering speed. This semiotic practice has little in common with music before the early modern period, but it continues unabated into

---

[16] See David Wellbery, *Lessing's 'Laocoon': Semiotics and Aesthetics in the Age of Reason* (Cambridge, 1984), pp. 24–30; and Victor Anthony Rudowski, 'The Theory of Signs in the Eighteenth Century', in Nancy Struever (ed.), *Language and the History of Thought* (Rochester, NY, 1995), pp. 83–90.

[17] Abbé Du Bos, *Réflexions critiques sur la poésie et sur la peinture* (7th edition, Paris, 1770; reprint Geneva and Paris, 1982), p. 124.

[18] For an exception that proves this rule, see Matthew Riley, 'Straying from Nature: The Labyrinthine Harmonic Theory of Diderot and Bemetzrieder's *Leçons de clavecin* (1771)', *Journal of Musicology*, 19/1 (2002), pp. 3–38.

[19] Thomas Reid, *An Inquiry into the Human Mind on the Principles of Common Sense*, ed. Derek R. Brookes (Edinburgh, 1997), p. 53.

the present. Wagnerian leitmotifs, Hollywood film cues and cellphone ring tones all rely upon a bank of stylistic and generic tags. Indeed, topical representation has paralleled the growth of modern political and economic liberalization, as composers have marketed French courtly dance in amateur keyboard suites or imported Kwela pennywhistles into pop songs. Topics allow musicians to extract repertories from their traditional enclaves, whether Versailles or a South African township, and commodify them as compact, malleable signs. Mozart's supple play with topics exemplifies that democratizing impulse that David Wellbery identified in Enlightenment theories of the literary sign: 'The desacralization of language is the extrication of language from its place within the ceremonies of religious and absolutist authority and its transformation into a medium of communication and debate among equal subjects.'[20]

Articulation, figurae and tropes

We can explore the similarities between topics and language, while still respecting the distinction between the two sign systems, if we pay closer attention to articulation. In linguistics, articulation refers to the way in which the phonological level structures sound to produce meaningful units. Topics also consist of shared features that combine to form signs. Topic theory has largely neglected articulation, focusing instead on semantics and formal disposition. A study of how topics are produced can enhance both areas of research, helping explain both the motivation of topical icons and the way they interact with fundamental structures of metre, harmony, texture and form.

Linguistic articulation occurs at two levels, a division known as 'dual patterning' or, in André Martinet's expression, 'double articulation'.[21] The first articulation consists of meaningful units, or morphemes and words. The second articulation comprises the meaningless elements that make up morphemes, that is, phonemes, distinctive features and prosody. Analyses of topics rarely venture beyond the first articulation. Standard accounts list the family of stylistic features that identify each topic; an inventory of the hymn topic would thus include chordal texture, *alla breve* rhythm, suspensions and the I–V^7–vi progression. All these features, however, belong to the genre or style imitated by the topical icon. They are meaningful units, like the curves of a human torso sculpted in marble or the gestures of grief pantomimed by a dancer. The double upbeat of gavotte, the syncopated rhythm of *stile antico*

---

[20] Wellbery, *Lessing's 'Laocoon'*, p. 36.

[21] See André Martinet, *Éléments de linguistique générale* (Paris, 1963), pp. 17–19.

suspensions, the circling melody of the *ranz des vaches* or the thrusting ascent of the Mannheim rocket are all meaningful units, the equivalent of morphemes.

To reach the second articulation, we must identify those meaningless structural features shared by multiple topics. For instance, both the double upbeat of gavotte and the syncopated rhythm of fourth-species arise from displacement, the shift of rhythmic grouping within the notated metre. The same structural feature accounts for the syncopation of *alla zoppa* and the offbeat accents of mazurka and polonaise. Similarly, both the circling *ranz des vaches* and ascending Mannheim rocket share the structural feature of arpeggiated melody restricted to the notes of the tonic triad, as do fanfare, pastorale and many *Teutsche*. Displacement and arpeggiation of the tonic triad do not signify any particular topic and they can be analysed as purely structural features. Yet they also generate features that identify multiple topics.

In order to avoid inexact comparisons with language, we shall call these features topical 'figurae', Louis Hjelmslev's term for all the non-signifying elements of language.[22] Figurae occur in other sign systems as well: the dot and dash of Morse code, the colours of national flags and the 0 and 1 of computer code are all meaningless elements that articulate meaningful units. Topical figurae will be indicated by slashes, the notation for the phoneme; hence, /displacement/ and /arpeggio/.[23]

The most important figura of the hymn topic is /homorhythm/. This figura comprises octave and chordal textures and helps articulate fanfare, *opera buffa, ombra*, march, hymn and fantasia, as well as rustic dances. While /homorhythm/ may seem overly capacious, its textures are functionally interchangeable within late eighteenth-century syntax. Octaves and chords play the same annunciatory role in opening gestures and they alternate freely in cadential passages. Octave and chordal textures function as a single paradigmatic class because both depart from the homophonic norm of late eighteenth-century style with its clear separation of melody and accompaniment. The topics articulated by /homorhythm/, including hymn, share not only a common feature but also a deeper structural relation to the style in which they appear.

---

[22] See Louis Hjelmslev, *Prolegomena to a Theory of Language*, trans. Francis J. Whitfield (Madison, WI, 1961), pp. 45–7.
[23] A fuller discussion can be found in my 'Topical Figurae: The Double Articulation of Topics', in Danuta Mirka (ed.), *Oxford Handbook of Topic Theory* (New York and Oxford, 2014), pp. 493–513. For a more

sceptical view of double articulation in music, see Marshall Brown, 'Origins of Modernism: Musical Structures and Narrative Forms', in Steven Paul Scher (ed.), *Music and Text: Critical Inquiries* (Cambridge, 1992), pp. 75–92; and Nicholas Meeùs, 'Musical Articulation', *Music Analysis*, 21/2 (2002), pp. 161–75.

Example 4.7 Mozart, *Eine kleine Nachtmusik*, 1st movement, bars 1–27.

The opening theme of *Eine kleine Nachtmusik*, K. 525 demonstrates the functional equivalence of two /homorhythm/ topics (see Example 4.7). The theme begins with a fanfare topic in octaves (bars 1–4), followed by a singing allegro (bars 5–10). The motoric quaver and semiquaver accompaniment lends the lyrical theme in bars 5–10 a sense of propulsion, as if the circling

Example 4.7 (cont.)

melody were hastening towards a goal. After six bars, however, a caesura checks the rhythmic energy and an *alla breve* theme prolongs the arrival of the cadence (bars 11–17). The lightly ornamented chordal texture, I–V⁷–vi progression (elaborated with an upper-neighbour motion) and touch of imitation identify the passage as a token of the hymn topic. The bustling accompaniment returns in bar 12, however, and fuels the drive to the medial caesura.

The octave fanfare and chordal hymn both act as foils to the propulsive singing-allegro theme. The fanfare with its gaping rests builds anticipation for a continuous theme, while the hymn with its measured chords dams the energy of the accompaniment. Both /homorhythm/ topics suppress the stratified texture that lends the symphonic style its rhythmic continuity and sense of forward motion. Semantically, fanfare and hymn belong to opposing categories – secular/sacred, bellicose/peaceful, outdoor/indoor,

Example 4.8 Mozart, Act 2 Quartet 'Ach Belmonte!', *Die Entführung aus dem Serail*, bars 193–6.

instrumental/vocal. Syntactically, however, they share an equivalent function. The /homorhythm/ figura helps explain the structural logic underlying the apparently random sequence of surface signs.

Because the hymn topic is articulated primarily through texture, it can join forces with all topics based upon rhythm and metre, that is, marches and dances. The hymn thus lends itself easily to 'troping', in Robert Hatten's sense, in which new meanings emerge from the strategic combination of disparate styles or genres.[24] The ceremonial *entrée* (*Aufzug*) can be heard as a trope of march with hymn; indeed, Heinrich Christoph Koch cited the march of the priests from *Die Zauberflöte*, which infuses the *alla breve* hymn with dotted rhythms foreign to sacred music.[25] Similarly, Don Alfonso's motto yokes the sacred genre to the festive accents and scoring of the ceremonial march. The chordal texture of hymn also accommodates the siciliano topic, as in the Act 2 quartet of *Die Entführung aus dem Serail*. The A major Andantino imitates the pastoral dance with its 6/8 metre and *sautillon* rhythm, while the four-part chordal texture and suspensions evoke the sacred genre (see Example 4.8). We can perhaps recognize a similar hymn-like texture in the famous siciliano theme of the Piano Sonata in A major, K. 331. The Andante of the Serenade in C minor, K. 388 provides a clearer example, with its suspensions and I–V^7–vi progression (see Example 4.9). The march-hymn trope of the exalted *entrée* evokes a divinely sanctioned authority. The siciliano-hymn, by contrast, suggests the quiet devotion of natural religion.[26]

Hymn can also be troped with sarabande, as in the Andante of the Piano Concerto in B flat, K. 450 (see Example 4.10). The moderate triple metre and accented second beat summon the courtly dance, while the strict four-part

[24] See Robert S. Hatten, *Interpreting Musical Gestures, Topics, and Tropes: Mozart, Beethoven, Schubert* (Bloomington, IN, 2004), pp. 68–89.
[25] Heinrich Christoph Koch, *Musikalisches Lexikon* (Frankfurt am Main, 1802; reprint Hildesheim, 1964), p. 178. Quoted in Andrew

Haringer, 'Hunt, Military, and Pastoral Topics' in Mirka (ed.), *Oxford Handbook of Topic Theory*, pp. 202–3.
[26] Mozart put this trope to comic use in the satiric hymn 'Eitelkeit!' from the *Gallamathius musicus*, K. 32.

Example 4.9 Mozart, Wind Serenade in C minor, K. 388, 2nd movement, bars 1–8.

Example 4.10 Mozart, Piano Concerto in B flat, K. 450, 2nd movement, bars 1–8.

writing and opening I–V^7–vi progression invoke the church genre.[27] The finale of Beethoven's Piano Sonata in E major, Op. 109 and the opening song of Schumann's *Frauenliebe und -leben* ('Seit ich ihn gesehen') provide nineteenth-century examples of the same trope. The hymn lends the stately Baroque dance an inner spiritual focus, suggesting both nobility and devotion. Appropriately, Wagner used the sarabande-hymn trope for the Valhalla motive in *Der Ring des Nibelungen*, where it represents both the sacred court of the gods and Wotan's entranced reverie.

Markedness and assimilation

The topical *figurae* proposed above all depart from stylistic norms of late eighteenth-century music. They exemplify 'markedness', a linguistic term

[27] See also the primary theme of the Andante from the Piano Quartet in G minor, K. 478. Ferrando's aria 'Un'aura amorosa' from *Così* *fan tutte* provides another example of a sarabande in 3/8, rather than the normative 3/4.

Hatten has applied fruitfully to music semiotics.[28] Markedness refers to an asymmetry within a linguistic opposition in which the marked term occurs less frequently and with greater specificity and salience than its unmarked opposite. Phonological examples include consonant voicing, nasality and vowel rounding. Grammatical tenses provide a semantic example: the unmarked present tense can refer to either present or past (as in the historical present), while marked past tense refers only to past events. Asymmetrical oppositions in late eighteenth-century style include major/minor (mode), string/wind (timbre), and tonic/non-tonic (key areas).

Topical articulation exhibits the same asymmetry. While unmarked duple metre can accommodate both marches and dances, marked triple metre hosts only dances. The ends of the metrical spectrum are similarly marked, as Allanbrook has shown.[29] While the intermediate metres (2/4, 3/4 or 4/4) accommodate a wide variety of topics, 2/2, at one end, and 3/8, 6/8, 9/8 and 12/8, at the other, correlate overwhelmingly with ecclesiastical and pastoral topics. Marked features heighten the salience of a topic: while listeners might confuse a march with a bourrée or a minuet with a passepied, they will easily recognize the displaced rhythms of gavotte and sarabande. Topical figurae thus preserve an etymological connection with rhetorical figures as expressive departures from normal stylistic usage.

Markedness depends, of course, on context. /Arpeggio/ is unmarked in the music of Swiss farmers or military trumpeters; transplanted into art music, in which conjunct motion predominates, the same figura becomes marked. /Homorhythm/ is unmarked in the *stylus a cappella* or military marches but marked in the homophonic late eighteenth-century style. Topics obviously share unmarked features (metrical definition for marches and minuets, major mode for fanfares and *ranz des vaches*), yet these features lack salience and serve little purpose in distinguishing topics. Indeed, those topics with few marked features tend to fade into the stylistic background; while marches, minuets and contredanses can function as topics, they also serve as default settings for entire movements.

Marked features tend to cluster together in certain contexts, a process known as 'markedness assimilation'. In phonology, assimilation occurs when a phoneme adopts the marked feature of a neighboring phoneme. For example, the final sibilant of *cats* is the unvoiced /s/; in *dogs*, however, the sibilant assimilates to the voiced /g/, becoming /z/. In markedness assimilation, marked terms from different categories occur together. For example, the marked past tense assimilates to the marked subjunctive mood

---

[28] See Hatten, *Musical Meaning in Beethoven: Markedness, Correlation, and Interpretation* (Bloomington, IN, 1994).

[29] See Allanbrook's metrical chart of topics in *Rhythmic Gesture in Mozart*, p. 23.

Example 4.11 Mozart, Serenade in E flat, K. 252, Trio, bars 1–8.

(*If only they were home!* or *We wish we could come*). Edwin Battistella has adduced the language of official utterances (*in witness thereof, by the power invested in me*), in which diction (formal) and speech act (illocutionary) assimilate to the marked context (ceremony).[30]

Late eighteenth-century music offers many examples of markedness assimilation. The slow movement of a sonata cycle is marked not only for tempo, but also key (non-tonic), dynamics (soft) and style (lyrical). Works in minor keys are frequently marked rhythmically (syncopation, offbeat accents), harmonically (chromaticism, Neapolitan and diminished-seventh chords), and dynamically (abrupt contrasts, *sforzandi*). The hymn topic is also marked across different structural categories, including texture (chordal), dynamics (soft), rhythm (*alla breve*) and often voicing (close). Markedness assimilation sharpens contrasts and reinforces the expression of a single affect.

This principle explains the occasional appearance of chordal textures in minuet trios (Beethoven's First Symphony provides a familiar example). As a marked formal position, trio attracts marked features to heighten contrast with the unmarked minuet. These can include soft dynamics, reduced scoring, concertante texture and mode shifts. /Homorhythm/ can also assimilate to the marked context, as in the trio from Mozart's Serenade in E flat, K. 252 (see Example 4.11). The fauxbourdon chords contrast with the lively homophonic texture of the minuet, although they do not suggest a clear topic. When combined with suspensions, however, as in the trio of the Sonata for Keyboard and Violin in E minor, K. 304, the chordal texture strongly suggests the hymn topic (see Example 4.12). In both trios, the

---

[30] Edwin L. Battistella, *The Logic of Markedness*
(Oxford and New York, 1996), p. 9.

Example 4.12 Mozart, Sonata for Keyboard and Violin in E minor,
K. 304, 2nd movement, bars 93–100.

textural shift enhances the expressive design of the form, heightening the contrast between the interior space of the trio and the more public world of the minuet. The E major hymn topic of K. 304 fleshes out this expressive design topically, suggesting a spiritual retreat amidst the troubled minuet with its *lamento* bass.

Markedness assimilation also spans the two articulations. Octave and chordal textures typically call attention to important events in the musical syntax. These 'stop-look-and-listen' textures, as Janet Levy called them, announce beginnings or confirm endings in the tonal and formal structure.[31] They function as 'introversive signs', in Kofi Agawu's terminology, indices that point to events in the musical syntax.[32] Yet the same indexicality also motivates their use in topics or 'extroversive' signs. Hymns turn the faithful inwards to spiritual devotion; fanfares call soldiers to attention; the eerie octaves of the *ombra* awaken a sense of foreboding. /Homorhythm/ functions both introversively and extroversively, as both formal signpost and topical *figura*.

Markedness thus reinforces the correlation of signifier and signified. The displaced rhythms of gavotte and accents of mazurka and polonaise correspond to their marked status as feminized or nationalist dances. The homorhythmic texture of the hymn corresponds to the marked status of the spiritual realm in Enlightenment culture. Markedness assimilation thus creates an analogical relationship between the structure of both sign and object. Using S and O for sign and object, and primes to indicate markedness, we may diagram this analogue as S':S::O'O. The relationship is iconic, resting upon resemblance between the form and content of the topic. It thus transcends one-to-one mapping and reinforces merely habitual associations between topics and cultural meanings.

The finale of Mozart's String Quartet in A, K. 464 provides a case study of markedness assimilation in the hymn topic. The hymn arrives midway

---

[31] See Janet Levy, 'Texture as a Sign in Classic and Early Romantic Music', *Journal of the* *American Musicological Society*, 35/3 (1982), p. 531.

[32] See Agawu, *Playing with Signs*, pp. 26–79.

Example 4.13 Mozart, String Quartet in A, K. 464, 4th movement, bars 112–35.

through the development, after the turbulent core has reached a half cadence in F sharp minor (see Example 4.13). Following this dramatic caesura, a deceptive cadence derails the conventional move to the relative major, unveiling a periodic theme in D major. The marked tonal progression attracts a host of marked features – *alla breve* rhythm, homophonic texture, *piano* dynamic and low register. The subdominant key, a harmonic centre normally reserved for the recapitulation, is also marked in this formal

Example 4.14 Mozart, String Quartet in A, K. 464, 4th movement, bars 204–13.

context. The cluster of marked features creates an effect of maximal contrast within the development.

The arrival of the hymn topic is particularly striking in the K. 464 finale, one of Mozart's most motivically relentless movements. The monothematic sonata form doggedly develops a four-note chromatic head motive, which undergoes imitation, inversion and both harmonic and schematic reinterpretation. A pervasive syncopated motive heightens the sense of headlong drive, as does the throbbing *Trommelbass* in the secondary and closing sections. The hymn topic through its sheer Otherness opens a portal onto a world beyond the frantic course of the Allegro.

Yet despite its right-angled contrast with the surrounding movement, the D major hymn recalls elements from earlier in the Allegro. The development begins with an equivalent deceptive cadence to G major, following a half cadence in B minor (bars 83–5). The hymn topic itself already surfaces at the end of the secondary area, where four *alla breve* chords beginning with a V^7–vi progression prolong the arrival of the cadence (bars 62–3). The recapitulation expands this passage to eight bars, dropping the chordal passage into the same low register as the development hymn (see Example 4.14). Moreover, the *alla breve* chords are introduced by a leisurely cadenza in running quavers that anticipates the second violin's countersubject in the development. Finally, the D

Example 4.15a Mozart, String Quartet in A, K. 464, 4th movement, bars 1–7.

Example 4.15b Mozart, String Quartet in A, K. 464, 4th movement, bars 40–5.

Example 4.15c Mozart, String Quartet in A, K. 464, 4th movement, bars 95–100.

major hymn echoes the head motive of the Allegro, retracing the chromatic descent from $\hat{5}$ to $\hat{3}$ (bars 118–19). The consequent phrase extends the chromatic line, descending from $\hat{6}$ to $\hat{3}$ (bars 129–34).

Yet the hymn transforms the head motive, stabilizing the restless chromatic motive. The primary theme of the Allegro embeds the motive within Robert Gjerdingen's Sol–Fa–Mi schema, where it triggers a move to F#, V/ii (see Example 4.15a).[33] The secondary theme recalls the motive

[33] See Robert O. Gjerdingen, *Music in the Galant Style* (New York and Oxford, 2007), pp. 258–60.

untransposed above a tonic pedal with the $\hat{5}$–#$\hat{4}$–$\hat{4}$–$\hat{3}$ line reinterpreted as $\hat{1}$–$\hat{7}$–$\flat\hat{7}$–$\hat{6}$. It now functions within Gjerdingen's Quiescenza schema (see Example 4.15b).[34] The first half of the development combines both versions (see Example 4.15c). The $\hat{1}$–$\hat{7}$–$\flat\hat{7}$–$\hat{6}$ line from the secondary theme passes into the bass, yet it begins with the I–V/ii progression from the primary theme. No longer confined within the periodic Sol–Fa–Mi, the applied dominant sparks a rising stepwise modulation from G major to C sharp major. The D major hymn anchors the restless motive. Mozart has harmonized each chromatic tone in the antecedent phrase with an applied dominant, creating a decisive progression to the half cadence (bars 118–19). The consequent phrase grounds the chromatic line even more firmly within a circle-of-fifths progression leading to a perfect authentic cadence in D major (bars 130–4). The soothing power of the hymn extends beyond rhythm and texture to the tonal structure itself.

This analysis of markedness structure and tonal function has laid solid foundations for a semantic interpretation of the hymn topic in K. 464. Meaning emerges through difference, and each token of a topic must be understood within its particular web of oppositions. In *Così fan tutte*, the solemnity of Alfonso's motive contrasts with the elegant frivolity of the surrounding music; in the Sonata for Keyboard and Violin in E minor, the beatific calm of the trio contrasts with the human pathos of the minuet. In the finale of the Quartet in A, the hymn topic provides a relief from the ineluctable drive of the Allegro. It suggests a numinous intervention, a *deus ex machina* that unknots the tangled plot. The formal position of the D major hymn enhances this dramatic role. It occurs midway through a development rotation, following the equivalent of a medial caesura. At this point in the exposition, the chromatic motive from the primary theme had returned over a *Trommelbass*, denying any respite to the manic Allegro. The development hymn breaks the cycle of repetition, interrupting the frantic pace and enfolding the motive in its serene embrace. In K. 464, we might say the hymn topic opens a keyhole onto the spiritual realm, revealing a pathway beyond human striving and intellect.

Neutralization

While markedness assimilation helps illuminate the formation of semantic structures, it does not explain the most original aspect of late eighteenth-century music, the systematic reconciliation of opposites. Assimilation accounts for the expressive redundancy of opera seria arias, in which topic,

---

[34] *Ibid.*, pp. 181–95.

figure, mode and tempo conspire to project a single unambiguous affect. In the newer style of Mozart's generation, however, meaning emerges more often from the juxtaposition of contrasting signs within the periodic phrase, theme group or sonata rotation. This new signifying practice is especially evident in Mozart's music, with its quicksilver play of topics and impertinent combination of opposing styles and genres.

'Neutralization', another concept borrowed from linguistics, can lend insight into the characteristically dialectical processes of late eighteenth-century music. Neutralization removes a markedness opposition in a particular context by suppressing the marked feature. For instance, word-final position in German neutralizes consonantal voicing. The opposition of /d/ and /t/ disappears in the words *Rad* (wheel) and *Rat* (advice, council), leaving only the unvoiced /t/. Likewise, the English opposition between lax and tense vowels (*lid, lead*) is neutralized in word-final position, leaving only tense vowels (*highly, glee*). Neutralization tends to push meaning to a more general level by removing contrast. Thus, the neutralization in French nasals that produces Jacques Derrida's famous homophones *différence* and *différance* calls attention to the wider opposition between speech and writing, *parole* and *écriture*.

The music of Mozart's age offers many examples of neutralization. The sonata recapitulation neutralizes the opposition of key areas, leaving only the unmarked tonic. The Picardy third, which can be expanded to a coda or even an entire movement (as in the finales of the String Quintet in G minor, K. 516 and the Piano Quartet in G minor, K. 478, or the final chorus of *Don Giovanni*), suppresses the marked minor mode. The sonata-form transition in symphonies and concertos provides another neutralizing context. Primary themes that begin with an anacrusis can create hypermetrical ambiguities, as in the Symphony in G minor, K. 550 or Haydn's 'Surprise' Symphony. The elision that typically initiates the symphonic transition precludes an anacrusis, neutralizing the marked feature.

In the case of /homorhythm/, any homophonic or polyphonic texture neutralizes the marked *figura*. Because octave and chordal textures normally punctuate the form as introductions, interruptions, or post-cadential material, we might say that the flow of the musical discourse itself neutralizes /homorhythm/. In *Eine kleine Nachtmusik*, as we saw, the stratified texture of the singing allegro neutralizes both the octave fanfare and the chordal hymn. Singing allegro belongs to the topics articulated by /augmentation/, a texture in which the melody moves in markedly slower values than the accompaniment. Its other topics include trio sonata and *stylus mixtus*, the blend of ancient and modern church styles. Vocal examples of /augmentation/ include the 'antichissima canzon' that concludes *Don Giovanni* ('Questo è il fin di chi fa mal') and the soprano solo 'Te decet hymnus' in the

Example 4.16 Mozart, Symphony in E flat, K. 16, 1st movement, bars 1–11.

Introitus of the Requiem. Mozart's novice Symphony in E flat, K. 16 provides an instrumental example (see Example 4.16). The opening period juxtaposes two /homorhythm/ topics: fanfare and *stile antico* homophony. The combination of the *alla breve* motive with its crochet accompaniment, however, neutralizes the homorhythmic texture, drawing the *stile antico* into the dynamic flow of late eighteenth-century style.

The role of neutralization in developing the syntactic and semantic implications of the hymn appears most clearly in the Clarinet Quintet, Mozart's most prominent use of this topic in his instrumental music. The quintet begins with an opposition between two structurally marked textures (see Example 4.17). The strings propose an *alla breve* hymn in strict four-part chordal texture, beginning with the characteristic I–[I⁶]–V⁷–vi progression. The clarinet, however, enters with a brilliant semiquaver flourish over a string pedal point. The clarinet's little cadenza exemplifies the figura /diminution/, the opposite of /augmentation/, in which the melody moves at an unusually rapid rate with respect to the accompaniment. Indeed, the

Example 4.17 Mozart, Clarinet Quintet in A, K. 581, 1st movement, bars 1–30.

clarinet's semiquavers stand in a 16:1 ratio with the strings' semibreve pedal. /Diminution/ articulates both the passagework of the brilliant style and the species counterpoint of the *stile antico*, as well as more vigorous strains of the contredanse. The combination of /homorhythm/ and /diminution/ figurae lend the opening period a discontinuous, fragmentary effect. The *alla breve* hymn and flamboyant cadenza also create a stark contrast between the string ensemble and solo clarinet.

Example 4.17 (cont.)

The process of neutralization begins in bars 5–6 as the first violin asserts its leadership. The lower instruments recede into an accompanying role, dissolving the chordal texture into unmarked homophony. This shift in texture leads smoothly into the clarinet's solo cadenza. The rhythmic values also unfold logically, progressing from minims (bars 1–2) to crotchets (bar 3) to quavers (bar 6) to semiquavers (bar 8). Moreover, this steady diminution of the rhythmic values clears up the metrical ambiguity of the opening bars. The *alla breve* rhythm of the opening

Example 4.18 Mozart, Clarinet Quintet in A, K. 581, 1st movement, bars 75–9.

four bars could suggest a slow introduction or andante; the rhythmic diminution and shift to homophony clarify the underlying allegro. Yet the theme has merely swerved from one marked texture to another, lurching from ponderous homorhythm to exaggerated 16:1 diminution. The consequent phrase abruptly restores the *alla breve* hymn in bar 9, as the playful clarinet collides with the impassive *stile antico*.

It falls to the transition to synthesize the opposing textures and topics. After the violins echo the semiquaver cadenza in bars 17–18, the clarinet introduces a flowing theme in quavers above descending minims in the violins. The /diminution/ figura also generates this new texture, but the strings and clarinet now move in the 4:1 ratio of Fux's third species. The repetition of the theme in bars 26–30 inverts the counterpoint, assigning the clarinet's melody to the cello. The transition thus neutralizes the *alla breve* hymn, nesting its homorhythmic minims within a contrapuntal texture. It also restores balance to the rhythmic texture, finding a happy medium between the note-to-note hymn and the clarinet's brilliant cadenza. The end of the closing section recalls this synthesis. As the strings reprise their opening hymn, the clarinet enters with its semiquaver cadenza, but now within a balanced contrapuntal texture (see Example 4.18).

The transition does more than simply neutralize marked features in the musical structure. The opening of the Clarinet Quintet also demonstrates the value of topical figurae in semantic analysis. The shift from the primary theme to the transition pivots around the /diminution/ figura, which articulates both the clarinet's cadenza and the following third-species theme. The opening page thus unearths the common ancestor of brilliant style and Fuxian counterpoint, the principle of rhythmic diminution. The progression of topics, we might say, performs a genealogical exploration of late eighteenth-century music, discovering a buried link between the archaic hymn and the modern virtuosic manner. Mozart's method runs counter to the rhetorical model of early eighteenth-century music, in which musical signs are chosen to express a predetermined affect, established at the beginning of the work. The Clarinet Quintet simulates a process of analytical discovery, in the spirit of Born or Lavoisier, as the sequence of topics brings to light hidden relationships within the composer's inherited style. But that level of meaning only appears when we dip below the lexical level and attend more closely to the way these signs are articulated within the musical structure.

Speaking *Ex Cathedra*

The hymn topic plays a further role in the Clarinet Quintet by reconciling opposing genres. As a concertante ensemble, the quintet straddles concerto and string quartet, mixing the public realm of the virtuoso with the more reserved world of the string quartet. Mozart's primary theme encapsulates this duality, pitting the intimate hymn against the flamboyant cadenza of the wind soloist. The opening period opposes not only instrument groups but also generic types. In the transition, the strings draw the clarinet into their *alla breve* orbit, integrating the soloist into the ensemble. The cultural authority of the *stile antico* hymn elevates the lighter concertante genre, even as its collective texture draws together the disparate forces.

The hymn topic does the same generic work in the Horn Quintet, K. 407, another combination of solo wind and strings. The quintet begins with a familiar gambit, juxtaposing a 'hammerblow' motive against a daintier idea (see Example 4.19). As the sentence continues in bars 5–12, the horn emerges as soloist. This new thematic idea has all the features of the hymn topic – *alla breve* chordal texture, the I–V^7–vi progression and sequential falling fourths in the bass line. The horn enters reverently on the second half of the bar, joining the strings' hushed choir; even the brief flourish at the end of the phrase does not ruffle the placid hymn. The development begins with a similar gesture as the horn now leads the ensemble in an *alla breve* point of imitation (see Example 4.20). The motive begins in minims and continues with a brilliant scalar figure, fusing sacred and virtuosic styles. As in the Clarinet Quintet, the hymn topic both knits together the heterogeneous ensemble and lends authority to the concertante genre.

Example 4.19 Mozart, Horn Quintet in E flat, K. 407, 1st movement, bars 1–12.

Example 4.20 Mozart, Horn Quintet in E flat, K. 407, 1st movement, bars 57–60.

The Oboe Quartet, K. 370, probably written the previous year in early 1781, may have provided the model for the development of the Horn Quintet. The first-movement development of K. 370 also begins with a point of imitation between the strings and wind soloist (see Example 4.21). The motive features the *alla breve* minims and sequential falling fourths

Example 4.21 Mozart, Oboe Quartet in F, K. 370, 1st movement, bars 64–75.

characteristic of the hymn. The oboe enters last, joining the choir deferentially before launching into a brilliant scalar passage. The oboe modestly reverses roles when the point of imitation repeats in bars 72–5; the wind soloist now initiates the polyphony and supports the violin's passagework. The sacred topic again elevates the lightweight genre, drawing the virtuoso soloist into the sacred embrace of the *stile antico*.

The hymn topic plays the same role in the Andante of the Piano Concerto in B flat, K. 450 (see Example 4.10 above). K. 450 is the first of Mozart's piano concertos to feature obbligato winds, a novelty he advertised in the opening theme with its antiphony of wind and string motives. The Andante hymn confers a spiritual unity on the heterogenous ensemble. The movement consists of three statements of a perfectly symmetrical thirty-two-bar theme in binary form (AABB), followed by a short coda. The symmetrical form, with its echoing phrases, allowed Mozart to balance the three elements of his new scoring – strings, keyboard and winds. The first time through the theme, the piano plays the even phrases, echoing the strings (bars 1–32). The second time, the piano and strings intermingle, as the soloist ornaments the strings' unchanging hymn on the odd phrases (bars 33–64). The winds enter on the third statement of the theme, echoing the piano and strings on the even phrases (bars 65–101). The serene hymn, repeating ritualistically, quietly integrates the diverse forces into a harmonious community.

Example 4.22 Mozart, Symphony in A, K. 201, 1st movement, bars 1–9.

The hymn topic perhaps performed a similar service for the audiences of Mozart's instrumental music. The echoes of the *stylus a cappella* may be heard as an aesthetic bid, an attempt to transform aristocratic divertissement into a high-minded pursuit tailored to the ideals and aspirations of bourgeois consumers. Mozart's Symphony in A, K. 201 certainly invites this more serious mode of aesthetic activity. The hushed intimacy of the opening bars demands a new level of attention from listeners accustomed to noisy fanfares and hammer blows (see Example 4.22). This introspective mood owes in no small part to the *alla breve* chords supporting the first violins' melody. The learned suspensions in bars 4–7, together with the canonic repetition of the theme that follows, confirm the ecclesiastical origins of the accompaniment. The subtle religious overtones encourage an attentive, even devotional response to this quiet utterance.

Mozart completed the Symphony in A in April 1774, within months of composing the 'Credo' Mass in F, K. 192, his most rigorous exercise in the strict church style (see Example 4.3 above). The *stylus a cappella* echoes in the opening bars of K. 201, as it will in so many of Mozart's later works, conferring its authority like Don Alfonso's greying temples. To the meanings of the hymn topic, then, we may add a sociological dimension. Like Mozart's other borrowings from sacred music, it lifted his instrumental music above mere entertainment and helped create the secular ritual that became the bourgeois concert. Despite its ancient origins, the hymn topic has a surprisingly modern ring.

5   A newly identified Viennese Mozart edition

Rupert Ridgewell

In November 1785, Mozart completed two vocal ensembles for performance as part of an adaptation of Francesco Bianchi's opera *La villanella rapita*: the quartet 'Dite almeno, in che mancai' for soprano, tenor and two basses (K. 479), which he entered in his *Verzeichnüss* on 5 November; and the trio 'Mandina amabile' for soprano, tenor and bass (K. 480), which followed on the 21st.[1] The author of the texts remains unknown, although Lorenzo da Ponte acted as the theatre's 'house poet' and has been suggested as a likely candidate.[2] The opera received its first Viennese performance at the Burgtheater on 25 November, with music by Bianchi interspersed with numbers by Mozart and other composers.[3] Mozart's ensembles were inserted after Act 1, scene 12 (K. 480) and Act 2, scene 13 (K. 479),[4] their presence recorded in the diary of the prominent court official and inveterate theatregoer Count Karl von Zinzendorf, who attended two performances: on 30 November he noted that 'the music contains several pieces by Mozart', while on 16 December he simply stated that 'the quartet is

Research for this chapter was made possible by the award of a Small Research Grant by the British Academy. An earlier version was presented at the Royal Musical Association Annual Conference at the Institute of Musical Research, University of London, on 21 September 2013. For their helpful comments, I am grateful to John Arthur, Dexter Edge, Ian Woodfield, Neal Zaslaw and Oliver Neighbour (1923–2015), to whom this chapter is dedicated in memoriam.

[1] British Library Zweig MS 63, f. 5v–6r. See Albi Rosenthal and Alan Tyson, *Mozart's Thematic Catalogue: a Facsimile* (London, 1990), p. 34. Mozart also included in his entry the names of the cast members involved in the first performances: Vincenzo Calvesi (Count), Celeste Coltellini (Mandina), Stefano Mandini (Pippo) and Francesco Bussani (Biaggio).

[2] This suggestion was put forward in NMA, II/7/3, p. xv. See also Maria Antonella Balsano Fiorenza, 'I due pezzi di Mozart per "La villanella rapita"', in Wolfgang Osthoff and Reinhard Wiesend (eds.), *Mozart e la Drammaturgia Veneta. Mozart und die Dramatik des Veneto. Bericht über das Colloquium Venedig 1991* (Tutzing, 1996), pp. 95–127.

[3] A score associated with the Viennese performances held in the Burgtheater collection of the Österreichische Nationalbibliothek (shelfmark KT 467/1–4) contains numbers attributed to Joseph Weigl, Franz Xaver Süssmayr and Giovanni Battista Borghi, as well as Mozart and Bianchi, although some of this material was probably added for the opera's 1794 revival. See Dexter Edge, 'Mozart's Viennese Copyists' (PhD thesis, University of Southern California, 2001), pp. 1340–1.

[4] The ensembles were originally numbered as 8½ in Act 1 (K. 480) and 8 in Act 2 (K. 479) in the Burgtheater score, although various erasures and amendments indicate that the ordering changed over time.

beautiful'.[5] The opera was briefly mentioned in the *Wiener Zeitung* on 2 December 1785, while reports in the Florentine journal *Gazzetta universale* on 10 December 1785 and 24 January 1786 singled out Mozart's contributions for special mention.[6]

La villanella rapita received a total of eight performances between 25 November 1785 and 17 February 1786[7] – a respectable initial run, even if it failed to enter the repertory over a longer period and was not revived in Vienna until June 1794. Mozart's ensembles nevertheless began to take on a life of their own. On 8 February 1786, the Viennese copyists Laurenz Lausch and Johann Traeg both placed advertisements in the *Wiener Zeitung* offering copies of the ensembles for sale independently of the opera.[8] Whether Mozart himself sanctioned their distribution is not known. 'Mandina amabile' later formed part of another pasticcio performed in Paris in 1789 and published there in full score by Jean-Georges Sieber in 1790. An arrangement for piano and viola *ad libitum* of K. 480 also appeared under Boyer's imprint.[9] The Leipzig publisher Breitkopf & Härtel subsequently issued vocal scores and orchestral parts for both ensembles in 1804 and 1805, as

[5] Dorothea Link, *The National Court Theatre in Mozart's Vienna: Sources and Documents, 1783–1792* (Oxford, 1998), p. 258: '30.Novembre: Au Specatacle. La villanelle rapita. Le spectacle est gai, la musique contient quelques morceaux de Moshart, les paroles beaucoup d'equivoques. Le souflet répeté' (a nearly identical transcription is given in MDL, p. 225); and p. 259: '16. Decembre: J'appris bientot du B. Reischach a l'opera, que sa Maj. avoit prit ce parti contre l'avis de tout le Staatsrath. L'opera, le Villanella rapita, le quartetto est beau.'

[6] *Gazzetta universale* (10 December 1785), no. 99, p. 788 and (24 January 1786), no. 7, p. 52. I am grateful to Ian Woodfield for bringing these notices to my attention. The texts are given in his forthcoming book on the reception of Mozart's operas. They are also transcribed and discussed in Dexter Edge, 'Report on the Viennese premiere of *La villanella rapita*' and 'Report on concerts of the Viennese *Tonkünstler-Societät*' in Edge and David Black (eds.), *Mozart: New Documents* (12 June 2014), https://sites.google.com/site/mozartdocuments/documents/1785-11-28-la-villanella-rapita and https://sites.google.com/site/mozartdocuments/documents/1786-01-07 (accessed 1 September 2014). The *Wiener Zeitung* notice mentions only Bianchi as composer and incorrectly gives the date of the premiere as 28 November. See *Wiener Zeitung* (3 December 1785), Anhang, p. 2793

(digital scans are available via the Österreichische Nationalbibliothek at http://anno.onb.ac.at/), and MDL, p. 225.

[7] Link, *The National Court Theatre in Mozart's Vienna*, pp. 72–7.

[8] *Wiener Zeitung* (8 February 1786), Anhang, pp. 295–6. See MDL, p. 231 (Lausch only) and MDB, p. 264. Lausch offered copies of the ensembles in keyboard reduction for 1 gulden 8 kreutzer (K. 479) and 48 kreutzer (K. 480) respectively, while Traeg does not specify the scoring or price. See also Alexander Weinmann, *Die Anzeigen des Kopiaturbetriebes Johann Traeg in der Wiener Zeitung zwischen 1782 und 1805* (Vienna, 1981), p. 22. K. 479 is also listed in Traeg's 1799 sale catalogue with the number 30 and priced at 2 gulden: see Alexander Weinmann, *Johann Traeg: Die Musikalienverzeichnisse von 1799 und 1804* (Vienna, 1973), col. 207.

[9] RISM Series A/I, M 5288 and M 5292/M 5341. Michel Noiray surveys the Parisian performances and proposes this newly revised dating for Sieber's edition (which was previously dated 1789), in 'La villageoise enlevée et l'édition du terzetto *Mandina amabile*, K. 480', in Cécile Reynaud, Herbert Schneider, Jacqueline Sanson and William Christie (eds.), *Noter, annoter, éditer la musique: Mélanges offerts à Catherine Massip* (Paris, 2012), pp. 369–86.

numbers III (K. 480) and VI (K. 479) of a collection of operatic numbers by Mozart.[10] K. 479 was also set to new words for performance as part of Pietro Guglielmi's opera *La pastorella nobile* in London and was published there by Robert Birchall in vocal score in about 1820.[11]

A hitherto neglected aspect of the dissemination of the two ensembles is represented by an arrangement for flute quintet, scored for flute, violin, two violas and cello, which survives in two sources in the Czech Republic: a set of printed parts in the castle archive of Český Krumlov (see Example 5.1); and a set of manuscript parts in Beroun (Example 5.2).[12] These sources are not entirely undocumented – both appear in RISM, and the printed parts are listed in a catalogue of Mozart sources in Bohemia published in 1982[13] – but they are absent from the various editions of the Köchel catalogue and have largely escaped scholarly attention. The scarcity and relative inaccessibility of these sources goes some way in explaining this neglect, and their obscurity is compounded by the absence of crucial pieces of information concerning the identity of the arranger or the date on which the arrangement was produced, copied, engraved and printed. Furthermore, the arrangement has not been associated with any known advertisement or sale catalogue issued by a music publisher, in Vienna or elsewhere, either before or after 1800. A manuscript copy is, however, listed in Johann Traeg's 1799 sale catalogue as number 110 under the rubric 'Quintetti aus Opern und Ballets für verschiedene Instr. arrangirt'.[14]

This relative dearth of information ultimately stems from the sources themselves, which betray no immediate sign of their origins: the identity of

---

[10] RISM Series A/I, M 7371. Copy consulted at the British Library, shelfmark Hirsch IV.991: *Operngesänge von W. A. Mozart welche zu seinen bekannten Opern nicht gehören, sondern von ihm einzeln geschrieben worden sind. Im Klavierauszug von C. Schulz* (Leipzig, 1804), Erster Heft, nos. III and VI (see also the orchestral parts of no. III at shelfmark h.321.x). For a description of Breitkopf's edition of K. 479, see Gertraut Haberkamp, *Die Erstdrucke der Werke von Wolfgang Amadeus Mozart* (Tutzing, 1986), vol. I, pp. 242–3.

[11] RISM Series A/I, M 5287: *Che dirò che far deggio. Quartetto, as sung in the opera of La pastorella nobile, but originally composed and introduced in the opera of La villanella rapita, with the words, Dite almeno in che maniera. Composed by Mozart* (London, c. 1820). Birchall also published an edition of K. 480 in 1814: see British Library shelfmark G.537.i.(11.).

[12] The printed parts are held by the Státní oblastní archiv, Český Krumlov, shelfmark No 222 K24. A second copy in the Fürstlich Waldburg-Zeil'schen Archiv, Leutkirch-Zeil (Bavaria), is now considered lost. See RISM Series A/I, *Einzeldrucke vor 1800* (Kassel, 1976), M 5340 and MM 5340. The manuscript parts are held by the Státní okresní archiv, Beroun, shelfmark CZ-BER/ HU 728. I am grateful to Dr Jana Vojtěšková (Národní museum hudby, Prague) for help in obtaining copies of these sources.

[13] Jitřenka Pešková and Jiří Záloha (eds.), *Českokrumlovská mozartiana: katalog skladeb W.A. Mozarta z hudební sbírky Státního oblastního archívu Třeboň, Pobočka Český Krumlov* (Prague, 1982), no. 165 (p. 41).

[14] '110 Mozart (La Villanelle Ràpita) à Fl. V. 2 Viole e B . . . g. 1.30'. See Weinmann, *Johann Traeg: Die Musikalienverzeichnisse von 1799 und 1804*, col. 59.

Example 5.1 Mozart, 'Dite almeno in che mancai' (K. 479), flute-quintet arrangement: printed flute part, p. 1. Reproduced with the permission of the Státní oblastní archiv, Český Krumlov: shelfmark No 222 K24.

the publisher is not stated anywhere on the printed parts, which lack a title page and imprint, and the manuscript parts likewise provide no further information beyond the titles of each piece. The two sources are nonetheless linked to a third item, an arrangement of Ofelia's aria 'La ra, la ra, che filosofo

Example 5.2 Flute-quintet arrangements of K. 479 and K. 480, manuscript parts: flute, p. 1. Reproduced with the permission of the Státní okresní archiv, Beroun, Czech Republic: shelfmark CZ-BER/ HU 728.

buffon' from Antonio Salieri's opera *La grotta di Trofonio*, scored for the same ensemble of flute, violin, two violas and cello. *La grotta di Trofonio* had been well received in Vienna following its first Burgtheater performance on 12 October 1785, in which Nancy Storace's return to the stage – following a period of illness and vocal crisis – helped to guarantee public success.[15] Indeed, Mozart himself apparently collaborated with Salieri and a composer named only as Cornetti in the composition of the cantata *Per la Ricuperata salute di Ophelia* (K. 477a), now lost, to words by Lorenzo da Ponte to celebrate the recuperation of 'Ophelia', the role assumed by Storace in the opera.[16] It is thought that Storace danced while singing 'La ra, la ra' in the Vienna performances, a feat that earned her considerable acclaim when she performed the aria in London in 1791.[17]

Unlike *La villanella rapita*, Salieri's opera entered the theatre's longer-term repertory, with another twenty-four performances scheduled up to 4 January 1788,[18] and was published in a lavish full score by Artaria in April 1786.[19] It also spawned various adaptations and related works by other composers, including published sets of keyboard variations based on 'La ra, la ra' by Joseph Sardi and Philipp Wschejansky, and on the trio 'Venite o donne meco' by Vanhal, as well as flute-quintet arrangements of 'Venite o donne meco' and the trio 'Ma perché in ordine il tutto vada'.[20] The latter appeared with no credit to the arranger under the imprint of Franz Anton Hoffmeister (1754–1813), who started publishing music in Vienna in 1784 and launched an ambitious subscription series in the summer of 1785. In this chapter I shall outline the case for associating the printed parts of the Mozart/Salieri arrangements held in Český Krumlov with the same

<hr/>

[15] See Dorothea Link, 'Nancy Storace's *annus horribilis*, 1785', *Newsletter of the Mozart Society of America*, 18/1 (27 January 2014), pp. 1–7 and Dorothea Link (ed.), *Arias for Nancy Storace: Mozart's First Susanna* (Middleton, WI, 2002), pp. x–xi. Link attributes Storace's crisis to the birth and death of her daughter that year.

[16] Artaria first advertised the cantata in the *Wienerblättchen* on 26 September 1785. See MDL, pp. 222–3. The identity of Cornetti is not known for sure, although the most likely candidate is Alessandro Cornetti, a vocal teacher and composer active in Vienna at the time.

[17] 'La ra, la ra' was included in Stephen Storace's pasticcio opera *The Siege of Belgrade*, which was first performed at the Theatre Royal, London with a cast including Nancy Storace on 1 January 1791. See John Rice, *Antonio Salieri and Viennese Opera* (Chicago and London, 1998), pp. 372–3.

[18] The performances are listed in Link, *The National Court Theatre in Mozart's Vienna*, pp. 69–118 (*passim*).

[19] Artaria's full score was advertised in the *Wiener Zeitung* on 26 April 1786. For a list of extant copies, see RISM Series A/I, S 520. The

aria 'La ra, la ra' appears in Act 2, scene 11 (pp. 290–4). For a facsimile reprint of the edition, see *La grotta di Trofonio, opera comica in due atti. Introduzione di Laura Callegari* (Bologna, 1984).

[20] RISM Series A/I, S 1070 (wrongly attributed to Giuseppe Sarti): Joseph Sardi, *Variazioni del minuetto La ra dell'opera La grotta di Trofonio, per cembalo con violino obligato* (Vienna [Artaria], 1786); Státní oblastní archiv, Český Krumlov, shelfmark 27/650 (not in RISM): Philipp Wschejansky, *VIII variazioni caratteristiche per il forte-piano sopra la cavatina la ra ra ra dell'opera Grotta di Trofonio* (Vienna [Hoffmeister], 1789); RISM Series A/I, VV 754a: Johann Vanhal, *Venite o donne meco, nell opera: La grotta di Trofonio, variées pour le clavecin ou piano-forte* (Vienna [Torricella], 1786); RISM Series A/I, S 526: *Deux airs de l'opera La grotta di Trofonio par M^n Salieri* (Vienna [Hoffmeister], 1786). The last of these editions was later reprinted by Artaria with a new title page attributing the arrangement to Hoffmeister himself (copy in Bibliothèque nationale de France, shelfmark A.34407), but the authority of this statement cannot be confirmed.

publisher. In doing so I shall validate a theory first put forward by Ian Woodfield in 2000, and further elaborated in my study of the publishing history of Mozart's piano quartets in 2010, even though the sources themselves were not accessible to either of us at the time of writing.[21] In the absence of any substantive documentary or contextual evidence bearing on their date, authorship or imprint, only the physical and textual content of the parts offer clues to their origins as part of Hoffmeister's series. Furthermore it will become clear that the music circulated in this adapted form even before copies of the full scores were made available by Traeg and Lausch, a sequence of events that raises questions about the sources upon which the arrangements were based and their authorship.

Hoffmeister's *Grosse Musiksammlung*

Hoffmeister was unique among Viennese music publishers operating at the end of the eighteenth century in offering most of his output via subscription, or to be precise through *Pränumeration*, or pre-payment. He announced the launch of what he called 'a grand music collection from Vienna available on pre-payment' ('Grosse Musiksammlung von Wien auf Pränumeration') in the *Brünner Zeitung* on 2 July 1785, followed by longer notices in the *Staats- und gelehrte Zeitung des hamburgischen unpartheyischen Correspondenten* on 22 July 1785 and the *Wiener Zeitung* on 6 August 1785.[22] These advertisements provide details of Hoffmeister's initial intentions for the series and its structure. Subscribers were invited to pay 1 gulden 40 kreutzer in advance for monthly *cahiers* divided into three categories according to instrumental genre: chamber music for strings, music for the piano, and flute music. Each *cahier* would contain several works – typically three or four, as it turned out – in each category. Hoffmeister also stressed that, besides original works, the series would include 'the best pieces from new German and Italian operas' ('die besten Stücke aus den deutschen und wälschen neuen Opern') and those included in the flute *cahiers* would be 'arranged for quintet or quartet' ('auf Quint- oder Quartetten übersetzt'). Based on this monthly offering, subscribers to all three strands in the series could expect to acquire

[21] See Ian Woodfield, 'John Bland: London Retailer of the Music of Haydn and Mozart', *Music & Letters*, 81 (2000), p. 214 and Rupert Ridgewell, 'Biographical Myth and the Publication of Mozart's Piano Quartets', *Journal of the Royal Musical Association*, 135 (2010), pp. 65–6.
[22] For the text of the *Wiener Zeitung* advertisement, see Ridgewell, 'Biographical Myth

and the Publication of Mozart's Piano Quartets', pp. 106–11. For partial transcriptions of the advertisements of 2 July and 22 July 1785, see NMA, Serie 10: Supplement, Werkgruppe 31: Nachträge, Band 2: *Mozart: die Dokumente seines Lebens: Addenda zusammengestellt von Cliff Eisen* (Kassel, 1997), p. 39.

up to twelve works per month and at least a hundred in a year, or as Hoffmeister put it, 'an entire library of original music over the course of several years' ('in etlichen Jahren eine ganze Bibliothek von Originalmusikalien anzuschaffen').

In order to fulfil these objectives, Hoffmeister needed not only to secure a regular flow of new works, but also music for particular instruments in order to fill each of the monthly *cahiers* in each category. Mozart and Haydn are among seven composers named as contributors, although the terms under which they agreed to supply material is not articulated in Hoffmeister's notices, or known from any other source.[23] Hoffmeister nevertheless claimed that 'all pieces will be completely new and taken from the master's hand' ('alle Stücke durchaus ganz neu von des Meisters hand weggenommen'). Each *cahier* was typically presented unbound inside a wrapper made of thick dark blue or grey paper, upon which the series title, month and contents were either printed or written by hand.[24] The wrapper therefore served as a title page for the *cahier* as a whole, so that individual title pages for the constituent works were not essential and a caption title often sufficed. Although in practice Hoffmeister usually provided a title page for more substantial works, at least eighty editions published as part of the series between 1785 and 1789 were presented without one.[25]

By highlighting his intention to publish operatic arrangements, Hoffmeister appears to have identified a gap in the market that the sub-scription series could potentially fill. Editions of the latest opera arias and ensembles were quite common in Mozart's Vienna, but they tended to appear in vocal score rather than in arrangements for chamber ensemble. While string and harmonie (wind band) arrangements of operas became increasingly popular in the 1780s and 1790s, they tended to circulate in manuscript rather than in print, suggesting that certain types of music were considered more suitable for manuscript dissemination than for publication. This comparative lack of activity was not unique to Mozart, but extended to other composers too. Artaria, for example, issued very few operatic adaptations for chamber ensemble of any kind in the 1780s,

[23] The other composers named in Hoffmeister's advertisement were Johann Baptist Vanhal, Johann Georg Albrechtsberger, Ignace Pleyel, Jan Adam František Míča and Karl von Ordoñez. In the event, neither Míča nor von Ordoñez contributed to the series.

[24] The constituent parts of the series were entitled 'Pr[a]enumeration pour la musique de la chambre', 'Pr[a]enumeration pour le Forte-Piano, ou Clavecin' and 'Pr[a]

enumeration pour la Flûte – Traversiere' respectively.

[25] These are editions with the plate numbers 20, 23, 25, 26, 29–31, 36, 39–41, 43, 44, 46–50, 58–61, 63, 67, 68, 70, 71, 73, 75, 81, 83–5, 87–9, 94, 95, 102–4, 106, 113, 114, 119, 121, 122, 127, 129, 131, 133–6, 139, 141, 145, 151, 152, 157, 162–5, 167, 170, 171, 174, 176, 177, 179, 180, 183, 184, 192, 193, 196, 204, 209 and 210.

Table 5.1 Opera arrangements published by Hoffmeister, 1785–9

Composer	Opera	Excerpts	Scoring	Plate number	RISM Series A/I
Mozart	*La villanella rapita*	Dite almeno in che mancai (K. 479) Mandina amabile (K. 480)	Flute quintet	31	M 5340
Salieri	*La grotta di Trofonio*	La ra, la ra, che filosofo buffon	Flute quintet	31	[M 5340]
Salieri	*La grotta di Trofonio*	Venite o donne meco Ma perche in ordine il tutto vada	Flute quintet	36	S 526
Dittersdorf	*Betrug durch Aberglauben*	Wer da will nach Mädchen ziehn Ja ich liebe Sie von Herzen	Flute quintet	77	D 3185
Dittersdorf	*Betrug durch Aberglauben*	Wer da will nach Mädchen ziehn Ja ich liebe Sie von Herzen	Piano, violin and viola	78	D 3186
Dittersdorf	*Betrug durch Aberglauben*	Nein du kennst nicht wahrer Liebe Liebe machet nur beherzt	Flute quintet	81	D 3187
Martín y Soler	*Una cosa rara*	Suite arranged by 'Mr Vent' (Johann Nepomuk Wendt)	Flute quartet	101	M 966
Martín y Soler	*Una cosa rara*	2 string quartets based on excerpts arranged by Hoffmeister	String quartet	108	H 5928 and M 964
Mozart	*Le nozze di Figaro*	Al desio di chi t'adora (K. 577)	Flute quintet	208	M 5344

although the firm did distribute such editions published elsewhere in Europe.[26]

But Hoffmeister's intentions were not, in this particular case, realized entirely by the publications that appeared under his imprint in the next few years. Excluding the Mozart/Salieri arrangements for now, only seven editions based on operatic excerpts can be associated with Hoffmeister's subscription series (see Table 5.1). These arrangements were scored for flute

---

[26] A notable exception was a string-quartet arrangement of Vicente Martín y Soler's opera *Una cosa rara*, which Artaria published in 1788. RISM Series A/I, M 878: *Una cosa rara ridotta in quartetti per due violini, viola, e violoncello dal Sig' V. Martin* (Vienna: Artaria, 1788). Artaria's sale catalogues of 1785 and 1788 include sections devoted to quartet arrangements of operatic overtures and arias, the majority of which were imported from abroad. See Otto Biba and Ingrid Fuchs (eds.), *Die Sortimentskataloge der Musikalienhandlung Artaria & Comp. in Wien aus den Jahren 1779, 1780, 1782, 1785 und 1788* (Tutzing, 2006).

quartet and quintet, string quartet, piano trio and solo piano, and were based on excerpts from Salieri's *La grotta di Trofonio*, Dittersdorf's *Betrug durch Aberglauben*, Martín y Soler's *Una cosa rara*, and Mozart's *Le nozze di Figaro*.[27] The last of these was a flute-quintet arrangement of the rondò for soprano 'Al desio di chi t'adora', K. 577, which was originally composed in July 1789 for the first Viennese revival of *Le nozze di Figaro*.[28] It appeared under Hoffmeister's imprint with the plate number 208.[29] This small corpus of pieces, only two of which are credited to a named arranger, is the context in which the arrangements of K. 479 and K. 480 may be located.

Physical characteristics

In at least four general respects, the printed parts of the Mozart/Salieri arrangements are entirely typical of music published in Vienna at the end of the eighteenth century. In common with the vast majority of Viennese editions, as well as most editions produced in London, Paris and many other centres in Europe at that time, it was printed on rolling presses from engraved pewter plates, rather than from movable type. Judging from the dimensions of the printed impressions the plates measured approximately 29.5cm by 22.0cm, while each page was ruled with twelve, thirteen or fourteen staves to accommodate the musical text.[30] Also in keeping with general practice, the music was published in parts in the upright format rather than in score, making the edition suitable to be used in performance, not least by the prime market of amateur musicians. The parts are identified by the instrumental designations engraved centrally at

[27] Hoffmeister additionally composed and published in the series a set of piano variations based on an air from Dittersdorf's *Betrug durch Aberglauben* (plate number 87, RISM Series A/I, H 6194).

[28] K. 577 was entered in the *Verzeichnüss* under the date 'Im Jullius [1789]' (British Library, Zweig MS 63, f. 21v–22r). See Rosenthal and Tyson, *Mozart's Thematic Catalogue: a Facsimile*, p. 50. It was included in performances of *Le nozze di Figaro* at the Burgtheater starting on 29 August 1789 as a replacement for Susanna's aria 'Deh vieni non tardar'. See also Janet K. Page and Dexter Edge, 'A Newly Uncovered Autograph Sketch for Mozart's 'Al desio di chi t'adora' K.577', *The Musical Times*, 132 (1991), pp. 601–6.

[29] RISM Series A/I, M 5344: *Quintette pour flauto-traverso, violino, 2 violes, è violoncello traduite de l'Opera Figaro composé par Mr.*

Wolfg. Amad. Mozart (Vienna: Hoffmeister, 1789). See Haberkamp, *Erstdrucke der Werke von Mozart*, vol. I, p. 328 (the title page is reproduced in vol. II, p. 300), and Ludwig von Köchel, *Chronologisch-thematisches Verzeichnis sämtlicher Tonwerke Wolfgang Amadè Mozarts*, ed. Franz Giegling, Alexander Weinmann and Gerd Sievers, 6th edition (Wiesbaden, 1964), p. 796 (Anh. B zu 577). K. 577 was first published in vocal score by Johann André in February 1790: see Haberkamp, *Erstdrucke der Werke von Mozart*, vol. I, p. 328–9 and RISM Series B/II: *Recueils imprimé XVIIIe siècle* (München and Duisburg, 1964), p. 190.

[30] Twelve staves: flute, pp. 1–2; violin, p. 1; viola 2, pp. 1–5; violoncello, pp. 2–4. Thirteen staves: flute, pp. 3–4; violin, pp. 2–3; viola 1, pp. 1–5; violoncello, p. 1. Fourteen staves: violin, pp. 4–5.

the top of each page: 'Flauto traverso', 'Violino', Viola I', 'Viola II' and 'Violoncello'.

The collation is also typical of the period, with each part consisting of a series of either two (flute and cello) or three (violin, violas) nested bifolios, paginated separately with the page numbers engraved in the outer corner at the top of each successive page. Two small holes in the top left-hand corner of each page are the only remnants of the original rudimentary string binding. There are no missing or blank pages where a title page might have been accommodated, strongly suggesting that the parts were presented in this way at the point of publication, which was common in Hoffmeister's output. The printing is generally clear, with no smudging or evidence of cracks in the plates, although the presence of faint offset impressions on pages 2 and 5 of the violin part indicates a degree of carelessness in assembling the parts before the ink was completely dry, a not uncommon defect in music printing at that time.[31]

The paper itself derives from the Veneto region of Italy, each page measuring approximately 35.3cm (height) by 24.5cm (width) with a watermark consisting of horizontal chain lines with three crescent moons countered by the letters 'GFA' over 'SOTO IPERIAL'.[32] Prized for its smooth surface and bright appearance, Italian paper was used by major Viennese publishers such as Artaria, Hoffmeister, Christoph Torricella and Leopold Kozeluch at the end of the eighteenth century, but very little is known about their consumption of paper over time, making it impossible to establish with any certainty the period in which any particular type or batch was used. Given the current state of knowledge, the watermark therefore does not help us to date the edition more precisely.

A printed label pasted on the bottom right-hand corner of the first page of each part offers the first clue to determining a *terminus ante quem* for the edition. The label bears the abbreviated name 'C. D'OETTING' surrounded by a decorative border, indicating that the parts were once in the possession of Count Philip Karl Oettingen-Wallerstein (1759–1826). The archive at Český Krumlov houses some 982 items bearing the count's label, among them many Viennese editions of the 1780s and 1790s. This provenance is important because the count must have acquired the parts by 1803, the year he sold the collection to his nephew, Arnošt Schwarzenberg (1773–1821). The collection was only transferred to

---

[31] The worn surface of page 1 of the flute part may be attributed to exposure or usage, rather than a printing defect.

[32] The full watermark is visible only in the flute part and the two viola parts (the violin and violoncello parts were printed on sections of paper showing only the chain lines

and the crescent moons). According to a proclamation issued in Venice in 1774, the designation 'Sott' imperiale' referred to the second largest paper format, the sheet measuring 739mm by 514mm. See Dexter Edge, 'Mozart's Viennese Copyists', pp. 331–2.

Example 5.3 Mozart, 'Dite almeno in che mancai' (K. 479), flute-quintet arrangement: violin, p. 1, staves 1–2. Reproduced with the permission of the Státní oblastní archiv, Český Krumlov: shelfmark No 222 K24.

Český Krumlov after Arnošt's death.[33] Items bearing the count's label therefore date from the period leading up to 1803, which means that the parts must have been printed at some point between the completion of Mozart's original ensembles in November 1785 and the sale of the collection in 1803.

While these attributes are all consistent with Hoffmeister's claim to the edition, none of them are exclusive to his output, or point definitively to him. The parts nevertheless reveal other defining characteristics of his 'house style' – distinctive textual and physical properties that reflect his particular methods of engraving and selling music – which help to determine when the edition was produced.

Engraving

The engraved musical text of the printed parts bears all the hallmarks of Hoffmeister's firm. A comparison between them reveals that the parts were produced by two engravers using distinct sets of engraving punches: Engraver 1 was responsible for the flute part and the two viola parts, while Engraver 2 produced the violin and cello parts. To illustrate the work of each engraver, the first two staves of the violin and viola 1 parts are shown in Examples 5.3 and 5.4. These examples demonstrate a common approach to the basic layout, with the first stave indented to make room for the tempo indication, the name of the instrument engraved in the centre directly above the music, and the page number in the top right-hand corner. The opening tempo markings for each piece are given as 'Allegro' (or All$^{\circ}$), 'Andante' and 'Allegretto' (or All^{to}) consistently in all the parts. Both the tempo indications

[33] For further information about the collection's history, see Jiří Záloha, 'Über die Herkunft der Musikalien mit der Signatur "C. d'Oetting" in der Schloßmusikaliensammlung in Český Krumlov, ČSSR', *Die Musikforschung*, 26/1 (1973), pp. 55–8.

Example 5.4 Mozart, 'Dite almeno in che mancai' (K. 479), flute-quintet arrangement: viola 1, p. 1, staves 1–2. Reproduced with the permission of the Státní oblastní archiv, Český Krumlov: shelfmark No 222 K24.

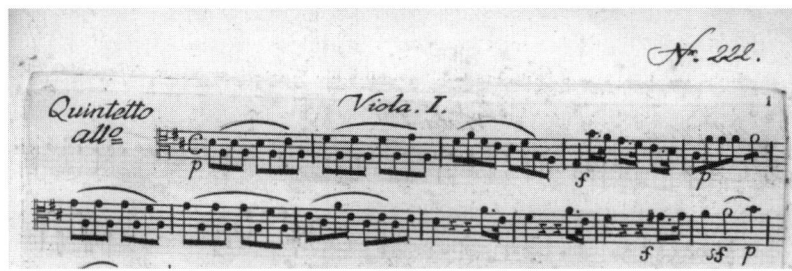

and instrumental designations were engraved freehand with the burin, rather than with letter punches, as were the titles that appear in various places. The title 'Quintetto' is given at the beginning of K. 479 in each part, directly above the tempo marking, while additional titles appear as follows: 'La Villanella Rapita :| Quartetto dite almeno di Mozart' engraved at the top of page 1 of the flute part;[34] 'Mandina amabile' in the flute part, page 3, and underlined in the viola 1 part, page 3; and 'La grotta di Trofonio del Salieri || lara lara.' in the flute part, page 4.

The placing of the note heads and stems is also quite similar in the two parts, but notable differences are apparent in the shapes of the punches used for the dynamic markings 'f', 'sf' and 'p'. The 'f' punch used by Engraver 1 produced a slightly more defined impression than that used by Engraver 2, while the horizontal crossbar is positioned around the middle of the stem in Engraver 1's punch and closer to the upper curl in Engraver 2's. The two engravers also made very different 'sf' markings: Engraver 1 used his 'f' punch in combination with a separate 's', whereas Engraver 2 employed a special 'sf' punch, in which the 'f' is considerably larger than the 's'. Although the punches used to engrave the 'p' sign look very similar in both parts, they too are distinct: the hook at the top left of the sign faces downward in the punch used by Engraver 1, but curls upwards in Engraver 2's punch. Another distinguishing feature is the positioning of the crotchet rest. The design of the punch employed by both engravers is practically identical, taking the form of a reversed 'Z', but Engraver 2 always places it at a 45-degree angle in relation to the middle stave line, whereas Engraver 1 places it in a vertical position between the second and fourth stave lines.[35]

[34] This was engraved on either side of 'Flauto traverso', implying that it was added at a late stage in the engraving process. See Example 5.1.
[35] For a detailed comparison of the punches used by the same two engravers in Hoffmeister's edition of Mozart's Piano Quartet in G minor (K. 478), see Ridgewell, 'Biographical Myth and the Publication of Mozart's Piano Quartets', pp. 88–94.

From the publisher's point of view there were clear benefits to be gained by employing two engravers to work on an edition simultaneously, not least to increase capacity to speed up the production process and to help minimize the risk of piracy.[36] No doubt by implementing this policy, Hoffmeister sought to maximize his ability to publish new editions according to the monthly schedule demanded by the subscription series. A study of his published output reveals that the same two engravers worked exclusively on the series in the first few months of production. Thus of the twenty-nine editions in the plate number range from 12 to 40, eight were engraved by either Engraver 1 or 2 working alone, while the remaining twenty-one editions were shared between them in a similar manner to the Mozart/Salieri arrangements (see Table 5.2). It is also worth noting that the engraving work was divided

Table 5.2 Hoffmeister's engravers: editions produced by Engravers 1 and 2

Plate number	Composer	Work	Engraver 1 number of plates	Engraver 2 number of plates	RISM number
12	Hoffmeister	Piano Sonata		11	H 6180
[13]	Hoffmeister	Duet for 2 flutes		8	H 6062
14	Hoffmeister	Flute Quartet [1]	15		H 5920
15	Vanhal	String Quartet [1]	8	8	V 386
16	Hoffmeister	String Quartet [1]	18	5	H 5922
17	Vanhal	Fugue for piano or organ	4		V 954
18	Hoffmeister	Flute Concerto	18	9	H 5844
19	Pleyel	String Quintet [1]	15	8	P 3025
20	Hoffmeister	String Trio 1		6	H 5971
21	Albrechtsberger	Piano Quartet	8	8	AA 748I, 75
22	Mozart	Piano Quartet (K. 478)	10	23	M 6306
23	Hoffmeister	Sonata for flute and violin	2	2	H 6116
24	Vanhal	Piano Concerto	22	9	V 353
25	Hoffmeister	Flute Quartets 2 and 3	7	16	H 5920
26	Pleyel	String Quintet 2	14	9	P 3027
27	Vanhal	9 Variations for piano	7		V 800

[36] For further discussion of the practice of shared engraving and a summary of the various stages in the publication process, see Rupert Ridgewell, 'Publishing Practice in Haydn's Vienna: Artaria and the Keyboard Trios Op. 40', in Richard Chesser and David Wyn Jones (eds.), *The Land of Opportunity: Joseph Haydn in Britain* (London, 2013), pp. 163–94.

Table 5.2 (*cont.*)

Plate number	Composer	Work	Engraver 1 number of plates	Engraver 2 number of plates	RISM number
28	Mozart	Violin Sonata (K. 481)	16	5	M 6543
29	Vanhal	Duet for 2 flutes 1		12	V 591
30	Vanhal	String Quartet 2	14	11	V 386
31	**Mozart**	**Flute-quintet arrangements of Mozart, *Dite almeno, in che mancai* and *Mandina amabile*, and Salieri, *La ra, la ra, che filosofo buffon***	**14**	**9**	**M 5340**
32	Haydn	String Quartet 1 (Hob. III/43)		14	H 3488–9
33	Haydn	Piano Trio (Hob. XV/10)	18	5	H 3672
34	Hoffmeister	Flute Concerto	17	24	H 5861
35	Hoffmeister	Duetti Concertanti for piano and violin 1	18	7	deest
36	Salieri	Flute-quintet arrangements of *Venite o donne meco* and *Ma perché in ordine il tutto vada* from the opera *La grotta di Trofonio*	3	12	S 526
37	Haydn	Overture (Hob. 1a/4)	4	8	H 3287
38	Sterkel	String Quintet	13	10	S 5898
39	Hoffmeister	String Quartet 2	11	12	H 5922
40	Hoffmeister	Flute Quartet 4	8	9	
Total			**284**	**260**	

fairly equally between the two individuals overall, as the totals given at the bottom of the table suggest: thus Engraver 1 produced a total of 284 plates, while Engraver 2's total was 260.

The only specific identifier on the edition is the plate number 31, which appears in the customary central position at the foot of each page. Hoffmeister's use of plate numbers has not yet been fully elucidated, but it seems likely that he introduced the system in the summer or autumn of 1785, around the time that he devised plans for the subscription series that would fuel a substantial increase in the number of new editions released over the next five years. By mid-1785, he had issued eleven editions in the previous eighteen months: ten were published jointly with the book publisher Rudolf Gräffer without engraved plate numbers, while a set of violin duets by Hoffmeister himself represented the first edition to appear under his sole imprint.[37] The latter was accordingly assigned the number 11 and each edition published thereafter was numbered sequentially, the number 210 being reached by the end of 1789. Within that sequence, 31 is one of several numbers that have not been previously associated with any known Hoffmeister editions, leading to the assumption that copies of these editions either do not survive or are yet to be identified.[38] The printed parts of the Mozart/Salieri arrangements therefore fill a gap in the sequence at that point.

Series chronology

The engraving of the Mozart/Salieri arrangements is therefore consistent with Hoffmeister's practice in late 1785 and early 1786, but the exact position they occupied in the series is not immediately obvious. After his initial announcements, the publisher rarely issued advertisements in the press and never specified the contents of the series in such notices. Furthermore, very few of the original wrappers have survived the passage of time, no doubt because they were not attached to the contents of each *cahier* and were therefore easily discarded (the wrapper associated with the printed parts in Český Krumlov, for example, is not known to survive). Despite these documentary and bibliographical lacunae, it is nevertheless possible to reconstruct the contents of the series by allocating Hoffmeister's editions to particular *cahiers* according to their instrumentation and plate numbers. Table 5.3 shows the contents of the first three monthly instalments, which together account for a total of twenty-eight editions in nine *cahiers*. The titles shown in bold are taken from extant wrappers associated with the first chamber music *cahier* and the third *cahiers* of chamber music and flute music.[39]

---

[37] RISM Series A/I, H 6063: *III duetti à violino primo et violino secondo composti dal Signore Franc. Ant. Hoffmeister* (Vienna: Hoffmeister, 1785). For a list of the editions published jointly with Gräffer, see Alexander Weinmann, *Die Wiener Verlagswerke von Franz Anton Hoffmeister* (Vienna, 1964), pp. 22–6. A collection of 'Vier Lieder für Gesang und Klavier. Von F. A. Hoffmeister. Wien 1785' printed from movable type may also have been issued upon his instigation: see Alexander Weinmann, *Wiener Musikverlag 'Am Rande': ein lückenfüllender Beitrag zur Geschichte des alt-Wiener Musikverlages* (Vienna, 1970), p. 98 (copy held in the Gesellschaft der Musikfreunde, Vienna, shelfmark VI 15168).
[38] The other editions so far not accounted for would have been assigned the numbers 80, 92, 93, 97, 107, 132, 137 and 156.

[39] A copy of the wrapper for the first chamber music *cahier*, from a private collection, is reproduced in Ridgewell, 'Biographical Myth and the Publication of Mozart's Piano Quartets', p. 60. An annotation in an unknown hand ('/P.t/ Mᵣ de Mozart Maitre de Chapelle') suggests that this copy was intended for Mozart himself. Exemplars of wrappers for the third flute and chamber music *cahiers* are held in the Bibliothèque nationale de France (shelfmark A-34410) and the Landesbibliothek Mecklenburg-Vorpommern, Schwerin (shelfmark Mus.2620), respectively. An annotation on the chamber-music wrapper makes clear that a fourth scheduled work, a symphony by Haydn (Hob. 1a:4; plate number 37), was held over to the following month ('Die versprochene Sinfonie des Hᵣⁿ Capellemeisters Joseph Haydn wird künftiges Monat folgen').

Table 5.3 Hoffmeister's subscription series: *cahiers* 1–3

	Cahier 1 for Nov 1785 (published Nov / Dec 1785)	*Cahier 2 for Dec 1785* (published Jan 1786?)	*Cahier 3 for Jan 1786* (published Feb 1786)
Piano	Albrechtsberger, Piano Quartet (21)	Mozart, Violin Sonata (28)	Haydn, Piano Trio (33)
	Mozart, Piano Quartet (22)	Vanhal, Piano Concerto (24)	Hoffmeister, Duetti Concertanti for violin and piano 1 (35)
	Hoffmeister, Piano Sonata (12) Vanhal, Fugue (17)	Vanhal, Variations (27)	
Chamber	**Vanhal, String Quartet [1] (15)**	Pleyel, String Quintet 2 (26)	**Haydn, String Quartet 1 (32)**
	Pleyel, String Quintet [1] (19)	Vanhal, String Quartet 2 (30)	**Sterkel, String Quintet (38)**
	Hoffmeister, String Quartet [1] (16)		**Hoffmeister, String Quartet 2 (39)**
	Hoffmeister, String Trio 1 (20)		
Flute	Hoffmeister, Flute Concerto (18)	Hoffmeister, Flute Quartets 2 and 3 (25)	**Hoffmeister, Flute Concerto (34)**
	Hoffmeister, Flute Quartet 1 (14)	Vanhal, Duet for 2 flutes 1 (29)	**Hoffmeister, Flute Quartet 4 (40)**
	Hoffmeister, Sonata for flute and violin (23)	Flute-quintet arrangements of Mozart, *Dite almeno, in che mancai* and *Mandina amabile*, and Salieri, *La ra, la ra, che filosofo buffon* (31)	**Flute-quintet arrangements of Salieri, *Venite o Donne meco* and *Ma perché in ordine il tutto vada* (36)**
	Hoffmeister, Duet for 2 flutes [13]		

The evidence of these early wrappers demonstrates that the plate number sequence was not designed to mirror the order in which works appeared within each *cahier* precisely. The first *cahier* of chamber music, for example, contained editions numbered 15, 16, 19 and 20, while numbers 17 and 18 were assigned to a keyboard fugue by Vanhal and a flute concerto by Hoffmeister – editions included in the piano and flute strands of the series respectively. Rather, it seems likely that numbers were allocated in the order in which works were engraved or prepared for publication, so that a full month's worth of editions would naturally cover a defined range of numbers in the sequence.

According to my deductions, the first three *cahiers*, scheduled for release in November 1785, contained twelve works accounting for plate numbers 12 to 23.[40] No wrappers survive from the next batch of three *cahiers*, intended for the month of December 1785, but their contents may be deduced by placing the next eight editions in the plate number sequence (24 to 31) into the appropriate *cahier* according to instrumentation. According to this schema, the Mozart/Salieri arrangements appeared in the second *cahier* of flute music, alongside two flute quartets by Hoffmeister and a flute duet by Vanhal.[41] Finally, the third instalments of chamber and flute music account for six editions in the plate number range 32 to 40, allowing us to allocate the two remaining editions – with plate numbers 33 and 35 – to the piano *cahier* for that month.

Dating

Had Hoffmeister been able to stick to his original plans, these first three instalments containing a total of twenty-seven editions would have appeared over three consecutive months starting in November 1785. However, it is clear that he fell behind schedule even at this early stage of the project. Hoffmeister acknowledged the delays in a short notice in the *Wiener Zeitung* on 16 February 1786, blaming them on a large number of retrospective subscriptions and a temporary lack of printing capacity during the winter months. As a result, he announced that the third *cahiers* of piano and flute music, which should have appeared in January, would only be available from 20 February, while the third *cahier* of chamber music would be delayed until the 25th.[42] Whilst the release dates of the first two instalments are not possible to establish with the same degree of accuracy, approximate dates may be surmised by tracking the series chronology in relation to Mozart's contributions.

[40] While no edition with the plate number 13 is extant, a copy of a duet in G major for two flutes by Hoffmeister held by the Bibliothèque nationale de France matches the style of engraving found in other editions produced by the firm in this period and fits into the first *cahier* of flute music. See RISM Series A/I, H 6062.

[41] A copy of the Hoffmeister flute quartets is held in Český Krumlov (shelfmark 119–23), but the Vanhal flute duet is not found there. During a visit to the Fürstlich Waldburg-Zeil'schen Archiv in the 1970s, Gertraut Haberkamp observed that the (now lost) copy of the Mozart/Salieri edition preserved there had a handwritten title and date 'Dec 1785', which must refer to the month in which the edition was scheduled in the series. Her transcription is preserved on a catalogue card held by the RISM office at the Bayerische Staatsbibliothek, Munich, reproduced in Ridgewell, 'Biographical Myth and the Publication of Mozart's Piano Quartets', p. 65.

[42] 'Hoffmeisters Musiksammlung', *Wiener Zeitung* (18 February 1786), p. 379. For the text of this announcement, see Ridgewell, 'Biographical Myth and the Publication of Mozart's Piano Quartets', p. 52.

The first work by Mozart to appear in the series was the Piano Quartet in G minor, K. 478, which formed part of the first *cahier* of piano music together with a piano quartet by Albrechtsberger, a fugue by Vanhal and a sonata by Hoffmeister himself. The latter was assigned the number 12, implying that it was the first work to be engraved, while Mozart's piano quartet was given the penultimate number, 22, which in turn suggests that it was among the last to be prepared for publication that month. The piano quartet was entered in the *Verzeichnüss* as one of a series of entries for July 1785, at the time that Hoffmeister's subscription venture was first advertised. Mozart's autograph manuscript is dated 16 October 1785, however, and it seems plausible to assume that Hoffmeister received the work soon afterwards.[43] We know from Leopold Mozart's letter to his daughter Maria Anna (Nannerl) dated 2–3 December 1785 that the edition was in production at that time, since the violin and viola parts are already mentioned as having been printed.[44] It therefore seems likely that the first *cahier* of chamber music (with plate numbers in the range 15 to 20) appeared on schedule in November 1785, and was followed by the piano and flute music *cahiers* in late November or early December.

Mozart's second contribution to the series, the Violin Sonata in E flat major, K. 481, was published in the second *cahier* of piano music with the plate number 28. Assuming the entry in Mozart's *Verzeichnüss* is trustworthy, the sonata was completed by 12 December 1785.[45] The sonata therefore cannot have been engraved before 12 December and it follows that the next three editions in the plate number sequence, from 29 to 31, were similarly engraved after that date. It therefore seems safe to assume that the three *cahiers* intended for December 1785 were not published before the end of that month, and probably did not appear until January 1786.[46] We can be sure that they were available by 16 February at the latest, when

---

[43] Mozart's manuscript of K. 478 bears on fol. 1r the autograph title and date 'Quartetto. di Wolfgango Amadeo Mozart^mpr Vienna li 16 d'Ottobre 1785'. See *Wolfgang Amadeus Mozart: Quartett in g für Klavier, Violine, Viola und Violoncello KV 478: Faksimile nach dem Autograph im Museum der Chopin-Gesellschaft Warschau mit einer Einführung von Faye Ferguson* (Warsaw, 1991). John Arthur (personal communication) has observed that the inks used in the manuscript appear to confirm the assumption that this inscription was added upon completion of the work. The inscription is similar in colour to the ink (or inks) found in various late additions and alterations to the work, including the foliation numbers and the tempo marking 'All°' in the first movement,

as well as in bars 33ff. of the slow movement and in bars 60ff. of the finale.

[44] See MBA, vol. III, p. 461; LMF, p. 894.

[45] British Library Zweig MS 63, f. 5v–6r. Rosenthal and Tyson, *Mozart's Thematic Catalogue: Facsimile*, p. 34.

[46] The eight editions that made up the three *cahiers* intended for December 1785 were engraved on a total of 165 plates: ninety-four produced by Engraver 1 and seventy-one by Engraver 2. It is not known how many plates a single person could engrave in a typical day, but if we assume a maximum of four, it becomes clear that the two engravers might have taken between about eighteen and twenty-four days to deliver all eight editions. The Mozart/Salieri arrangements accounted for twenty-three plates, which might have

Hoffmeister announced that the third set of *cahiers*, originally scheduled for January 1786, had been delayed. This would mean that the flute-quintet arrangements of K. 479 and K. 480 appeared in print between five and nine weeks after the first performance of *La villanella rapita*, and up to five weeks before Traeg and Lausch announced the availability of manuscript copies of the ensembles on 8 February 1786. Given this proximity to the first performance and the fact that Mozart had been announced as a regular contributor to the series in the summer of 1785, the question naturally arises as to the nature of his role, if any, in bringing the arrangements to the press.

Authorship

It is possible to conceive of two scenarios involving the composer directly. In the first, Mozart was himself responsible for the arrangements, acting perhaps in response to Hoffmeister's request or encouragement. In the second scenario, Mozart supplied scores of the two ensembles on the understanding that Hoffmeister would publish them in an adapted form, or perhaps with no particular expectation. Needless to say, no documentary evidence has come to light in favour of either option: the arrangements do not appear in Mozart's *Verzeichnüss*, nor are they mentioned in his only known letter to Hoffmeister, which is dated 20 November 1785, or in any other source. Such negative evidence does not offer conclusive proof that Mozart had no involvement in the creation or publication of the two arrangements. Indeed, one might reasonably point to the fact that Mozart failed to enter several other pieces in the *Verzeichnüss*: thus Alan Tyson identified sixteen works composed between 1785 and 1791 that were not included for one reason or another.[47] Similarly, the subject of the letter is a request for money and does not concern future publishing plans directly, though Mozart does allude to Hoffmeister's series by stating 'you know me, and are aware of how anxious I am for your affairs to go well'.[48]

It is equally possible that Hoffmeister acquired the ensembles from an independent source, even if the timeframe in which the edition was

taken only three or four days to make by dividing them between the two engravers.
[47] See Rosenthal and Tyson, *Mozart's Thematic Catalogue: Facsimile*, pp. 17–18. To these we might add Mozart's contribution to the Singspiel *Der Stein der Weisen*. See David J. Buch, 'Der Stein der Weisen, Mozart, and Collaborative Singspiels at Emanuel Schikaneder's Theater auf der Wieden', *Mozart Jahrbuch 2000*, pp. 91–126. Neal

Zaslaw similarly notes the absence of ten works from Leopold Mozart's 1768 list of Wolfgang's compositions in his article 'Leopold Mozart's List of His Son's Works', in Allan Atlas (ed.), *Music of the Classic Period: Essays in Honor of Barry S. Brook* (New York, 1985), pp. 323–58.
[48] See MBA, vol. III, p. 454; LMF, p. 894 (20 November 1785). My translation.

published somewhat limits the period within which he could have done so. Whoever undertook the arrangements must have completed them by the second half of December 1785, to allow time for the parts to be copied, engraved, printed and distributed in January 1786. It follows that the arranger must have obtained copies of Mozart's ensembles soon after the first performance of *La villanella rapita* on 25 November, and almost certainly by mid-December in order to complete the arrangements by the end of that month at the latest. The likely sources for the ensembles are therefore limited either to manuscripts supplied by Mozart himself, or to copies obtained from someone associated with the Burgtheater performances. Happily, Mozart's autograph manuscripts of both ensembles survive, while several other contemporary scores may be associated either with the first performances directly or with commercial copying firms in Vienna, making it possible to explore in some detail the early transmission of Mozart's text.[49] The principal secondary source is the Burgtheater's original performing score, which was prepared in large part under the supervision of the theatre's official copyist Wenzel Sukowaty, who also distributed Mozart's ensembles separately and supplied two early scores to the Vienna Hofkapelle, as Dexter Edge has shown.[50] Sukowaty therefore emerges as a plausible alternative source for Hoffmeister's acquisition of the ensembles in the period immediately after the first performance. Any scores associated with the copying shops of Johann Traeg and Laurenz Lausch can be excluded for the purposes of this investigation because they were prepared slightly later and were not advertised until February 1786.[51]

The scoring of the arrangements for flute quintet with two violas was itself somewhat unusual in 1785. There are no examples of Viennese published editions for this combination of instruments before 1785 and very few in other cities, though such works may well have circulated in manuscript.[52] While it is tempting to imagine that the scoring could reflect Mozart's own

[49] The autographs are held by the Staatsbibliothek zu Berlin – Preussischer Kulturbesitz, Musikabteilung mit Mendelssohn-Archiv, shelfmarks Mus. ms. autogr. W. A. Mozart 479 and 480.
[50] The Burgtheater score (Österreichische Nationalbibliothek, shelfmark KT 467/1–4) consists of four volumes: K. 479 appears on the sixth and seventh gatherings of volume 3 (fol. 69r–92v), and K. 480 on the last three gatherings of volume 2 (fol. 127v–146v). Dexter Edge identifies the copyists of K. 480 as Sukowaty 1a and Sukowaty 3, and the copyist of K. 479 as Sukowaty 1a. A copy of K. 479 bearing Sukowaty's name and address is held by the Mozarteum, Salzburg, shelfmark

M. n. 53 (d). See Dexter Edge, 'Mozart's Viennese Copyists', pp. 1402–6 and 1410–12.
[51] Dexter Edge identifies a score of K. 479 held in the archive of the Gesellschaft der Musikfreunde in Vienna (shelfmark VI 7349/Q 3774) as a product of Johann Traeg's copying shop. See Dexter Edge, 'Mozart's Viennese Copyists', pp. 901–5.
[52] A set of six flute quintets with two violas by Giuseppe Cambini were published in Paris by Boyer and Le Menu (RISM A/I, C 394) and listed in Artaria's sale catalogue of 1785. See Biba and Fuchs (eds.), *Die Sortimentskataloge der Musikalienhandlung Artaria & Comp. in Wien*, p. 110.

Example 5.5 Mozart, 'Dite almeno in che mancai' (K. 479), bars 1–12: flute-quintet arrangement (annotated to indicate the original scoring).

preference, evidenced in his string quintets scored for two violas, the arrangements themselves show no obvious sign of the composer's input. The opening bars of K. 479, shown in score in Example 5.5, are representative of the technique adopted throughout the two pieces. The music is divided between the five instruments in a fairly consistent way and remains largely faithful to the original text. The flute, violin and cello parts mostly follow the solo soprano, violin and cello parts in Mozart's original ensemble, while the violas are deployed in a flexible way with material drawn from the solo vocal parts and the accompanying string and wind parts.[53] There is no evidence of any serious attempt at recomposition and there are no changes to the harmony or structure of the two pieces. In these respects, the arrangements are similar to the other flute-quintet arrangements published in Hoffmeister's series.

Modifications to the text are nevertheless evident in various places. Perhaps the most significant change is the transposition of K. 479 down a semitone to D major, whereas K. 480 was kept in its original key of A major.

[53] Both K. 479 and K. 480 are scored for strings, two oboes, two clarinets, two bassoons, and two horns, while K. 480 also includes parts for two flutes.

The intention here was clearly to make the music more accessible to amateur flautists of the period, by lowering the range by a semitone and by transposing the music to a more orthodox key. According to Janice Dockendorff Boland, D major is the easiest key for players of the baroque and classical one-keyed flute, while flat keys are the most difficult owing to a need for cross-fingering, the preponderance of 'weak' notes and attendant intonation difficulties.[54] As a result of this transposition, the highest note for the flute in either arrangement is F sharp, two octaves above middle C (f#''').[55] Similarly, 'La ra, la ra' and the later arrangements of 'Ma perché in ordine il tutto vada' from Salieri's *Grotta in Trofonio* and of Mozart's 'Al desio di chi t'adora' (K. 577) were also transposed to D major from their original keys of B flat, C and F major respectively, while a disproportionate number of Hoffmeister's own flute compositions were in D major.[56]

Other changes to the text were made both for practical reasons and to exploit the individual characteristics of each instrument. In the passage shown in Example 5.6, the accompanying semiquavers in the two viola parts were simplified to iron out the rather awkward leaps in Mozart's original text. This is also an example of where Mozart's dynamic markings were not adhered to in the arrangement, with *sforzando* replacing the *piano* and *mezzo forte* markings in the autograph manuscript. Another notable departure from Mozart's text is found at the end of K. 480. Here, the flute plays an altered version of the original vocal line, with the introduction of a motive based on the falling sixth instead of a rising arpeggio (Example 5.7). This was clearly a practical alteration designed to bring about a gradual diminuendo in accordance with the instruction *perpendosi*, without playing at the extremes of the flute's range. Elsewhere, the vocal part is often transposed up an octave to exploit the flute's upper register. In a few instances the arranger also added material to fill out the instrumental texture. In Example 5.8 the accompanying triplets in the violin part are entirely new and bring forward momentum to an otherwise rather static passage of repeated chords. A similar passage is shown in Example 5.9. Here, the repeated semiquavers in the second viola part are new and help to generate additional volume and intensity at this point in the music.

None of these changes can be explained by alternative readings in the Burgtheater's performing score, or any other copies prepared by Sukowaty's

[54] Janice Dockendorff Boland, *Method for the One-Keyed Flute: Baroque and Classical* (Berkeley, CA, 1998), p. 30.
[55] The maximum range of flute parts for other works published in Hoffmeister's subscription series routinely extends to g'''. In a set of twelve variations for flute and string quartet by Hoffmeister himself (plate number 66, RISM A/I, H 6190), the highest note for the flute is a'''.
[56] See the thematic catalogue of Hoffmeister's flute pieces issued by the composer in 1800 and reproduced in Weinmann, *Wiener Verlagswerke von Franz Anton Hoffmeister*, after p. 252 (Bildteil).

Example 5.6 Mozart, 'Mandina amabile' (K. 480), bars 55–6: flute-quintet arrangement (score) and original scoring.

Example 5.7 Mozart, 'Mandina amabile' (K. 480), bars 195–200: flute-quintet arrangement (flute part) and original vocal line.

shop, which are all textually very close to Mozart's autographs.[57] Any differences between them are limited to minor issues, such as the placing of dynamics and details of articulation, which means that it is difficult to identify passages in the arrangements that favour one manuscript source

---

[57] Dexter Edge, 'Mozart's Viennese Copyists', p. 1408.

Example 5.8 Mozart, 'Dite almeno in che mancai' (K. 479), bars 48–50: flute-quintet arrangement.

Example 5.9 Mozart, 'Mandina amabile' (K. 480), bars 165–6: flute-quintet arrangement.

over another. For example, the opening motive of K. 480, scored for bassoons and clarinets in parallel sixths, is slurred in Mozart's autograph, but the slurring is missing in the bassoon parts in the Burgtheater score. In the arrangement of K. 480, the same motive is slurred and divided between the two viola parts (see Example 5.10). But this notation could just as easily have been copied from the clarinet parts in the Burgtheater score as it could from Mozart's autograph. Another example, as Dexter Edge has indicated, is the interpretation of Mozart's articulation in bars 15, 75, 107 and 112 of K. 480 as dots in the Burgtheater score, rather than strokes. In three of these four variant bars (75, 107 and 112), the arrangement offers no articulation markings at all, while in bar 15 they are notated as strokes. This might be seen as evidence of a different reading of Mozart's notation were it not for the fact that articulation markings are consistently rendered as strokes throughout the edition, surely as the result of a predetermined policy on

Example 5.10 Mozart, 'Mandina amabile' (K. 480), bars 1–2: flute-quintet arrangement.

the part of the arranger or the engravers. Indeed, strokes were also used exclusively in the other editions published in the first three instalments of Hoffmeister's series.

There are, however, a few indications that would appear to favour the autograph as the source for the arrangement, or at least a different copy to that prepared by Sukowaty's shop for the Vienna performances. Two mis-readings in the Burgtheater score of K. 480 are potentially significant in this regard. The first of these relates to the phrasing of the bass part in bars 146–7: in the autograph (fol. 8r), the phrase line extends from the B natural in bar 146 to the end of bar 147, whereas in the Burgtheater score (fol. 141v in vol. I) it covers the four notes in bar 147 only – perhaps because the beginning of the line partly merges with the word 'cavarmelo' (from the bass part) in Mozart's handwriting. The second misreading concerns the first violin part in bars 167–8, a passage of descending arpeggios that Mozart marks with strokes in the autograph. In the Burgtheater score, however, the copyist has slurred the last note of bar 167 to the first of bar 168 (A to F sharp, fol. 143v in vol. I). This is surely the result of a misreading of the autograph, where the two bars are notated over the page break between fol. 9r and 9v: the brace at the beginning of fol. 9v curls over the top of the beginning of bar 168, making it look like the end of a slur. In both cases, the equivalent passage in the arrangement follows the autograph, rather than the Burgtheater score (see Examples 5.11 and 5.12). Similarly, the instruction 'descresc[endo]' at bar 211 in the autograph of K. 479 (fol. 13v) is given as 'cresc[endo]' in the Burgtheater score (fol. 90v in vol. II), whereas the arrangement has the equivalent marking 'manc[ando]' at this point in the violin part (p. 3).

There are also occasional signs of slavish adherence to Mozart's nota-tion in some passages that the composer himself might have modified. Example 5.13 highlights an inconsistency in the way that the string parts

Example 5.11 Mozart, 'Mandina amabile' (K. 480), bars 146–7: autograph, Burgtheater score, and flute-quintet arrangement. Autograph reproduced with the permission of the Staatsbibliothek zu Berlin – Preußischer Kulturbesitz: shelfmark Mus. ms. autogr. W. A. Mozart 480, fol. 8r. Burgtheater score reproduced with the permission of the Österreichische Nationalbibliothek, Musiksammlung, Wien, shelfmark: KT.467/1–4 (vol. I, fol. 141v).

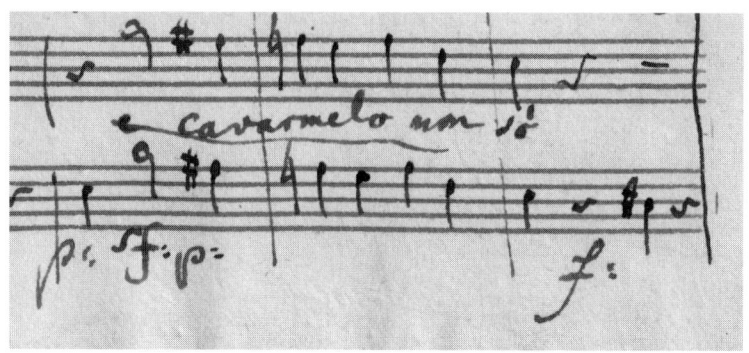

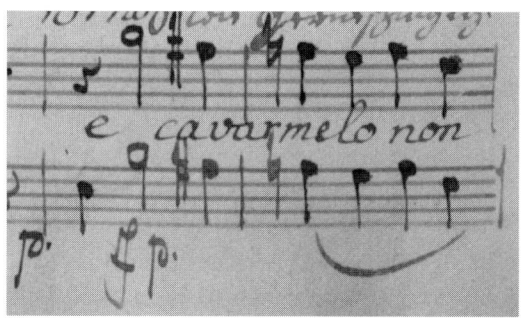

are articulated, with the slurring missing in the violin part but present in the first viola part – a tiny omission reflecting the vocal part in Mozart's autograph at this point. This detail perhaps implies that the arrangement was made in some haste, without considering all the implications of

Example 5.12 Mozart, 'Mandina amabile' (K. 480), bars 168–9: auto-graph, Burgtheater score, and flute-quintet arrangement. Autograph reproduced with the permission of the Staatsbibliothek zu Berlin – Preußischer Kulturbesitz: shelfmark Mus. ms. autogr. W. A. Mozart 480, fol. 9v. Burgtheater score reproduced with the permission of the Österreichische Nationalbibliothek, Musiksammlung, Wien, shelfmark: KT.467/1–4 (vol. I, fol. 143v).

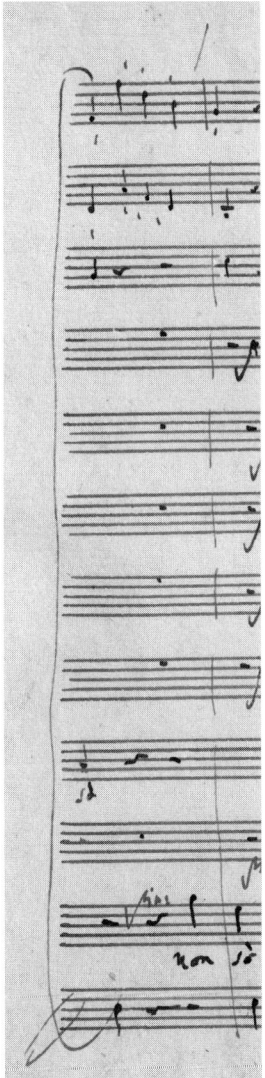

rendering the original notation in a new scoring. There are numerous other minor omissions or alterations for which *Vorlagen* can be found neither in Mozart's autograph nor in the early manuscript copies, but which were introduced either by the arranger or the engravers, thereby further obscuring the transmission history. In the arrangement of K. 480, these

Example 5.12 (cont.)

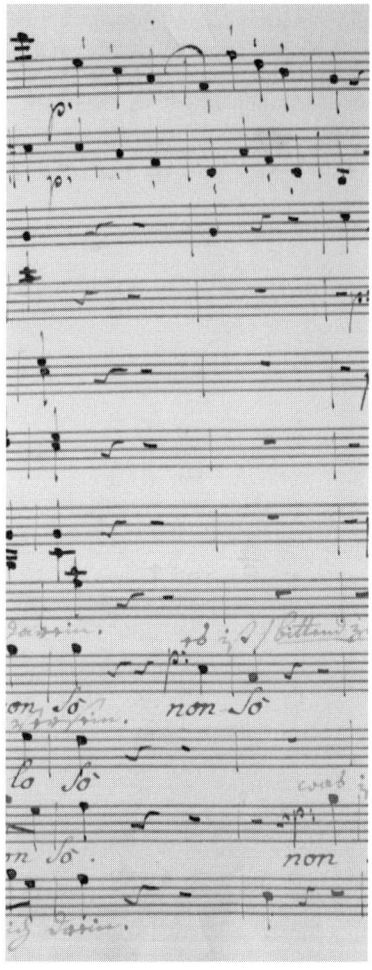

Example 5.13 Mozart, 'Mandina amabile' (K. 480), bars 9–10: flute-quintet arrangement (score) and autograph. Autograph reproduced with the permission of the Staatsbibliothek zu Berlin – Preußischer Kulturbesitz: shelfmark Mus. ms. autogr. W. A. Mozart 480, fol. 1r.

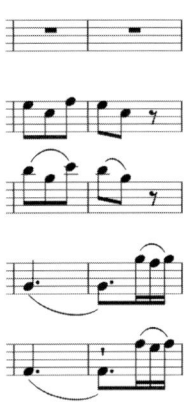

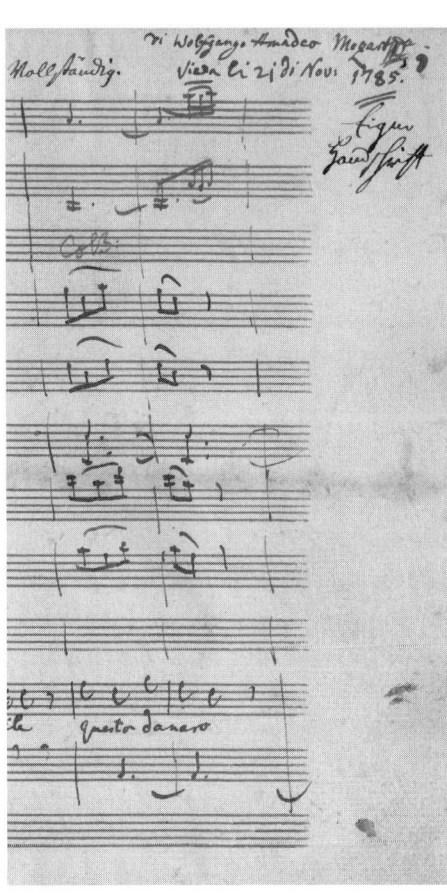

Example 5.14 Mozart, 'Mandina amabile' (K. 480), bars 31–3: flute-quintet arrangement.

include the omission of the opening tempo marking 'Andante', the addition of the expression marking 'Dolce' in bar 3 of the violin part, and the new dynamic markings 'p'–'f'–'p' together with new articulation in bars 31 to 33 (see Example 5.14).

Despite the evidence of creative thinking behind at least some of the changes, nothing points clearly to Mozart's own hand. Perhaps the most meaningful piece of evidence, however, is the order in which the pieces appear in Hoffmeister's edition, with K. 479 followed by K. 480. This mirrors the order of composition, rather than the sequence in which the ensembles appeared in the opera when it was performed at the Burgtheater. Had the arrangements been prepared from the first performance score, one might have expected the two pieces to be published in the order in which they appear there. This simple observation, while by no means conclusive in itself, might strengthen the case for thinking that the arrangements were based on sources obtained from Mozart himself, rather than being made independently of the composer from a score acquired from Sukowaty. But an alternative interpretation is even possible here. The arrangements as they appear in the edition effectively form a single quintet: an opening Allegro in D major (K. 479), followed by an Andante in A major (K. 480), and ending with an Allegretto in D major ('La ra, la ra'). Whether this was the publisher's intention is impossible to say with any degree of confidence. The title 'Quintetto' at the beginning of each part might point in this direction, or it may have been simply intended as a statement of instrumentation. Judging from the manuscript parts held in Beroun, however, it seems likely that the arrangements were at least perceived in this way. These parts were evidently copied directly from Hoffmeister's edition, a common practice in the late eighteenth century, although the copyist did not attempt to replicate the layout of the edition and sometimes failed to render details of articulation or phrasing precisely.[58] A significant new addition, however, is a title page in which Mozart is credited as the composer of the entire 'Quintetto' (see Example 5.15).[59]

Regardless of the true motivation behind the decision to bring the three arrangements together in this particular order, the musical evidence favours a scenario in which Hoffmeister (or an associate) was responsible for doing the arranging work itself. A plausible sequence of events is as follows: Mozart completed the two ensembles on 5 and 21 November 1785 and delivered them to the Burgtheater, or directly to Sukowaty, to be copied in preparation for the first performance on the 25th. Aware that Hoffmeister wished to include operatic numbers in the subscription series, Mozart also supplied manuscripts to him – perhaps the autographs once Sukowaty had finished with them – to be adapted accordingly. A score of the arrangement was assembled, which was then copied to produce a *Stichvorlage* consisting of five parts to be distributed between Engravers 1 and 2. Hoffmeister added a popular number from Salieri's *La grotta di Trofonio*, thus producing by accident or by design a manufactured work made up of three movements. The parts were engraved and printed in late December 1785 or early January 1786, and were added to the second *cahier* of flute music issued at some point in January. Hoffmeister's edition was never reissued, but manuscript copies of the arrangements circulated later and were offered for sale by Johann Traeg.

This scenario makes sense when viewed in relation to Mozart's initial engagement with Hoffmeister's series. As we have seen, two more works appeared in the early stages of the scheme, both of them in first editions: the Piano Quartet in G minor K. 478 and the Violin Sonata in E flat major K. 481. All three editions could have been part of a plan to include regular contributions from Mozart, as implied in Hoffmeister's preliminary advertisement in the *Wiener Zeitung*, an aim that was only sporadically realized over the following years.[60] Given this background, it seems unlikely that the

---

[58] The copyist's handwriting is itself more akin to German practice in the late eighteenth century rather than Viennese. Thus the treble clefs are formed without a lower stem, the bass clefs are open at the left, and the C clefs are made of two vertical lines, with a shape resembling a slanting '3' to the immediate right. For a general overview of handwriting types in relation to Viennese practices, see Edge, 'Mozart's Viennese Copyists', pp. 264–95.

[59] The title page appears on the cello part only: 'Quintetto in D | â | Violino | Flautotraverso | Viola Prima | Viola Seconda | & | Violoncello. | de Sig: Mozart'.

[60] Hoffmeister is now known to have published thirteen editions of Mozart's music before 1792. In addition to K. 478, K. 481, and the arrangements of K. 479/K. 480, he issued editions of K. 426, K. 496, K. 499, K. 501, K. 511, K. 521, K. 526, K. 533/494, K. 546 and the flute-quintet arrangement of K. 577. All these editions fit comfortably within the parameters of the subscription series, but their dates of publication and allocation to particular *cahiers* are not always self-evident.

Example 5.15 Flute-quintet arrangements of K. 479 and K. 480, manuscript parts: violoncello, title page. Reproduced with the permission of the Státní okresní archiv, Beroun, Czech Republic: shelfmark CZ-BER/ HU 728.

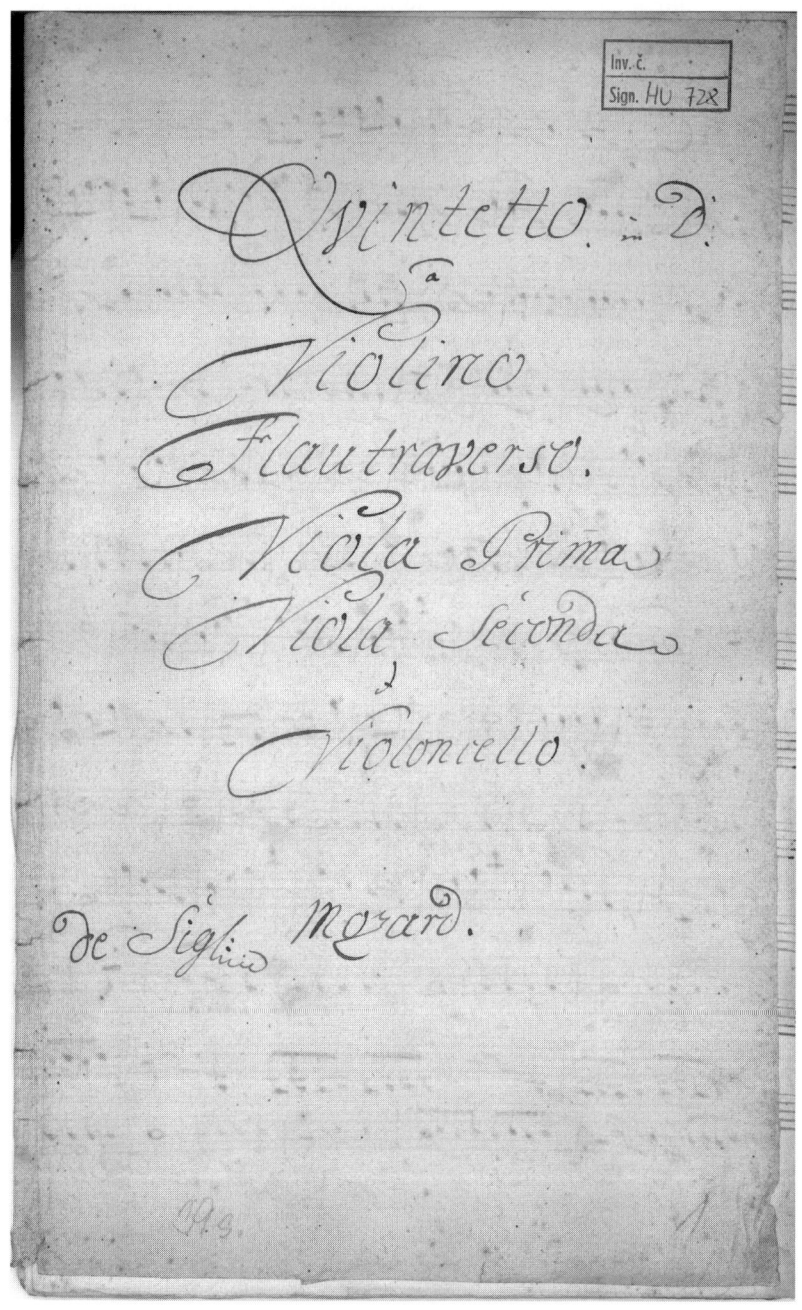

arrangement would have appeared without Mozart's consent. Perhaps Mozart himself will have felt less proprietorial about insertion pieces than about numbers from one of his complete operas. The publication also presumably offered some welcome additional publicity for his operatic activities in advance of preparations for the premiere of *Le nozze di Figaro* later in 1786. As things stand, Hoffmeister's edition represents not only a new addition to the roster of Mozart first editions, but also one of only a very few arrangements of his music for chamber ensemble to be printed in Vienna before 1792. It therefore constitutes a significant new strand in the rich tapestry of our knowledge of the dissemination of Mozart's music in his lifetime.

6   Composing, performing and publishing: Mozart's 'Haydn' quartets

Simon P. Keefe

The successes Mozart enjoyed as a performer–composer on the public stage in his first five years in Vienna were complemented by his well-developed profile as a composer of published instrumental music. A number of his works had appeared in print before 1781, but he made a concerted effort to publish only after moving to Vienna and while establishing himself as a freelance musician. After the sonatas for keyboard and violin K. 376, 377, 379 and 380 and the three piano concertos K. 413–15 written for publication and distribution in manuscript copies (as well as for his own performances) in 1781 and 1782–3 respectively, Mozart gained a considerable head of steam, bringing into the public domain old and new works alike. Artaria published the four-hand piano sonatas K. 381 (written 1772) and K. 358 (1773–4) in 1783[1] and the solo piano sonatas K. 330–2 in 1784; Torricella also issued the piano sonatas K. 333 and K. 284 (written 1775) and the accompanied sonata K. 454 in 1784. A flurry of publications followed in 1785: from Torricella, two sets of piano variations (K. 455 and K. 265); from Viennese copyists Johann Traeg and Lorenz Lausch, manuscript copies of a number of works; and from Artaria, the symphonies K. 385 (1782) and K. 319 (1779), the piano concertos K. 413–15, the 'Maurerfreude' Cantata K. 471, the fantasia and piano sonata K. 475/K. 457, and the six quartets dedicated to Haydn.[2] Anton Hoffmeister's Viennese subscription series, for which in his words he 'made agreements with our best local composers . . . as well as foreign masters . . . to receive new products'[3] also began in 1785, bringing out the piano quartet K. 478, the keyboard and violin sonata K. 481 and the rondo for piano K. 485 in the first few months. Mozart's father, Leopold, who saw announcements for Mozart's works during his Viennese

---

Earlier versions of this chapter were read at the Universities of Huddersfield and Manchester in January and March 2014 and at the Mozart Colloquium, Harvard University in April 2014. I dedicate this chapter to the memory of the wonderful violinist Peter Cropper (1945–2015), cherishing memories of our discussions of Mozart's chamber music.
[1] MDL, p. 191; MDB, p. 215. (All translations of MDL and MBA are my own, unless otherwise indicated.)

[2] For advertisements, see MDL, pp. 208–28; MDB, pp. 234–60 (*passim*). B. Schott in Mainz also published a keyboard arrangement of *Die Entführung aus dem Serail* in 1785, carried out by Abbé Stark and unsanctioned by Mozart, who at one stage worked on his own arrangement. See MBA, vol. III, p. 471; LMF, p. 895 (Leopold to Nannerl, 16 December 1785); MDL, pp. 219–20; MDB, pp. 249–50; NMD, pp. 40–2.
[3] NMD, p. 36.

sojourn from 11 February to 25 April 1785, reported to Nannerl later in 1785 the words of the Salzburg journalist Lorenz Hübner: 'it is quite astounding what quantity of things your son is publishing. In all music advertisements I always see nothing but Mozart. The Berlin advertisements, when announcing the [string] quartets, state only the following: "It is unnecessary to recommend these quartets to the public. It is sufficient to say that they are by Herr Mozart."'[4] It is tempting to dismiss as publisher's hyperbole Torricella's mention of the 'eagerness with which the works of this famous master are particularly yearned for by people on all sides'.[5] But Mozart's significant presence in the musical marketplace suggests that such 'eagerness' was perhaps a reality.

As a thoroughly practical musician, Mozart naturally would have brought to the table multifarious views as a performer and a performer–composer when writing works primarily for publication rather than for his own personal use. After all, markings in such works represented his only way of exerting influence on the interpretation of his music by players beyond his immediate control. In the set of keyboard and violin sonatas from 1781, the piano concertos K. 413–15 and the piano sonatas K. 330–32 and K. 333 written with public dissemination in mind, Mozart actively negotiated performance and compositional concerns, encouraging imaginative interpretation from his players.[6] In addition, Mozart included material in the first edition of the piano sonatas that does not appear in the autographs. Thus, it is important to try to determine how Mozart's creative processes were affected by the composing-performing–publishing dynamic in the 'Haydn' string quartets. Informal performances of the 'Haydn' quartets by Mozart and others in advance of publication apparently influenced materials Mozart provided to Artaria for publication. (The same also applies to the concert performance of the keyboard and violin sonata K. 454 in the Kärntnerthorteater with famous violinist Regina Strinasacchi, relative to materials provided to Torricella for publication.[7]) As we shall see, issues around performance and publication inform our understandings of Mozart's chamber works.

Composing the 'Haydn' quartets

The protracted genesis of the 'Haydn' quartets K. 387 in G, K. 421 in D minor, K. 428 in E flat, K. 458 in B flat, K. 464 in A and K. 465 in C includes two main

---

[4] MBA, vol. III, p. 439; LMF, p. 893 (letter of 3 November 1785).

[5] MDL, p. 522; MDB, p. 246.

[6] See my work in progress, *Mozart in Vienna: the Final Decade* (Cambridge University Press), and Keefe, '"Liebhaber und Kenner müssen sie selbst erst durchspielen":

Mozart's Early Viennese Instrumental Works for Publication, 1781–84, *Mozart-Jahrbuch 2014*, forthcoming.

[7] See Keefe, *Mozart in Vienna: the Final Decade*, and 'Mozart's Early Viennese Instrumental Works for Publication'.

phases of compositional activity from late 1782 to summer 1783 and November 1784 to January 1785. It is complicated by K. 458's appearance in both phases, by aborted sketches for several movements, and by near simultaneous work on non-adjacent movements (for example, K. 428/ii and K. 421/i, and K. 421/iv and an insert for K. 387/iv).[8] Mozart planned a set of six published string quartets at least as early as spring 1783. Writing to the Parisian publisher J. G. Sieber on 26 April 1783, he offered his piano concertos K. 413–15 and also six string quartets (of which only one was complete at that stage), presumably feigning displeasure at Artaria's printing of the keyboard and violin sonatas in 1781 in order to strengthen his pitch:

> I have already now been in Vienna for two years. You will probably know about my sonatas for piano with accompaniment for one violin that I have had engraved here by Artaria and Co. But I am not all that much pleased with the local engraving, and, even if I were, would like once again to give something to my fellow countrymen in Paris, so hereby let you know that I have finished three piano concertos . . . Further, I am now writing six quartets for two violins, viola and cello. If you would also like to engrave them, I will also give them to you. But these cannot be so cheap [as the piano concertos, for which 30 louis d'or was requested] – I cannot give you these six quartets for under 50 louis d'or. Consequently, if you can and will make a deal with me, you can just reply to me and I shall give you an address in Paris where you will receive my work in exchange for your payment.[9]

While Mozart's proposed fee was high, 50 louis d'or equalling approximately 550 florins,[10] it did not turn out to be wholly unrealistic. When he eventually sold them to Artaria in 1785, Sieber having apparently declined, he received 100 ducats (450 florins). The high financial value Mozart placed on the quartets transmogrified into the artistic value Artaria cited as justification for producing a lavish edition and charging a high price for it:

> Mozart's works need no praise, so giving some would be completely unnecessary; one can only affirm that here is a masterpiece. One can affirm this all the more since the author dedicated this work to his friend Joseph Haydn, Kapellmeister to Prince Esterházy, who has honoured it with all of the approval of which only a man of great genius is worthy. In view of this, the publishers have also spared no costs to put this work in the hands of amateurs and connoisseurs beautifully and clearly engraved

[8] See Alan Tyson, *Mozart: Studies of the Autograph Scores* (Cambridge, MA, 1987), pp. 83–93, 94–105. On the fragments, see also Christoph Wolff, 'Creative Exuberance vs. Critical Choice: Thoughts on Mozart's Quartet Fragments', in Wolff (ed.), *The String Quartets of Haydn, Mozart, and Beethoven: Studies of the Autograph Manuscripts* (Cambridge, MA, 1980), pp. 191–210. Stages of work on each quartet, as determined by different ink colours in the autograph, are discussed in the *Kritischer Bericht*, NMA, VIII/20/1–2 (1993), ed. Ludwig Finscher and Wolf-Dieter Seiffert, pp. 20, 47–8, 73, 92, 107–8, 133.

[9] MBA, vol. III, p. 266; LMF, p. 846.

[10] Daniel Heartz, *Mozart, Haydn, and Early Beethoven, 1781–1802* (New York, 2009), p. 74.

both in paper and in print, confident that the fixed price will not be considered too high when the quartets come to 150 pages and could not have been written out for less than 12fl.[11]

Clearly Haydn's approval and association with the quartets carried weight; but Mozart's own reputation also justified the price of purchase. By the time Artaria had printed the requisite copies of its 1785 edition and re-issues from 1787 and 1789, the original plates had worn out, and were re-engraved in 1791.[12] The quartets thus appear to have sold well during Mozart's lifetime.

After his death, Mozart's quartets secured a reputation as compositions for connoisseurs, Haydn pre-eminent among them. As Franz Niemetschek, one of Mozart's earliest biographers explained in 1798:

> Certainly Mozart could not have honoured Haydn with a better work than with these quartets, which contain a mine of precious thoughts and which are, indeed, models of composition. In the eyes of the connoisseur this work is of importance equal to any of his operatic compositions. Everything in it has been carefully thought out and perfected. One can see that he has taken the trouble to deserve Haydn's praise.[13]

Ignaz Arnold, in an early study of Mozart's music in 1803 considered the quartets to be the very best of Mozart's work in the genre, their beauties only coming properly to light after diligent listening and study.[14] He also claimed later (1810) that these 'excellent quartets show unmistakeable evidence of the trouble that he gave to their composition'.[15] According to Ernst Ludwig Gerber, a lexicographer writing in 1813, the chromaticism and dissonance in the finale of K. 464 required intricately skilled players, explaining 'why the honorable composer wrote ... [it] not for public performance by a full orchestra, but rather for the private music making of a quartet for musicians and educated friends of art'.[16] And George Nissen, reiterating Niemetschek's views in his biography of Mozart finished with the help of Constanze in 1828, thought Mozart

[11] MDL, pp. 221–2; MDB, p. 252 (17 September 1785). The announcement goes on to distance Mozart's new string quartets from K. 168–73, which had been advertised by Torricella one week earlier in the same publication, the *Wiener Zeitung*. See MDL, p. 220; MDB, p. 251 (10 September 1785).
[12] See *Kritischer Bericht*, NMA, VIII/20/1–2, pp. 6–7.
[13] Franz Niemetschek, *Life of Mozart* (1798), trans. Helen Mautner (London, 1956), p. 34.
[14] Arnold, *Mozarts Geist: seine kurze Biographie und ästhetische Darstellung seiner Werke* (Erfurt, 1803), p. 449. Other late eighteenth-century musicians such as

Thomas Attwood and Gaetano Latilla also recommended – and benefited from – repeated performances and repeated study of the 'Haydn' quartets: see H. C. Robbins Landon, *Haydn: Chronicle and Works. Haydn at Eszterháza, 1766–1790* (London, 1978), p. 511.
[15] Ignaz Arnold, *Joseph Haydn: seine kurze Biographie und ästhetische Darstellung seiner Werke. Bildungsbuch für junge Tonkünstler* (Erfurt, 1810), p. 53.
[16] Given in Gretchen Wheelock, *Haydn's Ingenious Jesting with Art: Contexts of Musical Wit and Humor* (New York, 1992), pp. 114–15.

worked specifically to elicit Haydn's approval.[17] Twentieth-century critics and biographers largely endorsed and built upon the view of the 'Haydn' quartets as connoisseur-orientated above all: the works reflect 'a special effort in view of his expert dedicatee'; they are '"music made of music", "filtered" art'; their creative energy is 'harnessed so effectively that it carries the quartets into an unearthly region of pure musicality'; they were 'meant for those who could play their way into them at home'; and they were primarily for private consumption, 'for the connoisseur, the denizen of the chamber', manifesting a wide array of sophisticated musical processes.[18] For writers old and new Mozart's own reference to the quartets as the 'fruit of a long and laborious study' in the dedication to Haydn for the Artaria edition perhaps offers clinching proof of orientation towards connoisseurs, as does Haydn's praise of Mozart's compositional abilities after performances of K. 458, K. 464 and K. 465, first quoted by Friedrich Schlichtegroll in his influential Mozart obituary from 1793 and originating in a letter from Leopold to his daughter Nannerl: 'I say to you before God and as an honest man that your son is the greatest composer I know in person or by name. He has taste and more than that the greatest compositional knowledge.'[19]

Few will disagree with the prevailing view that Mozart's 'Haydn' quartets are precisely and elegantly constructed works. In addition to collective perceptions of intrinsic musical quality, Mozart's numerous revisions to the autograph score attest to the chiselling of exquisitely crafted compositions, as well as (perhaps) to general difficulties encountered in writing string quartets later in life.[20] Deletions, alterations and corrections, large and small alike, assume rhythmic, harmonic, melodic and structural significance. Among countless examples, Mozart deleted one bar between 33 and 34 of K. 428/i (see Example 6.1), which, in emphasizing the dominant of the

---

[17] Georg Nikolaus von Nissen, *Biographie W. A. Mozarts* (1828) (Hildesheim, 1991), pp. 489–90.

[18] See Hans Keller, 'The Chamber Music', in H. C. Robbins Landon and Donald Mitchell (eds.), *The Mozart Companion* (London, 1969), p. 102; Alfred Einstein, *Mozart: His Character, His Work*, trans. Arthur Mendel and Nathan Broder (Panther edition, London, 1971), p. 192; Michael Levey, *The Life and Death of Mozart* (London, 1971), p. 180; John Rosselli, *The Life of Mozart* (Cambridge, 1998), p. 56; Wye Jamison Allanbrook, '"To Serve the Private Pleasure": Expression and Form in the String Quartets', in Stanley Sadie (ed.), *Wolfgang Amadè Mozart: Essays on his Life and Music* (Oxford, 1996), pp. 132–60, at p. 156.

[19] MBA, vol. III, p. 373; LMF, p. 886 (16 February 1785). See also Friedrich Schlichtegroll, *Johannes Chrysostomus Wolfgang Gottlieb Mozart* (1793), ed. Erich Hermann Müller von Asow (Leipzig, 1942), p. 15. For the complete dedication as published (in Italian) in the Artaria edition, see MDL, p. 220 and MDB, p. 250; MBA, vol. III, p. 404 and LMF, pp. 891–2.

[20] On the latter point, see Tyson, *Mozart: Studies of the Autograph Scores*, pp. 46–7. The autograph is housed at the British Library in London. For a facsimile, see Wolfgang Amadeus Mozart, *The Six 'Haydn' Quartets: Facsimile of the Autograph Manuscripts in the British Library, Add. MS 37763* (London, 1985).

Example 6.1 Mozart, String Quartet in E flat, K. 428/i, bars 33–40
(including Mozart's deletion).

Example 6.2 Mozart, String Quartet in D minor, K. 421/iv, bars 9–10
(including Mozart's deletion).

dominant, would have probably precluded further play on the A natural/A
flat conflict that characterizes both the main theme and the subsequent
discourse in the transition, symbolizing the respective pulls of dominant
and tonic. The cancellation of the original bar allows A flats a temporary
foothold once again (35–6) before a firm German Augmented 6–I$^6_4$–V^7–I
confirmation of the dominant B flat (37–40). Five quavers of a 6/8 bar are
also excised early in the second half of the theme section of K. 421/iv
(Example 6.2) presumably because their inflection to the relative major

Example 6.3 Mozart, String Quartet in E flat, K. 428/ii, bars 22–30 (including Mozart's deletion).

would have detracted from the perfect cadence in F at the midpoint of the section. In K. 428/ii, a four-and-a-half bar deletion (Example 6.3) provides not only material rebarred immediately after it in the autograph, but also a harmonic progression in its last six quavers (I^6–IV/II^6–I^6_4–V) that is prolonged in the finalized bars 26–30. A crotchet–quaver–quaver–crotchet–crotchet rhythm new to the finale of K. 387 is squeezed in to the second violin, viola and cello parts in bars 221–4 (Example 6.4), Mozart presumably realizing after first writing the fugue subject in the top line that the impact of the sidestep to ♭VI could be dramatically enhanced by the accompaniment. And the original order of the K. 464/iii variations – 1, 2, 3,

Example 6.4 Mozart, String Quartet in G, K. 387/iv, bars 220–6 (where the notation for v2, va and vc in bars 220–4 inclusive is compressed).

6, 5, Coda, with the *minore* variation 4 notated at the end – may have been revised to group the 'regular' and 'irregular' variations together, or to change the position of the 'luminous fifth variation . . . to create a convincing, even if more conventional, close'.[21] It is surely indisputable that 'Mozart was still shaping and reshaping [the 'Haydn' quartets] while writing [them] down', envisaging compositional improvements in the process.[22]

That said, our perception of Mozart's achievements in the 'Haydn' quartets is unnecessarily limited by consideration only of compositional connoisseurship and of a purported appeal exclusively to connoisseurs. The resulting impression is of a compositional endeavour carried out semi-abstractly, where fastidious work to perfect the quartets in order to impress the dedicatee Haydn and other musical connoisseurs took precedence over the reality of writing music for publication and for performance. In fact, Mozart may have decided to dedicate his quartets to Haydn only on seeing Ignaz Pleyel dedicate his op. 2 to Haydn for publication by the Vienna-based Graeffer in mid-December 1784.[23] More important, Mozart could not have ignored the need to sell his quartets to a publisher and for that publisher then to sell copies to the musical public; Mozart's remit

[21] Marius Flothuis, 'A Close Reading of the Autographs of Mozart's Ten Late Quartets', in Wolff (ed.), *The String Quartets of Haydn, Mozart and Beethoven*, pp. 154–73, at 158; Elaine R. Sisman, *Haydn and the Classical Variation* (Cambridge, MA), pp. 210–14, at 214.

[22] See Ludwig Finscher, 'Aspects of Mozart's Compositional Process in the Quartet Autographs: I. The Early Quartets, II. The Genesis of K. 387', in Wolff (ed.), *The String Quartets of Haydn, Mozart and Beethoven*, pp. 121–53, at 132. For more on Mozart's autograph revisions, see Flothuis, 'A Close Reading of the Autographs of Mozart's Ten Late Quartets'.

[23] See Mark Evan Bonds, 'Replacing Haydn: Mozart's "Pleyel" Quartets', *Music & Letters*, 88/2 (2007), pp. 201–25, at 218. Needless to say, this is not to deny the influence of Haydn – the pre-eminent composer of string quartets at that time – on the four earlier quartets in the 'Haydn' set that were already complete by December 1784, namely K. 387, 421, 428 and 458. On Haydn's influence, see in particular Bonds, 'The Sincerest Form of Flattery? Mozart's "Haydn" Quartets and the Question of Influence', *Studi musicali*, 22 (1993), pp. 365–409.

consequently extended beyond refined and talented connoisseurs.[24] It has recently been argued that Mozart accommodated the broader audience of listeners in the 'Haydn' quartets. Evidence comprises Mozart's famous letter about striking a happy medium in his piano concertos, where the 'default mode of writing ... is to appeal first and foremost to the non-connoisseurs and to create moments from which connoisseurs alone will obtain satisfaction', as well as individual movements from K. 387, 428 and 465, which try 'to balance ... contrasting modes of writing that will appeal to connoisseurs and amateurs alike' and to juxtapose 'the difficult and the clear ... inscribing both *Kenner* and *Liebhaber* into these works, just not necessarily at the same time'.[25]

Concern for prospective performers of the 'Haydn' quartets perhaps weighed more heavily on Mozart's mind than concern for prospective listeners, both because the published works were intended not for public concerts with large audiences but for private renditions in small, intimate gatherings, and because players naturally would have been expected to purchase more copies than listeners. The documented difficulties of playing and listening to the quartets in the fifteen years or so post-publication,[26] often cited in the secondary literature, have probably influenced our understanding of the works more than they should, since the corollary is that difficulties experienced even by connoisseurs at the end of the eighteenth century were difficulties Mozart deliberately intended, without finding it necessary to appeal to a broad spectrum of listeners and players. As will be shown, attention to performers and performances of the quartets significantly affected Mozart's path to publication and the publication itself.

[24] The sale of the quartets to Artaria took place late in their gestation period. On 22 January 1785, Leopold reported to Nannerl, receiving a short letter that very day from Mozart that stated inter alia that he had sold his quartets to Artaria for 100 ducats. See MBA, vol. III, p. 368; LMF, p. 885. (K. 464 and K. 465 were entered into the *Verzeichnüss* on 10 January and 14 January respectively.)

[25] See Mark Evan Bonds, 'Listening to Listeners', in Danuta Mirka and Kofi Agawu (eds.), *Communication in Eighteenth-Century Music* (Cambridge, 2008), pp. 34–52, at 41–3. Elaine Sisman argues in a similar vein that the reference to the 'happy medium' in Mozart's letter about K. 413–15 (28 December 1782) is more applicable to the 'Haydn' quartets than the piano concertos, to Mozart's 'challenge of *demonstrating art* for the Kenner demanding

satisfaction, while also *concealing art* for the Nichtkenner seeking more passive pleasures'. Thus, the string quartets from 1782–83 'represented Mozart's attempt to forge a new path between the Viennese Kenner scene, mediated by Baron Gottfried van Swieten's quartet sessions in fugal repertory, and the broader social world promised by Haydn's newly published op. 33 quartets.' See Sisman, 'Observations on the First Phase of Mozart's "Haydn" Quartets', in Dorothea Link and Judy Nagley (eds.), *Words About Mozart* (Woodbridge and Rochester, NY, 2005), pp. 33–58, at 41 and 42.

[26] For comments from the classical era, see Simon P. Keefe, *Mozart's Viennese Instrumental Music: a Study of Stylistic Re-Invention* (Woodbridge and Rochester, NY, 2007), pp. 89–90.

Performance and publication

As is well known, a lot of discrepancies exist between the musical text of Mozart's autograph of the 'Haydn' quartets and the parts published by Artaria for the first edition in September 1785, many of which can be attributed with near certainty to Mozart himself.[27] In one case in particular, the first eighteen bars of the development section of the K. 387 finale (125–42), Mozart made several revisions in his autograph, subsequently arriving at his final version only in the first edition.[28] Here, and elsewhere, Mozart would have notated changes intended for the published edition on performance copies generated from the autograph. In accordance with normal practice, Artaria would then have used marked-up copies rather than the autograph in preparing the musical text for the edition.[29]

In comparing the autograph and the first edition, the largest number of additions and alterations for the printed text involve dynamics.[30] Since Mozart probably made the adjustments either during or after one of the play-throughs of the quartets before publication, the practical effects of his works in performance presumably affected him above all when interpolating or changing markings. As has been pointed out: 'Mozart's lingering indecision on [dynamic signs and tempo indications] demonstrated in the autographs, was finally overcome in trial performances, in which he decided on the "final" text.'[31] Even though performance copies of the 'Haydn' quartets originating before the first edition are no longer extant, we know of their erstwhile existence from performances documented in Mozart's correspondence. Several took place in early 1785 (15 January, 12 February, 2 April), but also in 1784 before the set was complete, judging by Mozart's reference to the violinist Zeno Franz Menzel sightreading them better than anyone else in Vienna.[32] Leopold had also received K. 387, 421

[27] See Wolf-Dieter Seiffert, 'Mozart's "Haydn" Quartets: an Evaluation of the Autographs and First Edition, with Particular Attention to mm. 125–42 of the Finale of K. 387', in Cliff Eisen (ed.), *Mozart Studies 2* (Oxford, 1997), pp. 175–200. For the first edition see W. A. Mozart, *Sei Quartetti per due violini, viola, e violoncello composti e dedicati al Signor Giuseppe Haydn* (Vienna, 1785). The publication is given on the title page as Artaria's plate number 59 and as Mozart's op. 10.
[28] Seiffert, 'Evaluation of the Autographs and First Edition', pp. 176–90.
[29] *Ibid.*, pp. 194–5.
[30] There are also a lot of cautionary accidentals in the first edition that do not appear in the autograph: 'In all likelihood ... [they]

derive from the experience of specific performances before the engraving was begun.' Seiffert, 'Evaluation of the Autographs and First Edition', p. 194.
[31] Seiffert, 'Evaluation of the Autographs and First Edition', p. 195.
[32] See MBA, vol. III, p. 368 and LMF, p. 885 (letter of 22 January 1785 from Leopold to Nannerl); MBA, vol. III, p. 373 and LMF, p. 886 (letter of 16 February 1785 from Leopold to Nannerl); MBA, vol. III, p. 384 (letter of 2 April 1785; not in LMF); MBA, vol. III, p. 310; LMF, p. 874 (letter of 10 April 1784). Seiffert explains ('Evaluation of the Autograph and First Edition', p. 192): 'we can conclude from various documentary references that at least two complete manuscripts existed before the first edition appeared'.

and 428 before his trip to Vienna in early 1785, and doubtless played them in Salzburg.[33]

The Artaria first edition has various limitations, probably related for the most part to the mechanics of the engraving process. As is often the case in late eighteenth-century editions, slurs and phrase marks are imprecise in ways that Mozart would not have sanctioned in notating the performance copies: they are sometimes divided seemingly to accommodate changes in stem direction and only occasionally snake between segments with both upward- and downward-pointing stems; and their duration is frequently either unclear, or self-evidently too long or too short.[34] The positioning of dynamic marks is affected by the typesetting process: they are often moved to the left of their ideal location, for example, if a note on a leger line gets in the way. The standard indication for a crescendo, '*cresc:*', is only rarely elongated (such as by a broken line, _ _ _ _), its end thus being more open to question than at the corresponding points of Mozart's autograph. Since '*cresc:*' occupies a uniform amount of typeset space on every occasion, no doubt on account of the same steel punch being used for each engraving, the extent of the musical material covered by it depends on how compact or spread out the instrumental notation is at the moment in question.[35] There are also a number of errors in the edition, involving dynamics, slurs and absent accidentals.[36]

Nevertheless, close similarities between the autograph and the first edition in a number of revealing passages underscore Artaria's serious intention to

[33] MBA, vol. III, p. 373 and LMF, p. 886 (16 February 1785).

[34] On the latter point, see for example K. 458/i (cello), bar 180; K. 458/iv (viola), bars 42–3 and 109; K. 428/i (second violin), bars 19–20; K. 428/i (first violin), bars 65–7; K. 464/i (viola), bars 12–14, 145. For a rare instance of a slur snaking between eight semiquavers, four with the stems pointing upwards and four with stems downwards, see K. 428/i (second violin), bar 122. On the unreliability of phrasing in general in late eighteenth-century editions, see Christina Georgiou, 'The Historical Editing of Mozart's Keyboard Sonatas: History, Context and Practice' (PhD thesis, City University London, 2011), p. 67.

[35] Places where '*cresc:*' indications are *not* extended across a protracted passage in the edition and where the autograph indicates they should be extended, include: K. 464/i, bars 134–7, 191–3; K. 464/iii, bars 157–9; K. 465/i, bars 114–15 (second violin, viola, cello); K. 465/ii, bars 20–2, 40–2, 63–5; K. 465/iv, bars 382–6. Extended crescendi are given in (for example): K. 465/i, bars 100–2

(viola, but not in first violin and second violin); K. 465/ii, bars 69–71 (viola); K. 465/iv, bars 389–90 and 396–9 (both cello). On the steel punches used in the engraving process in late eighteenth-century Viennese publications, see Rupert Ridgewell, 'Biographical Myth and the Publication of Mozart's Piano Quartets', *Journal of the Royal Musical Association*, 135 (2010), pp. 41–114, at 87–8.

[36] See, for example, the following: K. 421/i (cello), bar 83, beat 3, *p*; K. 421/i (cello), bar 98, beat 3, *f* (which appears two bars early); K. 421/iv (cello), bar 31, *p* (which appears one bar late); K. 458/iv (first violin), bar 129 (a minim rather than a crotchet); K. 458/iv (second violin), bar 259 (absent slur, when the first violin receives one and the second violin is unnotated and marked 'in 8tava' in the autograph); K. 465/iii (cello), bar 59, *p* (against *f* in all the other instruments and given as *f* in the autograph); K. 464/iv (cello), bars 97, 120 (respectively lacking a g sharp altogether and a sharp sign); K. 465/iii (viola), bar 24 (lacking a flat sign).

Example 6.5 Mozart, String Quartet in E flat, K. 428/iii, bars 48–54 (with no staccati in bars 50–2 inclusive, in either the autograph or the Artaria edition).

reproduce Mozart's text accurately throughout the publication process (that is, from performance copies generated, in turn, from the autograph) and not to add material themselves. For example, in K. 428/iii (bars 48–54, Example 6.5), K. 428/iv (bars 82–7), K. 464/i (bars 33–5) and K. 464/iii (bars 126⁴–34), only the exact staccati given in Mozart's autograph appear in the edition, even though the clear implication is that the staccati should continue when unnotated: reproducing Mozart's text is more important to Artaria, then, than standardizing it editorially. Also in K. 428/iv, only a single *p* is given in the second violin in bar 27, as in the autograph, when an altered version of the first eight bars to round off the Rondo theme section implies a standardization to simultaneous *p*s for all four instruments. In the development section of K. 465/i (bars 107–55), the so-called 'Dissonance' quartet, the first edition adheres absolutely precisely to the staccati and strokes notated by Mozart,[37] even when continuations unnotated in the autograph are certainly implied. The fact that the first edition (and seemingly the performance copies as well) did not take even a small editorial liberty in these passages, indicates the seriousness with which copying and engraving were approached vis-à-vis the material provided by Mozart.

Thus, all things considered, it is unlikely that the Artaria edition deliberately incorporated material not sanctioned by Mozart via annotations to the performance copies. Put another way, dynamic indications in short and long passages of the first edition for which no dynamic markings exist in the autograph are likely to derive from Mozart himself, from his continued thoughts about the quartets arrived at when playing through performance copies that would ultimately generate the published edition.[38]

---

[37] With one exception, the viola in bar 137.
[38] For applicable segments and passages in the first three quartets in the published set, see, for example, K. 387/i, bars 17–19, 125–7, 150–2; K. 387/iii, bars 43–6, 98–9; K. 387/iv, bars 268–78; K. 421/iv, bars 49–52, 57–61, 65–71, 113–34; K. 458/i, bars 125–6, 137–8; K. 458/iii, bar 49; K. 458/iv, bars 30–6, 102–6, 115–20, 228–33, 297–300, 308–12. The NMA records them in footnotes to the printed musical texts of all six quartets.

Ink colours in Mozart's autograph show that he revised and added to his musical texts on at least two passes through the autograph before handing it over for copying.[39] In a number of movements, dynamics were inserted into the score at these later stages of work. Thus, where dynamics are concerned, continuity can be posited between work on the autograph and annotations to the performance copies that made their way into the edition: in some cases, Mozart revisited a movement to add dynamics before surrendering the autograph for copying purposes; in other cases; he apparently waited until he was working with performance copies to include them. Similarly, no hard-and-fast distinction can be made between 'compositional' and 'performance-orientated' phases in Mozart's creative process: plainly, he will not have started thinking about performance issues and stopped thinking about compositional aspects of his works when working with the performance copies, just as he will not have excluded thoughts about performance when working with the autograph.

Mozart added dynamics to both K. 421/ii (Andante) and K. 458/ii (Minuet and Trio) in one of his passes through the autograph after writing the music.[40] Dynamics in the second movement of K. 421 ultimately support expression in timbral, textural and especially harmonic-tonal domains. Over the course of the A section, Mozart adds gently to the effects requested of performers, inviting them progressively to intensify musical expression (see Example 6.6). For example, the *mf*s in bars 2–3, slightly increasing the initial volume, lead in turn to the crescendo to *f* at the reappearance of the same figure in bars 6–7. After the double bar, and perhaps responding to an expansion of the harmonic palette to include Cm and V/g, Mozart moves more quickly than in bars 1–8 between *p* and *f*, echoing bar 10 twice in *p* and *pp* increments (bars 11, 12). A thematic extension appended to the return of the opening material that brings the A section to a close (Example 6.7, bars 21–6), coincides with a kind of dynamic synopsis of the movement thus far in its alternation of *f*, *p* and *mf* dynamics (minus notated crescendos). In the B section, perhaps again to reinforce the (expected) expansion of the movement's harmonic profile, Mozart asks for the longest *forte* passages so far (two full bars on two occasions, 31–2 and 47–8) and three crescendi in quick succession (bars 36–41, in the A flat major passage). The consecutive crescendi written at the end of the movement in A' take a procedural lead from the B section, then, while extending dynamics-related activities from A. Judging by ink colours in the minuet of K. 458/ii (Example 6.8), four *p*s (bar 11, early in the B section) and four *f*s (bar 21, at the beginning of the reprise) were

---

[39] Seiffert, 'Evaluation of the Autographs and First Edition', p. 191.   [40] *Ibid.*

Example 6.6 Mozart, String Quartet in D minor, K. 421/ii, bars 1–12.

Example 6.7 Mozart, String Quartet in D minor, K. 421/ii, bars 21–6.

written into the autograph alongside the notes (see Example 6.8, bars 9–28.) At a later stage, indicated by the darker ink, Mozart deleted the four *p*s and two of the *f*s (first violin and cello) and added all of the Minuet's other dynamic markings (including the *sf*s and *crescendi*). While the *p*s are simply displaced by two bars from their original location in bar 11 to bar 13, adjustments to the *f*s apparently capture an important re-evaluation of the B section's link to the reprise. Initially, Mozart envisaged the first violin carrying a one-bar *crescendo* by itself into the reprise (bar 20). The revision, though, sees the original *crescendo* crossed out and a new one written for the first violin, second violin and viola in bars 18–19; an *f* is therefore reached at the beginning of bar 20. Moreover, this juncture of the minuet – with its multi-instrument *crescendo* – is now

Example 6.8 Mozart, String Quartet in B flat, K. 458/ii, bars 9–28 (including Mozart's deleted dynamics).

aligned with the corresponding run-up to the reprise in the trio. The late-stage *sf*s in the minuet (bars 3–5, 23–5) also bring it into line with *sf*s and *sfp*s given in the trio, including several placed distinctively on the weak beats of both minuet and trio.[41]

It is clear from K. 421/ii and K. 458/ii that Mozart contemplated performers' expressive contributions while still working on the autographs and

[41] Small differences between the autograph and first edition of K. 458/ii might be attributable to Mozart, including the clarification in the edition that the second violin and viola reach *f* by the end of their crescendo at the end of the Minuet B section, and the *f–p/fp* markings for second violin, viola and cello in place of *sf–p/sfp* in the trio (cello, bar 8).

that (in the case of K. 458/ii at least) his views evolved over time. Mozart naturally could not have expected absolute sound levels from his performers when writing *p, mf, f* etc. But his dynamic refinements, linked to harmonic-tonal and formal procedures, need to be actively interpreted by players in response to synergies he promotes between dynamic effects and harmonic-tonal effects.

Many dynamics not present in the autograph but included in the first edition also appear to support notable textural, harmonic and tonal procedures. In the concluding *Più allegro* of K. 421/iv (Example 6.9), Mozart added a number of markings to the single marking in the auto-graph (an *f* in bar 139 accompanying the *tierce de picardie* shift to D major three bars before the end). *Piano*s and *forte*s coincide with distinctive harmonic moments, as if to support the mutually reinforcing harmonic and dynamic effects for bar 139 conceived at the autograph stage: a *forte* coincides with chromatic intensification, *piano*s with consecutive and different diminished harmonies, a *forte* with a rescoring of the diminished passage, and a *piano* with the final D minor cadences of the work (bars 120–4, 124–8, 129–33, 134–8 respectively; Example 6.9). Similarly, the textural intensification of Variation 2 (bars 49–72), each instrument receiving its own discrete musical strand at the opening of each A–B–A section, is enhanced in the Artaria edition with *fp*s and *f*s for viola and cello. It is not surprising that Mozart almost certainly notated dynamic intensifications to the performance copies of this second variation – and indeed the *Più allegro* at the end of the movement – after hearing them played, for the ebb and flow conveys a special energy in performance that is augmented by additional dynamics. Pre-publication renditions of K. 421/iv and K. 428/i could have motivated other additions as well. An *f* accruing to the end of bar 38 of K. 421/iv in the edition creates a 4 (*f*) + 2 (*p*) + 2 (*f*) profile for the first eight bars of the second section of the first variation, rather than the 4 (*f*) + 4 (*p*) profile of the autograph; one can imagine Mozart hearing the variation in performance and desiring not only an increased emphasis on the modulation to F (*p* in the theme section and originally *p* in the first variation at bars 39–40) but also a quicker alternation of dynamics than initially envisaged, as a precursor to the change of dynamics in almost every bar in the second half of the section. Considerable energy also accrues to the development section of K. 428/i between the autograph and the first edition: *f, fp* and *p* dynamics added to the edition in bars 77–91 (Example 6.10) augment the *f–p* contrasts given in the autograph at the beginning and the end of the development. Each type of material in bars 77–91 receives its own discrete marking: the triplet arpeggios are *f*; sustained notes are *fp*; and semiquaver/quaver figures are *p*. All three types are then combined in bars 85–91, the back and

Example 6.9 Mozart, String Quartet in D minor, K. 421/iv, bars 120–42 (with Artaria dynamic additions in bold italics).

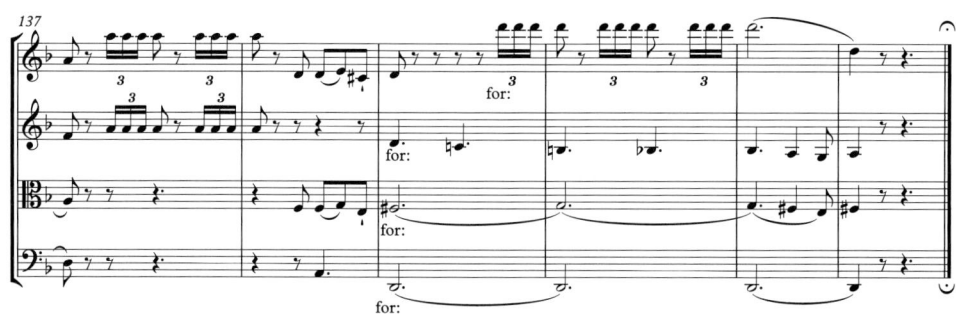

Example 6.10 Mozart, String Quartet in E flat, K. 428/i, bars 77–91 (with Artaria dynamic additions in bold italics).

Example 6.11 Mozart, String Quartet in E flat, K. 428/iii, bars 60–6 (with Artaria dynamic additions in bold italics).

Example 6.12 Mozart, String Quartet in A, K. 464/i, bars 157–62 (with Artaria dynamic additions in bold italics).

forth of different dynamics encouraging a vigorous performance not implied by the autograph.

Elsewhere in the 'Haydn', set dynamics accruing to the first edition accentuate existing musical drama. The passage from bar 60–6 in K. 428/iii (Example 6.11), already a climactic juncture of the minuet in the autograph with an *ff*, quick-fire imitation in the first violin, second violin and viola and *sf*s in the cello, becomes more climactic still: additional *sf*s in the upper three parts create a ripple of accented sounds (bars 60–3). The run-up to the recapitulation of K. 464/i is similar (Example 6.12). In the autograph Mozart includes two *sfp*s for the cello on the second beats of bars 158 and 159 to coincide with diminished harmonies that interrupt the E pedal preparing for the reprise; in the edition *fp*s accrue to the upper parts (*f*–*p*s in the viola), now emphasizing both dominant and diminished harmonies. The climactic moment in the B section of the minuet K. 464/ii, a *forte* half-diminished chord presented by a united quartet, acquires notes in the edition's cello part

Example 6.13 Mozart, String Quartet in A, K. 464/ii, bars 1–8 (all dynamics from Artaria edition).

(octave g/Gs rather than single gs, bars 42–3), lending further weight to the gesture.[42]

Dynamics notated only in the first edition of the entire trio of K. 464/ii also reinforce a prevailing compositional strategy (see Examples 6.13 and 6.14). Unusually for Mozart, A' comprises a modest decorative elaboration of A rather than a straightforward reprise, a process complemented by a dynamic adjustment to A in A': the *p–cresc* (A, Example 6.13) is replaced by the *forte* in bar 29 (A', Example 6.14). The combined *forte* and textural intensification in the last four bars of the trio thus support a moment of mild climax.

While the reinforcement of musical processes through dynamics is clearly a feature of the 'Haydn' string quartets, it by no means tells the full story. For on a number of occasions discrepancies between dynamics in the autograph and the first edition point to Mozart's views about performance evolving over time. Of course, in the absence of the actual performance copies Mozart used, it cannot be established for certain that specific differences between autograph and first edition originated with Mozart rather than creeping inadvertently into the first edition as a result of copying errors. But Mozart's potential involvement gains credibility where patterns of differences emerge, and especially once the seriousness with which Artaria went about the task of reproducing Mozart's text for the first edition is taken into account (see above).

The Andante cantabile K. 387/iii contains numerous discrepancies between dynamics written in the autograph and printed in the first edition. In bars 43–6 and 98–9, dynamics accrue to the edition (see Examples 6.15 and 6.16). Both segments contain markings that are unaligned among

---

[42] The NMA does not follow the first-edition cello part in bars 42–3, sticking with the autograph text instead.

Example 6.14 Mozart, String Quartet in A, K. 464/ii, bars 25–32 (all dynamics from Artaria edition).

Example 6.15 Mozart, String Quartet in G, K. 387/iii, bars 43–7 (with Artaria dynamics in bold italics and autograph dynamics above each stave).

Example 6.16 Mozart, String Quartet in G, K. 387/iii, bars 98–100 (with Artaria dynamic additions in bold italics).

instruments playing imitated material: an *sfp* and *f–p* for first and second violins in bar 46;[43] and an *fp* for viola, *sfp* for second violin and cello and nothing for first violin in bars 98–9. In bar 47, too, a uniform *forte* for all four instruments in the autograph becomes *fps* for first and second violin and *fs* for viola and cello in the edition. Such dynamic non-alignment becomes potentially significant once dynamics elsewhere in the movement are factored into the equation, including the cultivation of a degree of dynamic autonomy for individual instruments in both autograph and edition. For example, instruments are set apart dynamically, even if only slightly, in both the first-theme and the transition sections of the autograph. In the continuation of the first theme (bar 7ff., Example 6.17), the cello is asked to crescendo from *pp* to *p*, the first violin that imitates the cello presumably to play *p* (given in bar 4) and the second violin and viola presumably to retain the *pp* notated in bar 6,[44] Mozart indicating a little more prominence for the cello–first violin imitation than for the inner parts. Similarly, the cello triplet-semiquavers in bars 15–18 of the transition are *forte*, while the first violin and viola receive differently lengthened *f–ps* with corresponding material[45] and the second violin *fps*; in the second theme, the first violin has an *sf* accent (with a subsequent descrescendo) and the second violin, viola and cello *fps* (bar 36).

On account of the autograph of K. 387/iii, we need to give serious consideration as composer-endorsed readings to alterations in the edition that foreground non-alignments and re-alignments of dynamics among the

[43] Even if the second violin *f–p* in the first edition is an incorrect rendering of an intended *fp*, dynamics between the first and second violins remain unaligned.

[44] The NMA gives an editorial *p* for the second violin and viola in bar 8. But there is no reason to assume a standard *p* dynamic level for all four instruments at this moment.

[45] The viola's *ps* in the NMA are given on the fourth quavers in bars 15–16 to match the *ps* in the first violin, even though the markings clearly occur in the autograph on the third quavers.

Example 6.17 Mozart, String Quartet in G, K. 387/iii, bars 1–9 (from the autograph).

four instruments. The beginning of the first theme (bars 1–4, Example 6.18) is a case in point. Dynamic independence in line with the 1 + 2 + 1 texture is already evident in the autograph (see Example 6.17): an *f* is reached in the first violin in bar 3 via a crescendo in bars 1–2, when the second violin, viola and cello reach *f* only in bar 4; and the cello has no crescendo in bar 2, when both the second violin and viola receive one. The first violin in the edition has no crescendo at all, either as a result of a copying error or of Mozart crossing it out on a performance copy.[46] Potentially at least, the difference is no small matter in performance, affecting musical relationships among members of the group. With a crescendo in bars 1–2, the first violin aligns itself with the accompaniment in the second violin and viola, preparing for its *f* at the beginning of bar 3, but without one comes closer to the cello quavers, permitting (should a performer be so inclined) a more sudden arrival of a *forte* dynamic at bar 3.[47] Discrepancies between autograph and

[46] An instruction Mozart wrote at the beginning of the autograph score of K. 387/iii indicates that the first violin had already been copied ('schon geschrieben') by the time the second violin, viola and cello were to be copied.

[47] The presence of a first-violin crescendo in the edition at the corresponding point in the

recapitulation of K. 387/iii (bar 52) does not necessarily imply that the original absence of the crescendo was an error. Mozart may have envisaged a slightly different effect in performance at these two junctures of the movement.

Example 6.18 Mozart, String Quartet in G, K. 387/iii, bars 1–4 (from the first edition).

first-edition markings at corresponding junctures of the transition and in the secondary development (bars 15ff. and 70ff.) perhaps also demonstrate revised intentions on Mozart's part. The *f*s (first violin, second violin, viola) and *p*s (second violin, viola, cello) not in the autograph and added to the first edition in bars 17 and 19 result in an *f* dynamic for the first violin's demisemiquavers in bar 19ff. against a *p* in the lower parts in the edition, rather than a uniform *p* for all four in the autograph. The corresponding passage in the recapitulation (Example 6.19) has the first violin's demisemiquavers *p* in bar 74, following on from the *p* in bar 73. However, the placement of the *p*s in the first violin, second violin and viola in bars 72 and 73 is different in the autograph and first edition, namely synchronized in the first edition in bar 72, but not 73, and in the autograph in bar 73 but not 72.

In both autograph and first edition of the 'Haydn' set, dynamic non-alignments point to Mozart's concern for variety rather than regularity of sound.[48] The autograph of the first movement of K. 387 foreshadows the Andante cantabile in this respect. In bars 21–4 of K. 387/i (Example 6.20), the first violin figure is initially set *p* against *f*s in the other strings, the four instrumentalists then coming together with co-ordinated *fp*s and a *p*. We therefore hear the first violin as separate from the group dynamically as well as texturally at the outset and then aligned with it. Mozart originally thought to align them all dynamically from the start, demonstrated by the first violin *for:* crossed out at bar 21 in the autograph and replaced with a *pia.*; his ultimate desire for contrast at this juncture is confirmed by the alteration. The *fp*s for first violin throughout the corresponding segment of the recapitulation in the first edition (bars 129–32) support a different effect rather

---

[48] For an article making a similar point about Mozart's dynamic annotations to a manuscript copy of Haydn's string quartet op. 17 no. 6, see Cliff Eisen, 'Mozart Plays Haydn', *Mozart-Jahrbuch 2006*, pp. 409–21, at 413.

Example 6.19 Mozart, String Quartet in G, K. 387/iii, bars 70–4 (with Artaria adjustments to the autograph in bold italics above each stave).

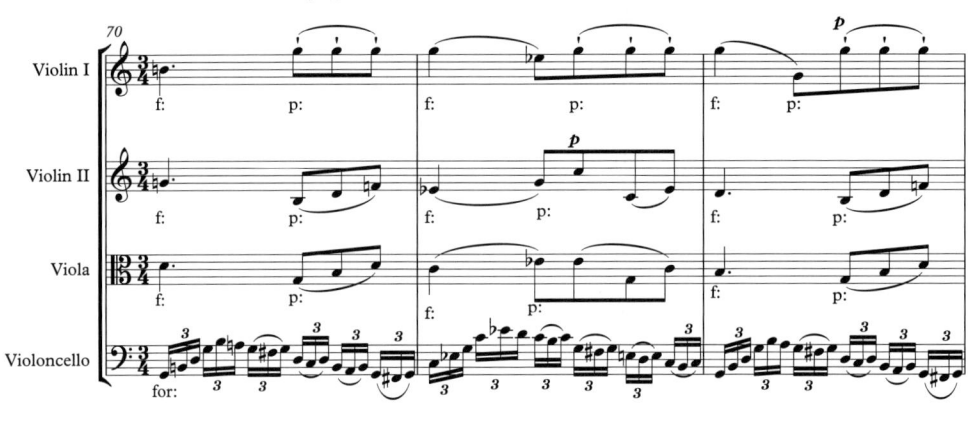

than justifying editorial intervention in the transition.[49] The edition's crescendo for first violin by itself in bar 19 (see Example 6.20) rather than alongside the second violin, viola and cello in bar 20 (as in the autograph) also supports the temporary non-alignment of the first violin and the rest of the ensemble. In the minuet and trio K. 387/ii, Mozart makes a particular feature of un-synchronized dynamics: the distinctive beat-by-beat alternation of *p* and *f* in the main theme, when heard simultaneously in second violin and viola, sets the two dynamics directly against each other on every crotchet of bars 14 and 16.

Elsewhere, too, discrepancies between the autograph and the edition point tentatively to Mozart seeking alignments of instrumental sounds and textures different from those originally envisaged, after experiencing the works first hand in performance. In the autograph of the trio of K. 458/ii, the first

[49] The NMA issues a cautionary *fp* for the first violin in bar 21[1] and 22[1] in spite of lacking support from autograph and first edition.

Example 6.20 Mozart, String Quartet in G, K. 387/i, bars 19–24 (including Mozart's deletion in the autograph and an Artaria marking in bold italics above the stave).

violin passes an *sfp* octave figure to the cello (bars 7–8) with uninflected *p*s in the second violin and viola accompaniment, whereas in the first edition *f*–*p*s are given to the second violin, viola and cello in bar 8 and no *sfp* to the cello. K. 428/ii opens *p*–*sf*–*p* in all four instruments in the autograph (bars 1–2), but *p*–*f*–*p* in the edition. (The *sf* markings are clear in the autograph, so are unlikely to have been misinterpreted in the copying process.) And the end of both sections of the third variation of K. 464/iii finishes with *fp*s in the violins and viola and *sfp*s in the cello in the autograph but *fp*s for all four instruments in the edition. Differences in articulation in the autograph and edition also suggest changed instrumental alignments. In the second theme of K. 387/i, the cello half-step oscillation (bar 30, see Example 6.21) is slurred in the autograph and aligned with the immediately preceding slurred semiquavers, but demarcated by strokes in the first edition that now foreshadow the semiquaver oscillations with strokes in the first violin and viola at the start of the restatement. Ultimately, neither articulation is 'better' than the other. Presumably after hearing the work played, Mozart came to prefer a presentiment of upcoming articulation (strokes) to an imitative rounding off of a previous one (slurs). The resulting impression is that the cello in the edition stands slightly apart from the

Example 6.21 Mozart, String Quartet in G, K. 387/i, bars 27–32 (with the articulation change for the cello in the Artaria edition in square brackets).

second violin and viola at the moment of delivery; the 1 + 3 texture that saw the first violin separated dynamically from the other instruments nine bars earlier in the transition (see Example 6.20) now morphs into a 2 + 1 texture in which the cello is momentarily distinguished by its different articulation. At the corresponding juncture of the recapitulation (bar 138), the autograph slur is retained in the edition, Mozart looking for a different alignment of instruments than in the exposition as he had done in the secondary development passage (bars 129–32) relative to the transition passage.

Conclusion

Practical decisions taken by performers today about the primacy of the autograph or first edition must be informed by the reality that the 'Haydn' quartets continued to evolve in their composer's mind after he had ceased working on the autograph. Responding to pre-publication performances by marking up performance copies, Mozart sometimes reinforced compositional processes by interpolating dynamics but sometimes changed his mind about renditions as evidenced by dynamic alterations. Such reactions would have been conditioned not only by Mozart's experiences of the quartets in performance but also (perhaps) by his perception of the needs and expectations of the customers purchasing the edition. Much more is at stake in Mozart's additions and alterations for the first edition than philological supremacy. Dynamics alone – their placement by Mozart and their interpretation by performers – create and refine relationships among quartet participants, shedding light on issues of interaction and individual and collective identity, on how (in short) the 'conversation' between individual participants is heard at a particular moment and over an extended period. Mozart's experiences of performance in the run-up to publication, the traces of which are communicated in the first edition, are therefore intrinsic to the identity, meaning and expression of the quartets.

Thus, the dominant historical view of the 'Haydn' quartets as exquisitely crafted compositions meticulously written and revised in order to please only a small, rarefied group of musicians, offers too narrow a critical perspective on their ontological significance. Mozart's opinions on performance evolved over time, affecting the published product, and perhaps continued to evolve beyond publication as well; they were 'live' works for Mozart, reinforced and altered after being contemplated in sound. And modern-day performers can capture this vibrancy. Ultimately, specific decisions about adopting autograph or first-edition markings on a case-by-case basis matter less than following Mozart's lead in thoughtfully and energetically interpreting the music in performance. The lively relationship between autograph and edition, mediated through performances Mozart experienced, can be reflected in our own animated renditions of the works, which might even take dynamic differences in the two principal sources as hermeneutic points of departure.

While Mozart's 'Haydn' quartets do not owe their existence to his dual status as performing composer and composing performer, their texts are as influenced by performance experiences and concerns as the piano concertos from 1782 to 1786 and the piano sonatas from *c.* 1783.[50] The spur to creative interpretation engendered by the concertos and sonatas, where the performer is encouraged to assume the imaginative mantle of the composer, again characterizes the 'Haydn' set; Mozart's mindset as a performer is ever present, then, even when he is writing instrumental music primarily for others rather than for himself. We owe it to these works and their composer to try to mirror in our own interpretations the intensely creative processes that led to their publication, whether we pay special attention to shaping the dynamic discourse of a particular movement or work; to correspondences and/or contradictions between markings in autographs and first editions; to inconsistencies as well as consistencies in dynamics and articulation; to relationships among participants; to the projection of an identity or series of identities for a work. Mozart's engagement with his 'Haydn' quartets in the moment can become the 'liveness' of our own interpretations. Mozart's product and the process that led to the creation of that product provide mutually reinforcing stimuli for our modern renditions.

---

[50] On the concertos and sonatas, see Keefe, *Mozart in Vienna: the Final Decade.*

7   The trouble with Cherubino . . .

Ian Woodfield

In his account of *Le nozze di Figaro*, Lorenzo Da Ponte recalled a crucial meeting with Joseph II during the course of which he succeeded in gaining permission to stage Mozart's new opera. In view of the recent ban on a German-language production of *La folle journée*, the conversation turned naturally to the question of censorship:

> But that Marriage of Figaro, returned he, I have forbidden to be performed in the National Theatre; you ought to have known that. Sir, answered I, as I had to write an opera, and not a comedy, I have been able to omit certain scenes, and shorten others, and I have carefully expunged whatever might offend the decency of a theatre over which your majesty presides. If that is the case, replied he, I rely on your opinion for the goodness of the music, and on your prudence for the choice of the characters; you may immediately give the parts to the copyist.[1]

In a perhaps rather surprising decision, Joseph agreed to allow the production to go ahead, but he insisted that Da Ponte take responsibility for ensuring the work's propriety.[2] With the apparent freedom of self-censorship, however, went increased responsibility. As it was obviously vital to avoid giving offence to the emperor, the informal scrutiny of contentious passages would have to be every bit as rigorous as anything that would have been demanded by a state censor in a formal review.

As he makes very clear in the preface to the libretto, Da Ponte's primary task in adapting *La folle journée* was a technical one: to reduce its length to fit 'the prescribed duration for dramatic representations'. He was well aware of the need to remove elements of political satire inappropriate for a musical genre, to which end the greater part of Figaro's diatribe was pruned. He passes rather lightly over other issues, merely alluding to certain 'prudent decisions' with regard to the exigencies of morality, location and audience. While there were many pedantic regulations as to what could or could not be represented on the Viennese stage, the critical issue with this work was the

[1] *An Extract from the Life of Lorenzo da Ponte* (New York, 1819); Daniel Heartz, 'Constructing *Le nozze di Figaro*', *Journal of the Royal Musical Association*, 112 (1986), pp. 77–98, at 80–1.

[2] Little information survives as to how Italian *opere buffe* texts were in general regulated. There was apparently no requirement for them to be submitted to the censor's office responsible for German drama.

168

question of moral decency; in particular, the impropriety of the Countess's feelings for an adolescent boy. In his preface, Beaumarchais revelled in the piquant persona of Chérubin:

> Excessively shy before the Countess, he is a charming rascal everywhere else; the root of his nature is a restless and undefined longing. He plunges aimlessly and ignorantly into puberty; yielding completely to every experience; in short he is the way every mother, at the bottom of her heart, would perhaps want her son to be, however greatly it would make her suffer.[3]

In the play itself, Chérubin's attraction to the Countess is as obvious as her reciprocal fondness for him. It would have come as no surprise when the third drama in the trilogy, *La mère coupable*, featured a love-child conceived during an illicit liaison between the two. An affair such as this, crossing ages and classes and undermining the high expectations of (female) marital fidelity, went far beyond the bounds of eighteenth-century Viennese theatrical propriety. From the start of his work on the opera, it must have been evident to Da Ponte that even a hint of such a relationship, let alone its full representation onstage, would be unacceptable. As if this was not difficult enough, he also had to take account of the issue of cross-dressing. Cherubino is played by a woman, adding erotic overtones to the scene in which 'he' is dressed and the whiteness of his arms admired.

As a prelude to a detailed discussion of how the authors of *Figaro* struggled to reconcile the requirements of dramatic coherence with words, acts and situations likely to cause offence, it will be useful to identify the main elements in the relationship between Chérubin and the Countess as they unfold in Acts 1 and 2. These are summarized in Table 7.1.

By general consent, Da Ponte succeeded brilliantly in fashioning a polished and coherent libretto out of an unusually complex play. In handling the contentious relationship between the Countess and Cherubino, his strategy was to remove from her role not only any suspicion of improper behaviour but also any awareness on her part of his feelings. In considering the character of the page, however, he concluded that the plot required his amorous interest to be convincing. He thus retained the page's fantasy of the dressing and undressing of the Countess, even drawing attention to it with rhetorically heightened language: 'You dress her in the morning, undress her at night, fix her pins, her laces . . .' ('Che la vesti il mattino, / Che la sera la spogli, che le metti . . . / Gli spilloni, i merletti . . .'). On the question of where to allow him to dramatize his state of mind more fully in an aria, Da Ponte

---

[3] *Le nozze di Figaro K.492: Facsimile of the Autograph Score* (Los Altos, CA, 2007), introductory essay by Norbert Miller, p. 9.

Table 7.1 Chérubin and the Countess in Acts 1 and 2 of *La folle journée*

Act 1, scene 7	Suzanne and Chérubin indulge in light-hearted banter. Chérubin reveals his feelings for his godmother, the only person who can help him avoid dismissal. Suzanne is fortunate to be in a position to dress her mistress in the morning and undress her in the evening, pin by pin. Chérubin snatches one of the Countess's ribbons and refuses to hand it back. In return he gives Suzanne a 'romance' he has written. In a febrile state, he confesses he no longer knows who he is. Every time he sees a woman his heart skips. Suzanne attempts to take back the ribbon, but Chérubin would rather die first.
Act 1, scene 9	With the Count and Chérubin in hiding, Bazile arrives and maliciously taunts Suzanne by reporting he has seen the page hanging around waiting to see her. The song the page is writing may be for her, but perhaps it is dedicated to the Countess? After all, it is common knowledge that at table Chérubin's eyes are fixed upon her. Hearing all this, the Count emerges in a rage and he confirms his decision to dismiss Chérubin.
Act 1, scene 10	In the crowd scene, Figaro asks why Chérubin is so downcast. Upon learning that the page is to be sent away, the Countess intercedes for him on the grounds of his youth. Chérubin offers a provocative and unconvincing apology to the Count: his behaviour may have been indiscreet but there has not been the least impropriety in his words! He kneels before the Countess but cannot speak. She is moved and the Count notices this, remarking in an aside that Bazile must have been right after all.
Act 2, scene 1	Suzanne reports Chérubin's favourable description of her mistress as well as his refusal to give back her ribbon. The Countess is eager to know what happened next, before suddenly realizing the improper direction her thoughts are taking: 'Laissons . . . laissons ces folies.'
Act 2, scene 3	Figaro has outlined his plot to have Chérubin dress up as Suzanne to take her place in the proposed assignation with the Count. The Countess waits for his arrival, dreamily staring at her small mirror.
Act 2, scene 4	When Chérubin arrives, Suzanne helps him out as he is hesitant with his words. His godmother is 'si . . . bonne!', to which she mischievously adds: 'Et si belle!' Chérubin agrees with a sigh. He blushes when asked about his song. It turns out to be a ballad featuring a soldier who has had to leave the godmother whom he will always adore.
Act 2, scene 5	Suzanne leaves to fetch a bonnet, and Chérubin and the Countess are momentarily alone. She is disappointed to learn that the page has already received his commission, and that there is therefore no excuse to delay his departure.
Act 2, scene 6	During the dressing scene with its erotic undertones, Chérubin is discovered wearing the Countess's ribbon, which he has used to bind a minor scratch. Suzanne is sent out.
Act 2, scene 7	The Countess stares at the ribbon. Chérubin 'devours her with his eyes'.
Act 2, scene 8	Suzanne returns and the Countess instructs her to find one of her own ribbons for a bandage, as she is intending to keep the ribbon with Cherubin's blood on it.
Act 2, scene 9	Again alone with the Countess, Chérubin kneels before her, eyes lowered. The Countess's ribbon would have healed him better.
Act 2, scene 10	In a panic at the sudden arrival of her husband, the Countess refers to Chérubin's state of semi-undress with his arms and shoulders naked.

decided that Chérubin's remark 'I no longer know who I am' ('Je ne sais plus ce que je suis') (Act 1, scene 7) would provide the perfect sentiment for an aria text. Skilled dramatist that he was, he sensed that it would be necessary to prepare the ground rhetorically, and he added in lines of his own to depict the page's near delirium before he embarks upon 'Non so più cosa son, cosa faccio'. When Susanna asks what she should do with the canzonetta he has just given to her, he replies: 'read it to my lady, read it yourself, read it to Barbarina, to Marcellina, to every woman in the palace' ('Leggila alla padrona: / Leggila tu medesma: / Leggila a Barbarina, a Marcellina; / Leggila ad ogni donna del palazzo'). In other words, broadcast my feelings to the whole wide world!

In Act 2, Beaumarchais presents the Countess struggling with her attraction to Chérubin. In reformulating these episodes, Da Ponte went as close to the boundary of taste as he dared. It was obviously necessary to abandon the text of Chérubin's ballad about his adored godmother with its fervently personal message. The replacement canzonetta 'Voi che sapete' expresses his feelings but only on a general level; there is nothing in it to arouse any personal suspicion on the part of the Countess who merely compliments him: 'Bravo! What a lovely voice!' ('Bravo! che bella voce!') As the dressing begins, Suzanne leaves repeatedly on errands for the Countess. Brief though these exits are, Da Ponte decided to retain them but not as separate scenes, perhaps with a view to forestalling numbering problems in the event of excisions being required later on. In Susanna's aria 'Venite inginocchiatevi', he demonstrated his penchant for teasing. Its punchline runs: 'if women love him [Cherubino], they certainly have their reason' ('Se l'amano le femmine, / Han certo il lor perchè'). The insinuation played on the fact that the Viennese audience would have been well aware that in the play the Countess harbours feelings for the page. With so provocative an allusion at the climax of her maid's aria, it was necessary for the Countess to disassociate herself from it, which she does very briskly: 'What utter nonsense!' ('Quante buffonerie!') Abrupt recitative beginnings were part of the stylized comic language of *opera buffa*, allowing the librettist to cut off moments that in a play might have hung in the air – a moving-on-swiftly formula. Responding to the delicate matter of the token, Da Ponte decided to retain the revelation that Cherubino has been wearing the Countess's ribbon to staunch the flow of blood from a minor wound, although there was no structural necessity to do so, as the resolution of this subplot at the end of the letter-writing scene (Act 4, scene 3) when the ribbon with Chérubin's blood on it accidentally falls out of the Countess's costume, was of course removed from the opera. This decision might well have been questioned on the grounds of decency, but Da Ponte had no wish to go too far in dulling a character so deliciously poised between innocence and knowledge.[4] Yet having retained the initial discovery of the ribbon, he had little choice but to allow Cherubino to explain to the Countess why he so valued it, which is a very revealing moment. In response, she once again has to remain brusque, almost wilfully unobservant: 'what is this nonsense?' ('cos'è questa follia?') Cut off from any recognition of the page's feelings, the Countess exudes an aura of isolation. Cool and aloof, she engages with the developing imbroglio only through her relationship with Susanna.[5]

Der närrische Tag

There is plenty of evidence that the problem of Cherubino's character was central to the Viennese reception of the new Figaro drama well before Da Ponte started work. In the first months of 1785, several German editions of *La folle journée* were on sale in the city. On 16 February, for example, a new version was advertised with the justification that *Le mariage de Figaro* had been defaced through the circulation of 'so many inauthentic editions' ('so viele unächte Auflagen').[6] On 9 March, *Der lustige Tag*, the most popular translation, was offered to the public with the selling point that it was the only German version with authorial approval.[7] With an irresistible tide of copies sweeping into Vienna, there was no possibility of controlling access to the text or of censoring detailed knowledge of its scandalous plot. Theatre, though, was a different matter. On 31 January 1785, Joseph II, referring to plans to stage the play in the Kärntnerthortheater, instructed the censor to review it on the grounds that it contained 'much scandalous material' ('viel Anstössiges').[8] Having made his view clear, he placed responsibility for the actual decision firmly in the censor's hands, and it is thus hardly

---

[4] Many years later, he was scornful of an English translator's desire to neutralize Cherubino's feelings, awarding his efforts three exclamation marks: 'You who know what love is, ladies fair, see whether it is in your heart ... I sigh, I lament without desire!!!'. *An Extract*, p. 20.

[5] In Acts 3 and 4, the encounters between Cherubino and the Countess take place in public and were therefore considered less controversial. Disguised as one of the girls who have come to present flowers, Cherubino receives a kiss from the Countess, but of course she is unaware of his identity. His verbal reaction – that kiss missed its mark! – was omitted by Da Ponte. As the imbroglio builds up in the Act 4 Finale, Cherubino thinks he has finally got the

chance to embrace the Countess, but it is only Susanna in disguise, and farce reigns when the Count interposes himself and inadvertently receives the kiss.

[6] *Wiener Zeitung* (16 February 1785), p. 13.

[7] *Wiener Zeitung* (9 March 1785), p. 15.

[8] Heartz, 'Constructing *Le nozze di Figaro*', p. 79: 'Ich vernehme, dass die bekannte Komodie *le Mariage de Figaro* in einer deutschen Übersetzung für das Kärntnerthortheater angetragen seyn solle; da nun dieses Stück viel Anstössiges enthält; so verstehe Ich mich, dass der Censor solches entweder ganz verwerfen, oder doch solche Veränderungen darinn veranlassen werde, dass er für die Vorstellung dieser Piece und den Eindruck, den sie machen dürfte, haften werde könnten.'

surprising that the production was banned almost immediately. The prohibition of the most popular play in Europe was so idiosyncratic a decision that it received news coverage outside Vienna. The *Bayreuther Zeitung*, for example, noted that the reason for the ban was that the play contained very many 'suggestive' elements.[9] The decision infuriated Johann Rautenstrauch, author of *Der närrische Tag*, the translation that was apparently to have been the basis of the stage production, and when he published his work (as permitted by the censor), he did so with a highly provocative title-page, citing an epigram from the play itself: 'published follies gain credence where their free circulation is hindered' ('Gedruckte Dummheiten haben nur da einen Werth, wo man ihren freyen Umlauf hindert').[10] It was dedicated with heavy irony 'to the memory of two hundred ducats' ('Dem / Andenken / von / Zweyhundert Dukaten / gewidmet'), the money presumably lost through the late cancellation.

Der närrische Tag is an established part of the pre-history of the opera, but little attention has been paid to the possibility that Rautenstrauch's translation was itself an influence on Da Ponte. As he began work, it is highly likely that the librettist would have consulted the text at the centre of the recent theatrical controversy. In some instances, credit for sowing the seeds of a memorable idea in Da Ponte's fertile imagination should probably go to Rautenstrauch rather than Beaumarchais alone. At the end of *La folle journée* (Act 2, scene 2), Figaro leaves the stage with the offhand comment: 'and then, Sir, you will dance' ('et puis dansez, Monseigneur'). Rautenstrauch developed this into a rhetorically heightened statement, well on the way towards 'Se vuol ballare': 'and this very night, you, my dear Sir, will be the one dancing, you will be dancing. (exits)' ('Und diesen Abend – Tanzen Sie nur gnädiger Herr, tanzen Sie nur! (ab)').[11] Rautenstrauch (Act 2, scene 25) incorporates in the Countess's short soliloquy sentiments about her husband which in the original play (Act 2, scene 24) she confides to Suzanne. Da Ponte in turn made much of the idea that Almaviva's behaviour should provide the occasion for her anguished soliloquy.[12] Most significantly of all, Rautenstrauch came up with the idea of the repetitions in the letter-writing scene so memorably exploited in 'Che soave zeffiretto'. In *La folle journée*

[9] *Bayreuther Zeitung* (10 February 1785), No. 18, Anhang, p. 119: Wien 4 Feb: 'Beaumarchais Hochzeit des Figaro ist allhier verbothen worden, weil er gar viele anzügliche Stellen darinnen enthalten.'
[10] *Der närrische Tag, / oder die / Hochzeit des Figaro; / ein / Lustspiel in fünf Aufzügen, aus / dem Französischen des / Herrn / Caron von Beaumarchais* (Vienna, 1785). A copy is in the Internationale Stiftung Mozarteum, Biblioteca Mozartiana, Rara Lib Foll 5.

[11] In *Der lustige Tag* (Berlin, 1785) this is rendered: 'Und dann, gnädiger Herr, geht der Tanz los.'
[12] *La folle journée* (Act 2, scene 24): 'Avoir puni sa jalousie et lui prouver son infidelité'; *Der närrische Tag* (Act 2, scene 25): 'Mein kleiner Entwurf ist ein wenig kühn. Seine Eifersucht bestraft zu haben, und ihm seine Untreue zu beweisen – ach ich vergaß mein liebes Band.'

(Act 4, scene 3), the Countess pronounces the message and then repeats its beginning as in a school language class. Suzanne merely adds the conclusion. In *Der närrische Tag* this is developed as follows:

COUNTESS	Write: song to the air: the evening is so gloriously beautiful.
SUSANNE	writes – so gloriously beautiful.
COUNTESS	In the garden under the Linden trees.
SUSANNE	Under the Linden trees – and then?
COUNTESS	That's where lovers can meet –
SUSANNE	Lovers can meet –
COUNTESS	And, without witnesses, find –
SUSANNE	Find –

(Gräfinn: Schreib: Lied auf die Arie: der Abend ist so herrlich schön! – / Susanne: (schreibt) – so herrlich schön. / Gräfinn: Im Garten unter Linden. – / Susanne: Unter Linden – hernach? / Gräfinn: Da können sich Verliebte sehn – / Susanne: Verliebte sehn – / Gräfinn: Und, ohne Zeugen, finden – / Susanne: Finden –)

Either Mozart or Da Ponte spotted the potential of this idea for a duettino in which musical imitation reflects onstage action.[13]

Rautenstrauch made his feelings abundantly clear on the issue of censorship, but necessarily in a coded fashion. He points out that although for the most part a literal translation, his work contains a few changes to lines through deletion or addition. The reader is urged to judge whether these are necessary or not.[14] A decision is soon required. Perhaps the first seriously controversial passage in *La folle journée* occurs when Chérubin fantasizes about Suzanne's role in dressing and undressing the Countess. Rautenstrauch (Act 1, scene 7) interpolates a series of exchanges so ludicrous in character that their function as a petulant response to officious interference is obvious. As he conjures up in his mind the removal of successive garments from the Countess, Chérubin can hardly bear the thought of not being present in the room. He offers to forfeit increasingly vital parts of his anatomy in exchange for the chance of a daily swap with Susanne. As she points out, soon nothing will be left of him at all:

PAGE	Pin for pin, ribbon for ribbon, gradually coming apart, until finally – I would give a finger [everything] to be in your position.
SUSANNE	How many fingers do you have, you rascal?

---

[13] Although he adopted the idea of the repetitions, Da Ponte could not risk ending in such a suggestive fashion. Moreover, in a musical duettino, he needed to come up with a final line that both women could sing.

[14] 'Hier ist es, beynahe wörtlich; denn die kleine Veränderung, mittelst Weglassung oder Zusetzung weniger Zeilen, ist von keiner Bedeutung, und der Leser mag urtheilen, ob sie nöthig oder unnöthig war.'

PAGE	Eight fingers and two thumbs.
SUSANNE	These would be lost in a few days. What would you give up afterwards?
PAGE	Arms and legs and all remaining limbs.[15]
SUSANNE	Even your head with the eyes? You poor boy, what would you look like in fourteen days?
PAGE	Like the front half of a frog which one throws away – but what have you got there?
SUSANNE	The ribbon –

(Page: Nadel für Nadel, Band für Band, allgemach los zu machen, bis endlich – ich wollte allemal einen Finger darum geben, an deiner Stelle zu seyn. / Susanne: Wieviel hast du Finger, schelmischer Junge? / Page: Acht Finger und zwey Daumen. / Susanne: Die wären also in etlichen Tagen verloren. Was gäbst du hernach darum? / Page: Arm und Beine und alle übrigen Glieder. / Susanne: Also auch den Kopf mit den Augen? Armer Knabe wie würdest du in vierzehn Tagen auszehen? / Page: Wie die vordere Helfte von einem Frosch, die man wegwirft. Aber was hast du da? / Susanne: Das Band ...)

The joke is obvious: the pettifogging bureaucrats in the censor's office will be satisfied only when this richly suggestive moment has been turned into farce, pandering to the famed Viennese taste for low comedy.[16] Da Ponte was not tempted to emulate this jest, but he did allow Cherubino to express a willingness to defend his possession of the ribbon: 'I will only give it up with my life' ('Io non tel renderò che co la vita'). This line (not in Beaumarchais) was set by Mozart, but the cliché was evidently regarded as somewhat controversial as it does not appear in all sources. A further jibe against the censor's office occurs (suitably enough) in the dressing scene (Act 2, scene 6) which is amended to lighten the emotions on display; the page is no longer shy ('honteux') while the Countess responds to Suzanne's saucy admiration of the whiteness of Cherubino's arm with vivacity ('mit Lebhaftigkeit') rather than in a glacial tone ('d'un ton glacé'). An additional stage direction introduces a note of withering satire as a strict limit is placed on how far Susanne is allowed to raise the sleeve: '(lifts the arm of the page and exposes it to the elbow)' ('(hebt den Arm des Page auf, und entblößt ihn bis auf Ellbogen)'). The Viennese were evidently going to have to make do with an erotic wrist!

Rautenstrauch's aim of ridiculing the petty nature of censorship in Josephinian Vienna turns the delicate moment when Cherubino performs

---

[15] Possibly a lewd reference to the one unmentionable male 'member' – there being no others! – was intended.

[16] An interesting, though unanswerable question is whether these lines would have been performed in the stage production.

his romance (Act 2, scene 4) into a travesty. The intimate ballad in which the page betrays his true feelings for his adored godmother, told in the first person in Beaumarchais, is rewritten in the neutral third person: 'There was a poor young wretch' ('Es war ein armer junger Wicht'). But this sensible precaution is completely undermined when the young man proves to be very forward in confessing his love: 'Once he fell to his knees and cried with rapture: I love you' ('Einst stürtzt er nieder auf sein Knie, und rief entzükt: ich liebe Sie'). An asterisk here directs the reader to a sarcastic explanation for the appearance of the new text: 'The arietta in the original would possibly have been less effective in German' ('Die Ariette des Originals würde vermutlich im Deutschen wenig gewirckt haben'). Susanne, who is either a decent sight-singer or who has retained and studied the copy of the song shown to her in Act 1, offers to accompany the page – quite literally. There is no mention of a guitar, but she will form a mini-chorus with him: 'I will sing along. (The page and Susanne sing)' ('Ich werde mitsingen. (Page und Susanne singen)'). Many in the Vienna audience would have known that this was a solo romance in the original play. The suggested manner of performance, however, negates any possibility of a personal message.

As a final shaft against those who would protect the oh-so-delicate sensibilities of Viennese maidenhood, Rautenstrauch decided to censor the name Cherubino itself, the mere mention of which was sure to inflame passions. In the cast list, the page is named 'Liebetraut': love-trust or more likely love-dare, drawing attention to the very strand of the plot that had to be downplayed.[17] In the text itself, however, no name is used, the character being described simply as 'Page'. Bazile's memorable characterization of him as 'Cherubino di amore' (Act 1, scene 9), retained by Da Ponte (Act 1, scene 7) as 'Cherubin d'amore', becomes the prosaic 'kleinen Pagen'.[18] Nameless he may remain but not faceless; a picture being worth a thousand words, Rautenstrauch commissioned a vignette showing the garden scene (see Figure 7.1). It is placed immediately above the motto taken from Figaro's monologue (Act 5, scene 3) in which he inveighs against the futility of censoring 'sottises imprimées' which thereby merely gain currency. Yet the figure centrestage under the spreading chestnut trees is not Figaro, described in the play as being attired rather ostentatiously with a large coat over his shoulders and a slouch hat: 'un grand manteau sur l'épaules un large chapeau rabattu'. Instead, Rautenstrauch shows the source of his own troubles with the censor: the pageboy himself, with

---

[17] My thanks go to my colleague Dr Franziska Schroeder for comments on the satirical aspect of this name and other observations on the nuances of the German text.

[18] In *Der lustige Tag* (Berlin, 1785) the names Fanchette and Cherubin are retained. In *Der lustige Tag* (Kehl, 1785) they are Hannchen and Cherubim.

Der

närrische Tag,

o d e r d i e

Hochzeit des Figaro;

e i n

Luftspiel in fünf Aufzügen, aus
dem Französischen des

Herrn

Caron von Beaumarchais.

Gedruckte Dummheiten haben nur da einen Werth,
wo man ihren freyen Umlauf hindert. Fünfter Aufzug,
dritter Auftritt.

Wien, 1785.

Figure 7.1 Cover page, *Der närrische Tag, oder Die Hochzeit des Figaros*
(Vienna, 1785).

tunic and military sash just visible, but more importantly shapely legs fully revealed, ready to cause havoc in the hearts of the fairer sex. In claiming that the 'amorous butterfly' will no longer be able to disturb the peace of every maiden with his curls, with his airs and graces, and with his roseate womanly colour, Figaro was indulging in wishful thinking; that is just what the irrepressible page continues to do.[19]

Die Hochzeit des Figaro

Da Ponte, who probably began work on *Le nozze di Figaro* in the spring of 1785, was no doubt well aware of the Rautenstrauch affair. One lesson would have been clear to him: he would have to review the character of Chérubin with great

[19] The *Wienerblättchen* covered the story of Schikaneder's attempt to stage Rautenstrauch's German translation of *La folle journée* and Joseph II's decision to forbid the production (4 February 1785, pp. 35–6). The same paper subsequently published an extended review-article of the play under the title 'Ueber Figaro' (28 February 1785, pp. 235–40; 1 March, pp. 7–12; 2 March, pp. 19–24). During the preparation of this chapter, the *Wienerblättchen* was unavailable, pending digitization, but it has since appeared online in ANNO, the searchable database of newspapers maintained by the Austrian Nationalbibliothek. Careful consideration will have to be given to the idea that it was reading this detailed discussion that first prompted Mozart to ask Da Ponte if it would be feasible to fashion an *opera buffa* libretto out of the play. The author of the article prudently sidesteps the controversial decision to prohibit Schikaneder's production. Concerning Cherubino, it is fascinating to see that in his detailed synopsis of the plot, he deliberately excises the role of the page, one reference to 'ein Page' excepted: 'Die Episode mit dem Pagen, die ich mit Bedacht von dem Hauptinnhalt des Stückes abgesöndert, weil er mit demselben in keiner besondern Verbindung steht, will ich dann erst anführen, wann ich den Karakter des Pagens besonders behandeln werde' (28 February 1785, p. 240). When, as promised, he considers the role of the page – like Rautenstrauch he evidently regarded the name Cherubino as unmentionable – he makes the extraordinary statement that this character might well have been omitted altogether, as it has little to do and has not the slightest connection (!) to the main thrust of the plot: 'Dieser Page scheint mir hätte ganz weg bleiben können, den außer einigen verwickelten Scenen, hat er nichts zu thun, und er hat auf den Hauptinnhalt nicht den mindesten Einfluss' (2 March 1785, p. 19). A synopsis of the scenes involving Cherubino is presented separately, albeit with heavy self-censorship of risqué elements. It was hardly possible to ignore his presence in the Countess's dressing room, but no mention is made of the erotic dressing scene or indeed of the reasons why he is there. The page is in the room as the Count approaches, a statement immediately qualified with a footnote pointing out that this is entirely innocent: 'Hier ist der Page in der Gräfinn Zimmer *) als der Graf kommt. (*) Doch aus den unschuldigsten Absichten' (2 March 1785, p. 20). All this leaves very little room for doubt that the censor's prime concern (reflecting the views of Joseph II) was the character of Cherubino. The potential detachability of this subplot was noted by Allanbrook, who commented on Cherubino's extraordinary ability to insinuate himself into the drama, as though he were writing his own role: 'he seems at first to be only a minor character, a member of a detachable subplot. Yet he gradually acquires transcendent importance as a touchstone for all the other characters in the opera.' Wye Jamison Allanbrook, *Rhythmic Gesture in Mozart: 'Le nozze di Figaro' and 'Don Giovanni'* (Chicago and London, 1983), pp. 84–5.

care, focusing especially on his Act 1 fantasy of the Countess, his performance of the romance, and above all his participation in the dressing scene. No drafts of the Italian libretto survive, but an important source of evidence is the German prose translation on sale to members of the audience at the premiere. It contains numerous variants of the stage instructions and several textual omissions relating to Acts 3 and 4, but there are also a few distinctive readings in Acts 1 and 2, some of which clearly reflect the ongoing debate as to how far the censorship of the role of Cherubino needed to go. Variants relating to the character of the page are listed in Table 7.2 with a brief commentary.

Although they cannot be precisely dated, the German readings certainly demonstrate the continuing obsession with the issue of Cherubino. There

Table 7.2 Variant readings relating to Cherubino in Acts 1 and 2 of *[Die] Hochzeit des Figaro*

	Italian libretto	*German libretto*	*Comments*
Act 1, scene 4	*Marcellina, poi Susanna con cuffia da donna un nastro, e un abito da donna.*[20] [Marcellina, then Susanna, with a lady's bonnet, a ribbon, and a lady's dress]	Marzellina, alsdenn Susanna. [Marcellina, then Susanna.]	Given that Cherubino's subsequent exchanges with Susanna over the dressing and undressing of the Countess were causing difficulty, it is interesting to see the reference to items of her mistress's clothing removed from her earlier scene with Marcellina.
Act 1, scene 5	*(con un sospiro).* [(with a sigh).]	(mit Freude) [(with joy)]	The stage direction for the much censored moment when Cherubino is dreaming of the daily scenes in the Countess's dressing room replaced his explicit sigh with a more generalized joyous state of mind.
Act 1, scene 5	Io non tel renderò che co la vita! [I will only give it up with my life!]		The line inserted by Da Ponte possibly as a result of reading Rautenstrauch's translation was at some point omitted. Even this cliché seemingly represented too strong an expression of the page's interest in the ribbon.
Act 1, scene 8	*(con passione, e sospirando).* [with passion, and sighing]	(seufzend) [sighing]	At the moment when Cherubino finally accepts that he is going to have to leave to serve as an officer, the German version tones down the stage instruction.

[20] In the Italian libretto, stage instructions are given in italics, with or without parentheses, often with only an opening bracket. In these cases, a closing bracket is supplied silently.

Table 7.2 *(cont.)*

	Italian libretto	German libretto	Comments
Act 2, scene 2	Perchè? questo è migliore! [Why? this one is better!]	Warum den? Dies ist ja besser (weiset ihm den Taffet.) [Why? This one is better (shows him the ribbon.)]	At this very sensitive moment with Susanna offstage and the Countess briefly alone with Cherubino, the German text has her showing him the ribbon as in *La folle journée* (Act 2, scene 9), which has '(Lui montrant le taffetas)'. This moment of physical interaction is not in the Italian libretto, although the Countess's subsequent action in wiping Cherubino's eyes is in both.
Act 2, scene 2	Or piange! . . . (*con affanno, e commossione*). [So, crying! (breathless and with emotion).]	Itzt weinet er . . . [He cries.]	Still alone with Cherubino, the Countess is very moved when he appears to cry. The instruction (not in Beaumarchais) is omitted.
Act 2, scene 2	Oh Ciel! perchè morir non lice! [Heavens! why can I not die?]	O Himmel! Warum darf man nicht sterben! (mit rührendem Tone.) [Heavens! why can I not die! (in an affected tone.)]	The addition of the stage direction ('in an affected tone') is interesting as it appears neither in the Italian libretto nor in *La folle journée*.
Act 2, scene 5	nudo il petto [bare chest]	Bloßer Brust (zitternd und erschrocken) [bare chest (trembling and frightened)]	The *risqué* moment when the Count learns that Cherubino (known to the audience to be being played by a woman) is inside with 'a bare chest' is accompanied in the German text (Act 2, scene 6) by the direction for the Countess 'trembling and shocked'.

were repeated changes of mind, especially in his critical scenes in Act 2 with the Countess, the stage directions for which were considered with particular care. Enough emotion had to be on display to make the encounter dramatically credible without implying anything improper.

Musical sources

Scores relating to the early development of *Figaro* also reflect the preoccupation with Cherubino as the drama progressed from libretto to score, from first draft to revision, and from premiere to early performances. Its authors seem to have been dogged by the fear that they had not gone far enough in muting the sprightly persona of the adolescent pageboy. It is striking that without exception the materials reflecting these concerns relate to performances of the opera in the Habsburg domains. Elsewhere the character of the page seemed to cause no difficulty at all, appearing uncensored for everyone to enjoy. There are two variant versions of the opera, each of which incorporates a phase of censorship. Version A, based on a retrenchment of the page's character in Act 1, was under consideration in Vienna and was performed in Prague in 1786. It was also given over two nights in June 1788 for Leopold, Grand Duke of Tuscany and next in line of succession to Joseph, a consequence of the selection of *Figaro* as the gala opera to celebrate his daughter's arrival in Prague. The sources for this version include:

1. An annotated copy of the 1786 Vienna libretto in the Library of Congress.
2. The Prague libretto of 1786.
3. The Donaueschingen score of Acts 1 and 2.
4. The Florence libretto of 1788.[21]

Version B, incorporating amendments to Acts 3 and 4, was given in Monza on 18 November 1787 for Ferdinand, the third Habsburg brother. Its sources include:

1. A layer of changes made to the Vienna Court Theatre score K.T.315.
2. The Monza libretto of 1787.
3. An early Viennese copy, annotated in Monza but later transferred to the collection of Elector Maximilian Franz, the youngest of the Habsburg brothers.[22]

While it is plain that both versions embody stricter censorship, they are not alternatives; each focuses on a specific section of the opera and no source has come to light that combines the two readings. There is some evidence to suggest that Version B came into existence in two stages: the first removes Barbarina from the opera, other than at the start of Act 4; and the second completes the process by omitting her character entirely as a stage presence. Further censorship of the role of Cherubino in Act 2 was entered in the Vienna Court Theatre score O.A.295, but these readings (with one exception) do not appear to have been transmitted elsewhere.

---

[21] For full details of these sources see: NMA, II/5/16, *Kritische Berichte*, ed. Ulrich Leisinger (Kassel, 2007): N[1] (90); N[3] (91); I (84–5); N[6] (92).
[22] *Ibid.*: B[2] (72–4); N[4] (91–2); D (79–80). I am grateful to Dr John Wilson, University of Vienna, Institut für Musikwissenschaft, for the suggestion (based on the paper-type used for the additional material) that it was edited in Monza rather than Bonn.

In his article on the Prague *Figaro* (Version A), Tyson identified two series of revisions, related to concerns over: i) Cherubino's erotic interest in the Countess; and ii) comments made by or about Basilio potentially inappropriate to his status as a priest.[23] These alterations, along with several cuts, the addition of a short cavatina for Marcellina, and a series of changes to the relative tessituras of the roles of Susanna and the Countess, constituted in his view a distinct version of the opera, the responsibility for which lay with the Bondini troupe in Bohemia. It is clear, however, that some of the cuts that define this revision originated in Vienna. A useful source of evidence is the list of pieces from the opera advertised for sale by Lorenz Lausch on 1 July 1786. As illustrated in Table 7.3, two items not on sale were also omitted in the Prague libretto.

A further cut, that of Cherubino's 'Non so più', was also under consideration in Vienna as shown by the deletion in the Library of Congress libretto, but seems not in the end to have been instituted, as the aria appears in the orchestral parts with no sign of any instruction to omit, except for a small internal abbreviation.

A still closer connection exists between the recitative revisions in the Prague version and the passages lightly marked in the libretto. In character these annotations represent work in progress – lines to be considered for possible deletion – rather than the bold mandatory crossings out of an official censor. There are several indications that this was a working document: on the

Table 7.3 Evidence for the cutting of pieces / sections in Acts 1 and 2 of Version A

Not advertised by Lausch on 1 July 1786	Marked for deletion in the Library of Congress libretto	Omitted in the 1786 Prague libretto	Commentary
No. 5: Via resti servita	No. 5: Via resti servita	No. 5: Via resti servita	'The evidence of the musical sources is . . . equivocal . . . the duettino is marked to be cut in a few of the orchestral parts.'[24]
	No. 6: Non so più	No. 6: Non so più	
No. 16: Conoscete Signor Figaro	No. 16: Conoscete Signor Figaro	No. 16: Conoscete Signor Figaro	'Marked to be cut in all of the original orchestral parts.'[25]

[23] Alan Tyson, 'The 1786 Prague Version of Mozart's "Le Nozze di Figaro"', *Music & Letters*, 69 (1988), pp. 321–33.

[24] Dexter Edge, 'Mozart's Viennese Copyists' (PhD thesis, University of Southern California, 2001), p. 1605.

[25] *Ibid.*, p. 1608.

title-page, the names of the Viennese cast were added in; in Act 4 all solo passages to be sung 'in an altered voice' were marked with a grey cross; and several missing but necessary stage directions were supplied.[26] The link connecting this copy of the libretto and the Prague version was almost certainly the Court Theatre score of Act 1. No longer extant, it must at some stage have been annotated with the 'Prague' revisions, before acting as the exemplar for the material sent to Bondini in Bohemia. These recitative cuts may well have formed part of the text of the opera as given at the Vienna premiere, a possibility hidden from view because of the loss of this score and all the original role-books. Bohemian copyists working on the score for commercial purposes quickly realized that this was not the text of the opera as first conceived by Da Ponte, and an exemplar of the full version was soon acquired. Of the two keyboard arrangements originating in Prague, that by Maschek was based on Version A, that by Kuchař on the standard text.[27]

The clear goal of the Act 1 censorship was to replace a hormonally charged teenager, feverishly aware of his newfound desires, with a beguiling but presexual boy who could with propriety still (just) enter the Countess's chamber to take part in the plan to deceive the Count. The textual changes in Version A are listed and analysed in Table 7.4. Not all are directly related to Cherubino but the overall conception seems unambiguous.

The overall effect of this re-shaping of Cherubino's character early on in the drama is to remove any indication that he is sexually 'on-heat'. To this end, his fantasy of the Countess in a state of semi-undress, the report of him prowling around waiting to see Susanna, and above all his aria in which he reveals that he can scarcely control his blushing and racing heartbeat in the presence of women are all taken out. What remains is his light-hearted banter with Susanna revealing his crush on the Countess.

In matters of fine detail as well as overall structure, the Florence text of *Figaro* was based on the Prague libretto, yet it was no mere duplicate. All the cuts relating to Cherubino remain, but Susanna's description of Basilio as a procurer is put back in, as is her duettino with Marcellina. That this was a restoration is demonstrated by the manner in which the text of 'Via resti servita' is given. Unlike the other arias and ensembles, it is shorn of its (many) stage directions, which suggests that the source of this replacement text was a musical score rather than the Vienna libretto.[28] The role of Cherubino, however, remained fully censored and no attempt was made to

[26] The emendations are listed in NMA, II/5/16, *Kritische Berichte*, pp. 312–14.

[27] Milada Jonášová, 'Le nozze di Figaro: Kuchař' unbekannte Partiturabschrift und sein Klavierauszug', in Klaus Aringer and Ann-Katrin Zimmermann (eds.), *Mozart im Zentrum: Festschrift für Manfred Hermann Schmid zum 60. Geburtstag* (Tutzing, 2010), pp. 141–75.

[28] Further evidence of this is that the Florence text of 'Via resti servita' includes two of Mozart's textual readings 'i meriti' and 'l'abito' rather than Da Ponte's 'il merito' and 'il titolo'.

Table 7.4 Textual revisions associated with Version A

Location (bar numbers)	Lines omitted (1786 libretto text)	Commentary
ACT 1		
Or bene, ascolta (19–24)	*Sus.* Chetati: or viene il meglio: Don Basilio / Mio maestro di canto, e suo mezzano, / nel darmi la lezione mi ripete ogni dì questa canzone. *Fig.* Chi? Basilio? Oh birbante! [Susanna: wait: there is better: Don Basilio, my singing teacher and his procurer, repeats this same tune daily in my lesson. Figaro: Who? Basilio? The rogue!]	These five lines contain Susanna's description of Basilio as a 'procurer' on the Count's behalf. Their excision led Tyson to suggest that this may have been regarded as 'somewhat insulting a role to be assigned to a priest'.
Tutto ancor (11–14)	[*Mar.*] Con quegli occhi modesti, / Con quell'aria pietosa, / E poi . . . / *Sus.* (Meglio è partir.) / *Mar.* Che cara sposa! [Marcellina: With those modest eyes and pious expression, and then . . . Susanna: (I'd better go!) Marcellina: What a sweet bride!]	This cut does not appear to be related to issues of censorship. Together with the loss of the following duettino, it removes the meeting between Marcellina and Susanna. In Prague, the ending of the recitative was revised to lead into Marcellina's cavatina.[29]
Via resti servita	CUT	
Va' là, vecchia pedante (21–23)	[*Cher.*] Che la vesti il mattino, / Che la sera la spogli, che le metti . . . / Gli spilloni, i metterli . . . [Cherubino: You dress her in the morning, undress her at night . . . fix her pins, her laces . . .]	Tyson commented: 'Cherubino's cut lines prais[e] Susanna's luck in having the job of dressing the Countess in the morning, undressing her in the evening, and putting on her brooches and ribbons. Could it be that it was desired to minimize Cherubino's erotic interest in the Countess?'[30]
Non so più cosa son, cosa faccio	CUT	In this quintessentially feverish aria, Cherubino demonstrates that he is moving beyond the age of innocence and is becoming aware of his uncontrollable reactions in the presence of women.
Ah son perduto! (59–63)	*Bas.* A Cherubino! Al Cherubin d'amore / Ch'oggi sul far del giorno / Passeggiava quì intorno, / Per entrar . . .	Tyson suggested that Don Basilio's four cut lines denouncing Cherubino, and claiming that the young man had tried to get access to Susanna's room 'prevents a priest from being insulted,

[29] In Florence, Cherubino's aria was replaced by an unknown piece, on this occasion an aria for Susanna entitled 'Senza speme ognor s'aggira'. See Michael and

Christopher Raeburn, 'Mozart Manuscripts in Florence', *Music & Letters*, 40 (1959), pp. 334–40.
[30] Tyson, 'The 1786 Prague Version', p. 331.

Table 7.4 (*cont.*)

Location (bar numbers)	Lines omitted (1786 libretto text)	Commentary
	[Basilio: To Cherubino, the cherub of love, who this morning at daybreak was walking about trying to get in . . .]	and reduces the insinuations about Cherubino's eroticism once more'.[31]
ACT 2		
Quante buffon-erie! (1–4)	*La con.* Quante buffonerie! / *Sus.* Ma se ne sono / Io medesma gelosa; ehi, serpen-tello, / Volete tralasciar d'esser sì bella!/ *(Prende pel mento Cherubino.)* / *La con.* Finiam le ragazzate: or quelle maniche. . . .	Susanna takes Cherubino by the chin, remarking that he is so pretty that she is almost jealous herself. The revision diverts attention away from Cherubino altogether, focusing briefly on the behaviour of Susanna:
	[Countess: What silliness! Susanna: I'm almost jealous myself. You little serpent, would you please not look so pretty! (She takes Cherubino by the chin.) Countess: Enough of this childishness. Now those sleeves . . .]	*La Con.* 'Quante lepidezze, / E bizzarie! / Ell'é tanto vivace, e manierosa, / Che s'ella é amata non é strana cosa, / Ehi, Susanna, Susanna? *(Susanna sorte).'* [Countess: What pleasantries and oddities! She is so lively and man-nered that if she is loved, it's no strange thing. Hey, Susanna, Susanna? (Susanna exits.)]
Conoscete Signor Figaro	CUT	In this section of the Act 2 Finale, the subplot concerning the letter sent to the Count to alert him that his wife has agreed to an assignation, reaches its climax. Perhaps even a malicious rumour about the infidelity of the Countess was thought to be too much. There is no evidence of any systematic attempt to remove this strand of the plot, but without the denouement seen in 'Conoscete Signor Figaro', the letter would remain in the background.

restore 'Non so più'. Indeed, in the following recitative, additional changes to the stage directions demonstrate that this character's agitated state of mind was still the focus of attention: i) having seized the ribbon, 'he repeatedly kisses it' ('Bacia, e ribacia il nastro'); ii) his outburst over his song is accompanied by the instruction 'with transports of joy' ('con trasporti di gioia'). Both these stage

---

[31] *Ibid.*, p. 331.

directions survived in Version A and are seen in the Prague libretto, but the Florence text omits the latter altogether and removes from the former the words 'e ribacia' so that Cherubino kisses the ribbon once only. (Da Ponte had already eliminated the *risqué* identification of the ribbon as a 'ruban de nuit'.) The rationale behind these further minor revisions was that of Version A as a whole: to cool down displays of feverishness.

In view of the care taken with Cherubino's character in Act 1, it is rather surprising that the scenes involving him with the Countess and Susanna in Act 2 survive in Version A without much intervention. A possible explanation for this apparent contradiction is that the censorship of the page's role was an ongoing process, the constituent phases of which were transmitted in a random fashion. It is clear from Viennese sources that Act 2 received an equivalent level of scrutiny, the changes for some (probably arbitrary) reason not being incorporated in the materials sent to Bondini in Prague. The censorship of Cherubino in Act 2 is seen in a series of annotations in the Vienna Court Theatre score O.A.295, some of which Edge tentatively ascribed to Mozart himself. These are listed and discussed in Table 7.5, except for one case that will be discussed later in relation to Version B.

Table 7.5 Censorship of the role of Cherubino in Act 2 as seen in O.A.295

Location (bar numbers)	Lines omitted (1786 libretto text excluding stage directions)	Commentary
Quante buffonerie! (17–22)	[*Sus.*] Non è mal: cospetto! ha il braccio / Più candido del mio! Qualche ragazza ... *La Con.* E siegui a far la pazza? [Susanna: It's not too bad: look! His arm is whiter than mine, like a girl's ... Countess: Are you going to continue with this folly?]	An apparent requirement to censor these lines referring to the whiteness of Cherubino's arm had already been mocked by Rautenstrauch. Concerning the implementation of the musical alterations, Edge commented: 'The bass notes in mm. 17–18 and 21–22 are altered with a tan-coloured crayon (possibly by Mozart?).'[32]
Quante buffonerie! (23–38 and 39–45)	[*La con.*] ch'è sulla scrigno: / inquanto al nastro ... inver ... per il colore / Mi spiacea di privarmene. / *Sus.* Tenete, / E da legargli il braccio? / *La con.* Un altro nastro / Prendi insiem col	These cuts address two sensitive moments that Da Ponte – pushing his luck – had allowed to remain: the passages in which the Countess is left alone with Cherubino.

---

[32] Edge, 'Mozart's Viennese Copyists', p. 1637.

Table 7.5 (*cont.*)

Location (bar numbers)	Lines omitted (1786 libretto text excluding stage directions)	Commentary
	vestito. / *Cher.* Ah più presto m'avria quello guarito! / *La con.* Perchè? questo è migliore! / *Cher.* Allor che un nastro . . . / Legò la chioma aver toccò la pelle / D'oggetto . . . / *La con.* Forastiero / E' buon per le ferite non è vero? / Guardate qualità ch'io non sapea! / *Cher.* Madama scherza; ed io frattanto parto: / *La con.* Poverin! Che sventura!	Susanna exits twice, first to fetch a plaster and then a second ribbon. It was by no means only a question of avoiding her absence. The cut also removes from the plot the Countess's recognition of her own ribbon, and even more to the point Cherubino's explanation of why it matters to him so much.
	La con. Or piange . . . *Cher.* Oh ciel! perchè morir non lice! Forse vicino all'ultimo momento . . . questa bocca a seria! *La con.* Siete saggio; cos'è questa follia?	
	[Countess: . . . which is in my box: as for this ribbon . . . truly . . . to judge by its colour . . . I'm sorry it is lost. Susanna: Here, now what to bind his arm with? Countess: another ribbon; bring me one with my dress. Cherubino: Ah, the other one would have healed me more quickly. Countess: Why? This one is better. Cherubino: If a ribbon has touched the hair or brushed the skin of someone . . . Countess: unknown. It is good for wounds, is it not so? That's a quality I was not aware of. Cherubino: My Lady is joking. I must leave. Countess: Poor boy, how unfortunate!	
	Countess: So, crying . . . Cherubino: Heavens, would that I could die! Perhaps at the last moment these lips would dare . . . Countess: Wise up! What is this folly?]	
Tutto è come (5–17)	[*La con.*] Mi credete capace / Di mancare al dover? / *Il con.* Come vi piace. / Entro quell gabinetto / Chi v'è chiuso vedrò. / *La con.* Si lo vedrete . . . / Ma uditemi tranquillo. / *Il con.* Non è dunque Susanna! / *La con.* No ma, invece e un oggetto. / Che ragion di	The Countess now knows that her husband has received Figaro's letter alerting him to her planned assignation. As she is unaware of Cherubino's feelings for her (already censored), she has no reason to suppose that the Count

Table 7.5 (*cont.*)

Location (bar numbers)	Lines omitted (1786 libretto text excluding stage directions)	Commentary
	sospetto. / Non vi deve lasciar; per questa sera ... / Una burla innocente ... / Di farsi disponeva ... / ed io vi giuro ... / Che l'onor ... l'onestà ... [Countess: Do you believe I could fail in my duty? Count: As you please. I will see who is in that room. Countess: Yes, you will see ... but listen to me calmly. Count: It's not Susanna then. Countess: No, but it's someone you could not suspect. I have prepared an innocent diversion for tonight, and I swear to you ... that honour ... honesty ...]	might be worried about the role of the page in this assignation. In the cut passage, she prepares the ground for revealing Cherubino by claiming she is involving him in 'an innocent diversion' ('una burla innocente'), unaware that this revelation will confirm her husband's worst suspicions.

The Act 2 revisions have the overall effect of further strengthening the barrier between the Countess and Cherubino, already constructed with such care by Da Ponte.

Version B (with one major exception) is concerned with the revision of Acts 3 and 4. What appears to be an initial phase of this reading is seen in a series of annotations in the Viennese Court score K.T.315. The role and character of Barbarina now come into question: i) as a potential consort for Cherubino, thereby implying that he is ready for one; and ii) in her own right as the willing recipient or unwilling victim of the Count's atrocious behaviour. The elements of this phase of revision are listed and discussed in Table 7.6.

The Estense score was marked up to incorporate the changes seen in the Monza libretto. A further and quite telling indication that 'Andiam, andiam' was indeed cut at one point in Vienna is a segue indication in the first-desk violin 1 part, which bypasses this recitative. The effective removal of Barbarina from Act 3 results in a substantial diminution of her role as stage partner to Cherubino. The Count still has to report his discovery of the page in her room in order to provide a pretext for the dismissal, but no trace remains of his scandalous treatment of her.

In the Monza libretto, the censorship of Barbarina is taken to its logical conclusion: she is removed entirely from the opera as an onstage character, although references to her remain in the text. This further level of revision necessitated a significant rewrite at the start of Act 4 with Antonio taking responsibility for the pin motif, as outlined in Table 7.7.

Table 7.6 Version B: the removal of Barbarina (phase 1)

Location (bar numbers)	Lost elements of the plot	K.T.315	Monza (1787)
ACT 3			
Andiam, Andiam	Barbarina invites Cherubino to her house. He will be dressed up as a girl in order to present flowers to the Countess.	The recitative is cut with rust-coloured crayon and there are also signs of missing paste-overs and stitching.[33]	The recitative is cut and the scenes are thereafter renumbered.
Queste sono (7–12)	Barbarina presents flowers to the Countess. In the cut section, she is told that the shy girl (Cherubino) is Barbarina's cousin. After the cut material, the recitative restarts with the Countess asking the girl to present her flowers.	The cut was implemented using a rust-coloured crayon, perhaps representing the earliest layer of changes.[34]	The scene heading is revised to remove Barbarina altogether. Her introduction of the girls is therefore cut as well.
Ehi! cospettaccio! (30–41)	Barbarina mentions that the Count has often kissed her and offered her anything she wants. After the cut material, the recitative restarts with Count's aside to the effect that he is constantly thwarted. This comment now acts as a further manifestation of his growing exasperation with Cherubino.	Various markings indicate the cut passage.[35] The Count's aside (41–4) is also cut. At the restart, Figaro enters, addressing the Count as 'Eccellenza' rather than 'Signor', thereby neatly stitching up the join, as Barbarina had also addressed him as 'Eccellenza' at the start of the cut. Edge suggested that the musical revision to facilitate 'eccellenza' could be in Mozart's hand.[36]	The Monza libretto makes this cut but leaves in the Count's aside.
Nel padiglione (CUT, except for 1–2?)	Barbarina is alone on stage waiting for Cherubino.	As implemented, the cut appears to allow	As Barbarina is removed completely, Figaro's opening words in the

---

[33] Edge, 'Mozart's Viennese Copyists', p. 1639.
[34] *Ibid.*, p. 1640.
[35] *Ibid.*, p. 1640.
[36] *Ibid.*, p. 1644.

Table 7.6 (*cont.*)

Location (bar numbers)	Lost elements of the plot	K.T.315	Monza (1787)
		Barbarina's initial statement in bars 1–2.[37]	following scene (Act 4, scene 6) which refer to her are amended to: 'E questo il sito'. [This is the place.]

Table 7.7 Version B: the removal of Barbarina (phase 2)

	Lost elements of the plot	Monza (1787)
ACT 4		
L'ho perduta	Barbarina enters in a state of anxiety, having mislaid the pin from the Count she was entrusted with giving to Susanna.	Antonio enters and tells Figaro he has lost the pin.
Barbarina cos'hai?	Barbarina admits she has lost the pin. Figaro takes a pin from Marcellina's dress and gives it to Barbarina who then exits.	The stage direction is revised so that Figaro hands the pin to Antonio. Barbarina's final words are replaced by 'Io non so più di questo, Vo da Susanna, ed ella saprà il resto.' [I don't know more than this. Go to Susanna, and she will know the rest.]
Signora ella mi disse		The stage direction at the end omits the reference to where Barbarina had gone in ('dove entrò Barbarina') [where Barbarina went in].
Perfida! e in questa forma		Cherubino's words 'Ove entrò Barbarina' are replaced by 'Dentro di questa nicchia' [inside this alcove]. The stage direction 'Il P[agio] entra da Barb.' is replaced by 'entra in una nicchia'. A niche or alcove had to be identified to substitute for references to Barbarina's place of exit.
Gente, gente		Antonio can no longer refer to his daughter and his exclamation 'mia figlia' is replaced by 'che veggo' [What do I see].

[37] *Ibid.*, p. 1641.

The revisions to the Estense score follow the Monza libretto consistently but the final change is overlooked. It is unclear if this phase of revision originated in Vienna. There are no hints of it in K.T.315 and 'L'ho perduta' was on sale from Lausch, yet there are many indications in the orchestral parts that the first section of Act 4 was cut in its entirety, the drama resuming with Figaro's *scena*. It is hard to date this radical abbreviation but it would certainly have obviated the need for further changes at the start of Act 4. It is possible that the fate of Barbarina in the opera was a compromise, allowing her to remain only at the start of Act 4 as the unwitting source of further aggravation for Figaro. There are two signs that her role was decided at the last minute: i) the list of performers added to the annotated libretto omits the name of the singer, the word 'Tedesca' (German) being added subsequently in a different hand; ii) her Act 4 aria is written on a paper type not otherwise seen in the opera.

Although the focus in Version B was on Acts 3 and 4, one major and very surprising change was made in Act 2, addressing the question of Cherubino's romance. In a drastic move, 'Voi che sapete' was taken from its usual position and re-allocated to the Count as an entrance aria in Act 1. In the Monza libretto (Act 1, scene 6), Almaviva enters and performs the aria without as yet noticing the others. As a man of the world, he sings a slightly different text.[38] At the end of his song, he spots Susanna and then continues with his usual lines, observing that she seems out of sorts: 'Susanna, you appear to me to be agitated and confused' ('Susanna, tu mi sembri / Agitata e confusa'). The loss of 'Voi che sapete' from Act 2 necessitated revisions to the recitatives surrounding it, as references to the canzonetta would be meaningless in its absence. Accordingly, the Monza libretto makes a large cut from the end of the preceding recitative, removing Susanna's teasing exchange with Cherubino over the word he had used to describe the Countess in Act I: 'Cherubino: … so good; Susanna: so beautiful! Cherubino: ah, yes, for sure' (*Cher.* … 'tanto buona' *Sus.* tantobella! *Cher.* Ah … si … certo'). In front of the Countess these words were evidently now thought inappropriate.

In O.A.295, 'Voi che sapete' remains in place as indeed it does in the orchestral parts, yet there are signs of the associated recitative revisions. The opening dialogue at the beginning of the following recitative refers to the performance of the song and is therefore cut. At the restart, the part label 'Susa' is written in dark ink. Edge comments: 'Again it is not out of the question that the hand in this inscription might be Mozart's.'[39] More

---

[38] According to Raeburn and Raeburn, 'Mozart Manuscripts in Florence', p. 335, two pairs of lines were suitably amended to reflect the Count's greater experience: 'Ei non m'è nova / Capir lo so'; and 'So chi lo tiene / So che cos'è'.

[39] Edge, 'Mozart's Viennese Copyists', p. 1642.

puzzling are the fragmentary revisions before the start of the arietta. Several attempts were made to edit Cherubino's words: 'but if Madam wishes' ('Ma se Madama vuole'). A paste patch probably containing a revision is now missing. In the score, the word 'Madama' is crossed out and 'Susanna' written below. A more substantial revision also appears: 'but if Susanna wishes me to sing' ('Ma se Susanna cantar per me vuole') with a new musical setting to provide the necessary twelve notes. Edge thought it 'not out of the question' that the musical handwriting was Mozart's.[40] Following this, the response 'I do wish it' ('Lo vuole') is reassigned from Susanna to the Countess. Although the new part label ('Con') implies that the Count is on stage, the clef is not changed. Edge suggested that the part label was simply a mistake and that the textual changes were 'to mitigate the sexually provocative situation'. With the revision in place, Cherubino no longer addresses the Countess directly. In general, it is interesting to note how regularly Edge proposes that the revisions relating to the censorship of Cherubino – he does not explicitly identify this connection – are early in date, a judgement often based upon the rust-red colour of the crayon. His tentative attributions of certain annotations to Mozart's hand are also linked firmly to this material.

There is very little evidence to suggest that 'Voi che sapete' was actually cut in Vienna (or removed to Act 1) and it is therefore worth considering a different explanation for the curious revisions just before its start. A charming and popular number, the arietta was offered for sale by Lausch on 1 July 1786, but when early in 1789 he advertised it among the individual pieces in *L'ape musicale*, he listed it as being for tenor voice.[41] Its attribution to a man is correct in a sense and provides an interesting echo of the sensitivities surrounding the cross-dressing of Cherubino in 1786. The Vienna Court Theatre score is likely to have been the source of the musical text for this *pasticcio*, a copying process that could well have generated small changes hard to explain in the context of the opera as a whole.[42]

With his recitative text under constant review, suggestions for arias for Cherubino seemed paradoxically to proliferate. As Edge points out, it is unlikely 'that Mozart and Da Ponte would have planned to give a secondary character three solos in an opera in which Susanna and the Countess are clearly the central female roles'.[43] Four arias (including a short reprise) were considered:

[40] *Ibid.*, p. 1642.

[41] *Wiener Zeitung* (28 March 1789), pp. 763–4.

[42] This function of the Vienna Court Theatre scores has yet to be studied systematically. In K.T.315, 'Che soave zeffiretto', incorporated in *L'ape musicale rinnuovata* in 1791, is marked in a manner seen nowhere else in this score.

[43] Edge, 'Mozart's Viennese Copyists', p. 1595.

Act 1   Non so più cosa son, cosa faccio
Act 2   Voi che sapete
Act 3   Se così brami
Act 4   Voi che intendete

The subject matter of Cherubino's arias in Acts 1 and 2 is essentially the same: a portrayal of his state of mind. But while in 'Non so più' he exhibits a fair degree of self-awareness, realizing only too well the source of his uncontrollable feelings in the presence of women, in 'Voi che sapete' he is merely puzzled as to the source of his emotion. The arietta text thus appears to reflect Da Ponte's decision that the pageboy had to be presented at an earlier stage of puberty. It may even have been conceived as a replacement for 'Non so più', if its loss really was under consideration as in Version A.[44] Without question, Cherubino's second arietta 'Se così brami' was to have been part of the opera until very late on; its text appears in the Italian libretto, while the autograph has continuity directions referring to it: 'Segue l'arietta di Cherubino' and 'dopo l'arietta di Cherubino viene'. These instructions were replicated in the Court Theatre score.[45] Nothing remains of any musical setting of 'Se così brami', nor is there any concrete evidence to suggest that it reprised (or replaced) the Act 2 arietta, despite its identical metrical structure.[46] Shortly before the Act 4 Finale, Cherubino enters singing: 'la, la, la, la, la, la, la, la, lera'. Although not notated musically, these syllables were probably intended to be sung to a melody already associated with him: his 'signature tune'. As it happens, the number of syllables matches the line 'Non so più cosa son, cosa faccio' as does the stress pattern.[47] Nonetheless, it is evident that what Mozart had in mind was a melody that the Countess could immediately recognize. He incorporated a fully scored reprise, although curiously with a different first line 'Voi che intendete'.[48]

---

[44] 'Non so più' is written on an 'early' paper type, but a single replacement sheet at the start is on one of the 'late' papers, which is at least consistent with a reinstatement.

[45] The German translation points to the existence of a draft version in which Cherubino refers in the second stanza rather more directly to the Countess as 'my beauty' ('meine Schöne').

[46] The bar missed out at the end of the first page of the autograph of 'Voi che sapete' is certainly consistent with the idea that Mozart was re-copying its beginning at least from a draft. The revision of the preceding recitative in which the composer seems to sense the need to move towards the key of B flat major more quickly is interesting but is probably indicative only of the late insertion of the arietta.

[47] The Copenhagen score of Version A has the nonsense syllables evoking the rhythms of 'Non so più' even though the original is not in its text. NMA, II/5/16, *Kritische Berichte*, H (84).

[48] The difference seems minimal, although possibly 'sapete' (know) is slightly less impersonal than 'intendete' (understand). The German translation has 'wisset' for both, although with a different salutation at the head of the first stanza: 'Ihr Schönen' (Act 2) and 'Ihr Weiber' (Act 4). 'Voi che intendete' survived in the role book for Cherubino produced for Eszterháza, though not in the full score. NMA, II/5/16, *Kritische Berichte*, M^1 & M^2 (89–90).

This was copied in all the orchestral parts but was then cut, almost certainly before the premiere.[49] If the original was under threat, so would be the reprise, but there is no direct evidence that this was the reason for its loss. It is difficult now to reconstruct the series of decisions that led up to the final choice of arias for Cherubino, but clearly the following were in some way interrelated: i) the apparent removal of 'Non so più' and its late reinstatement; ii) the late insertion of 'Voi che sapete' with a different first line from its reprise; iii) the retention until very late on of 'Se così brami'; and iv) the orchestration of a reprise of the Act 2 arietta followed by its early abandonment. To judge by the number of changes made, Cherubino must indeed have been a troublesome role to get right.

A wealth of evidence in the early sources points to the exceptional care taken over the development of the page's character. Da Ponte, acting as his own censor, was constantly walking a tightrope between credibility and propriety. By the time of the 1789 revival, the issue had been settled. None of Mozart's revisions relates to the role of Cherubino, and there is no mention of the page in a review in the *Pressburger Zeitung* (2 September 1789). It seems that Da Ponte took particular pride in the resulting creation, one of the most memorable characters in all opera. When many years later he needed to cite examples to demonstrate the felicity of his arrangement of *La folle journée*, his choice of five aria texts included both 'Non so più' and 'Voi che sapete', the latter placed at the head of the list. He took the opportunity to place on record his view that 'the song of Cherubino' was 'perhaps the happiest effort in the piece'.[50]

---

[49] Edge, 'Mozart's Viennese Copyists', pp. 1596–8.

[50] *An Extract*, p. 20.

8   Mozart's spirit from Seyfried's hands

David Wyn Jones

'Also sprach Mozarts Geist'

On 2 January 1813 musical life in Vienna was enlivened by a major initiative, the first issue of a new journal, the *Wiener musikalische Zeitung*. Edited by Ignaz Franz von Schönholz, it appeared weekly every Saturday, a challenging schedule that the editor was able to maintain for only a year; the last issue appeared on 29 December 1813. Modelled on the *Allgemeine musikalische Zeitung* published by Breitkopf & Härtel in Leipzig and, after fifteen years, now firmly established as the leading music journal in German-speaking Europe, its Viennese counterpart had eight pages per issue, featuring two or three major articles or reviews plus shorter anecdotes (typically a paragraph or two) and the occasional musical supplement. Unlike Leipzig, London, Paris and other cities, Vienna in the early nineteenth century had no sustained tradition of musical writing and this single volume offers a rare, often surprising snapshot of musical life in the city in a particular year.[1]

Beethoven's name figures only intermittently: a performance of the first movement of the Fourth Symphony in Pierre Rode's concert in January; an enthusiastic review of a performance in the Augarten of the Fifth Symphony directed by Ignaz Schuppanzigh; an account of the two charity concerts in the university on 8 and 12 December organized by Beethoven and Johann Nepomuk Maelzel that included the first public performances of the Seventh Symphony and *Wellingtons Sieg*; and a review of a benefit concert in the Theater an der Wien on 23 December that opened with an overture in C major by the composer (probably *Prometheus*).[2] While major works by other living composers, such as Louis Spohr's *Der jungste Gerichte* and Maximilian Stadler's *Die Befreiung von Jerusalem* feature

---

[1] *Wiener allgemeine musikalische Zeitung* (1813). Facsimile edition *Wiener Musikwissenschaftliche Beiträge*, vol. XIV (Vienna, 1986). (Hereafter *WAMZ*.)

[2] *WAMZ* (1813), col. 193; cols. 293–4; cols. 747–60; cols. 813–16.

prominently,[3] the columns of the *Wiener musikalische Zeitung* are more consistently concerned with music by two composers from the past.

The very first article was a review of the charity performance of Handel's *Alexander's Feast*, retitled *Timotheus oder Die Gewalt der Musik* (*Timotheus or The Power of Music*), that had taken place on 29 November 1812, a resounding demonstration by nearly 600 performers of the social and political power of music in Vienna, and an event that led directly to the foundation of the Gesellschaft der Musikfreunde.[4] The oratorio was performed in the version with added instruments by Mozart, originally prepared for Baron Gottfried van Swieten in 1790; the conductor and Handel enthusiast Ignaz von Mosel tinkered with Mozart's scoring as well as substantially augmenting the number of players. Exploiting the success of the performance the review promised a biography of Handel, which duly appeared spread across two issues;[5] there was also a subsequent review of a piano reduction of the oratorio, published by Carlo Mechetti.[6]

As the memory of this performance, plus several repeat ones, reverberated in the musical imagination of the Viennese, it coincided with a run of performances of Mozart's *Don Giovanni*, given in German at the Theater an der Wien. This, too, elicited an extended critical response in the *Wiener musikalische Zeitung*, comprising twenty columns across two issues.[7] In what would now be termed a review article, the anonymous author first discusses the opera itself, approaching it through each of the eight characters followed by an account of almost every number in turn, before commenting on the recent performances. A few months earlier the journal had included a brief account of the state of music in Vienna by an unknown visitor, 'Ein Wort über den Zustand der Musik in Wien', in which Mozart's popularity as an opera composer is noted, especially *Die Zauberflöte* and *Don Giovanni*; more generally, the composer is referred to as the musical Schiller whose work is owned by the Viennese and whose pre-eminence is currently unequalled in the city.[8] A later short article claiming to be from a group of new composers in Vienna frankly admits that there is no 'Mozartian genius' amongst them, before going on to complain in a mundane way about the performing standards of the orchestras in the main theatres.[9]

[3] *WAMZ* (1813), cols. 66–75 (Spohr); cols. 281–8 (Stadler).

[4] *WAMZ* (1813), cols. 2–5. For the significance of this event see Otto Biba and Ingrid Fuchs, '*Die Emporbringung der Musik*'. *Hohepunkt aus der Gesellschaft der Musikfreunde in Wien* (Vienna, 2012), pp. 12–13; David Wyn Jones, *The Symphony in Beethoven's Vienna* (Cambridge, 2006), pp. 138–9; and Nicholas Mathew, *Political Beethoven* (Cambridge, 2013), pp. 103–4.

[5] *WAMZ* (1813), cols. 43–6, 82–5.

[6] *WAMZ* (1813), cols. 33–4.

[7] *WAMZ* (1813), cols. 397–406, 407–16.

[8] *WAMZ* (1813), cols. 186–9, 382–4.

[9] *WAMZ* (1813), cols. 375–80.

Laudatory comments of this kind, whether considered or casual, are not extended to other Viennese composers, dead (such as Haydn) or alive (such as Beethoven), and were borne out of a heightened idolatry for Mozart that occasionally drifted into the bizarre. In August 1813 the journal included a short article headed 'Mozart as art critic in Elysium' ('Mozart als Kunstrichter in Elysium') in which the composer appears from beyond the grave as the spokesman for Apollo, the god of music and poetry: 'Gentlemen, In the kingdom in which I continue my ever more beautiful, ever more kindly existence, Apollo has given me the authority to examine and to judge you, far more successful new composers, on his behalf.' No composers are named in this spoof oration but five general, if rather elusive, precepts are articulated for those who wish to emulate the speaker's example. It ends: 'Thus spake Mozart's spirit in the presence of Apollo' ('Also sprach Mozarts Geist im Angesichte Apollos').[10]

Twenty-two years after his death – that is, within the living memory of many musicians in Vienna – Mozart had become a composer whose gifts were recognized as unparalleled, as in *Don Giovanni*, whose reputation was equalled only by a composer from an earlier epoch, Handel, and whose continuing presence in musical life was as much otherworldly as anecdotal. Although these images are from a single year, they were not fleeting, passing ones. The director of the run of performances of *Don Giovanni* was Ignaz von Seyfried, a leading figure in the musical life of the city for more than thirty years. As a working musician his devotion to Mozart was informed by a consistent engagement with the music itself: and what that music meant to him was entirely in keeping with the outlooks encountered in the *Wiener musikalische Zeitung*.

Ignaz von Seyfried (1776–1841)

Seyfried, who was born twenty years after Mozart and died fifty years after him, was a pervasive and respected presence in the musical life of Vienna in the first half of the nineteenth century, as a composer, music director, teacher and writer. His links with Beethoven have long been appreciated but the publication in 1990 of Bettina von Seyfried's comprehensive reference volume, a thematic catalogue with associated chapters, has enabled the extraordinary industry of the man across nearly half a century to be fully appreciated:[11] over 400 compositions (original works and arrangements)

[10] *WAMZ* (1813), cols. 503–5.
[11] Bettina von Seyfried, *Ignaz Ritter von Seyfried. Thematisch-Bibliographisches*

Verzeichnis. Aspekte der Biographie und des Werkes (Frankfurt, 1990). The factual information in the following account of his life is

and some 180 literary items (reviews, dictionary entries and edited volumes). From this material Seyfried's fondness for Mozart's music emerges as an abiding characteristic, one that helped shape the composer's reputation in the first decades of the nineteenth century, in Vienna and beyond.

Seyfried was a native Viennese, born a few minutes away from St Stephen's Cathedral, in the Rotenturmstrasse. His father, Joseph, was a court apothecary who in 1788 was elevated to the nobility. It was at about this time that Joseph took his young son, already a competent pianist, to visit Mozart. These visits continued up until Mozart's death in 1791, but as Seyfried was to make clear in his own memoirs, the visits were part of a social acquaintanceship between Mozart and his father, and any teaching that occurred would have been on an ad hoc basis; it was not a formal course of instruction, such as the one Thomas Attwood had enjoyed. The visits occurred several times a week, particularly one imagines when the Mozart family lived in the inner city; the composer often played the piano, something that left an indelible impression on the teenage boy. After Mozart's death, Seyfried received formal piano lessons from Leopold Koželuch (1747–1818) and Franz Dussek (1731–99). From 1792 to 1794 he studied philosophy at the university in Prague, where he established lifelong friendships with Wenzel Johann Tomaschek (1774–1850) and, especially, Dionysius Weber (1766–1842). On his return to Vienna he began a course of study in jurisprudence at the university, combining it with a period of theoretical study with Johann Georg Albrechtsberger (1736–1809). With his formal university education and his father's connections, a career in the complex bureaucracy of the Habsburg court beckoned but, much to the disappointment of his father, Seyfried was increasingly drawn to a musical career. The friendship of two people proved decisive: the librettist and impresario Emanuel Schikaneder (1751–1812) and the composer Peter Winter (1754–1825). Schikaneder was the manager of the Theater auf der Wieden where in June 1796 Winter's most successful stage work, *Der unterbrochene Opferfest*, received its first performance. The Kapellmeister at the theatre was Johann Baptist Henneberg (1768–1822). Either singly or together, he and Schikaneder decided that the theatre needed a resident musician who could help adapt existing scores of German opera, contribute

taken from this volume. For further information on particular aspects of Seyfried's life and music see David J. Buch, 'Three Posthumous Reports Concerning Mozart in his Late Viennese years', *Eighteenth-Century Music*, 2 (2005), pp. 125–9; Stephan Punderlitschek, 'Das Freyhaus-theater auf der Wieden: das Tagebuch von Ignaz Ritter von Seyfried 1795 bis 12. Juni 1801' (University Diploma diss., University of Vienna, 1997); John Rice, *Empress Marie Therese and Music at the Viennese Court 1792–1807* (Cambridge, 2003), *passim*; and Harald Strebel, 'Der Briefwechsel von Friedrich Rochlitz und dem Mozartschüler Ignaz von Seyfried im Lichte zeitgenössischer Kritik und Konzertpraxis', *Mozart Studien*, 19 (2010), pp. 224–79.

to the pasticcio operas that formed part of the repertory and assist with the preparation of entirely new works. In 1797, at the age of twenty-two, Seyfried signed a six-year contract with Schikaneder, the first phase of a career in German opera that was to last until the mid-1820s. Since Seyfried had no previous experience of writing for the theatre and, indeed, composition of any kind, the early years in the theatre were very much a type of informal apprenticeship for him. This general experience had a distinctive Mozartian element. The many performances of *Die Zauberflöte* in the 1790s led Schikander to commission what he termed 'the second part of *Die Zauberflöte*', for which he wrote the text and Winter the music. *Das Labyrinth, oder der Kampf mit den Elementen* was first performed in June 1798, receiving thirty-three further performances in the remainder of 1798 alone. For Seyfried, this sustained experience of working with an original composition by Mozart and with a work written in response to it created an outlook of intense admiration and hopeful emulation that was to remain with him for the rest of his life.

This high-minded outlook figured alongside a more pragmatic, utilitarian attitude to Mozart's music. In December of the same year, 1798, the Theater auf der Wieden gave the first, and probably the last, performance of a one-act opera, *Drei Väter und zwei Kinder*. The music has not survived but, in the practised tradition of pasticcio, Seyfried provided some original music to sit alongside music taken from works by Mozart and Franz Anton Hoffmeister (1754–1812). In 1801 Schikaneder moved to a brand new theatre, Vienna's largest, the Theater an der Wien, where one of the first operas to be performed was a German version of *La clemenza di Tito*, for which Seyfried wrote new recitatives.

Seyfried had already achieved success with two full-scale operas of his own, *Der Löwenbrunn* and *Der Wundermann am Rheinfall*, and increasing confidence as a theatre composer combined with the move to the new theatre led him to become an influential presence in the city's musical life. By 1810 he had composed eighteen original operas on a variety of subject matter: comic, historical and magical. Other stage works included two melodramas (*Montezuma* and *Saul, König in Israel*) and two three-act quodlibets, including *Rochus Pumpernickel*, a work that remained in the repertory for much of the nineteenth century; it quotes 'Se vuol ballare' from *Le nozze di Figaro* alongside music by Anton Diabelli, Carl Ditters von Dittersdorf, Étienne Méhul, Giovanni Paisiello and others. In addition, Seyfried contributed music to thirteen pasticcios, provided insertion numbers for the same number of operas, including three by Méhul, adapted two works by André-Ernest-Modeste Grétry (*Les mariages samnites* and *Richard Coeur-de-Lion*) and composed incidental music for twenty-four plays, including Schiller's *Die Räuber*.

From 1811 onwards Seyfried began to devote himself to sacred music for various churches in Vienna and later for the Benedictine abbey in Melk, ranging from the shortest of works, such as the *Trauergesang* for men's voices and trombones (BvS IX/6), an arrangement of Beethoven's three Equale (WoO 30) prepared for the composer's funeral service on 29 March 1827, to sixteen settings of the mass and four settings of the requiem. Although the balance in his compositional output was shifting, Seyfried continued to compose stage works until 1822, when a serious illness forced him to relinquish his connection with the Theater an der Wien, a connection that had lasted exactly a quarter of a century if its predecessor the Theater auf der Wieden is added into the equation. As an experienced composer of German stage music and of church music, Seyfried hoped that he would succeed Antonio Salieri as a court composer following the latter's death in 1823; in the event, that position was given, as so often, to an insider, Joseph Eybler (1765–1846).

Seyfried had already turned his hand to literary work, utilizing his university education in philosophy and jurisprudence. Between 1819 and 1821 he was the editor of the new local music journal, the *Allgemeine musikalische Zeitung mit besonderer Rücksicht auf den österreichischen Kaiserstaat*, and he may have contributed to the Leipzig *Allgemeine musikalische Zeitung* too. More ambitiously Seyfried devoted himself to assembling the collected writings of his former teacher, Albrechtsberger, on thorough bass, harmony and composition, and published them in 1825. A similar collection based on the writings of the Viennese church composer Joseph Preindl (1756–1823) came out in 1827/8, and was dedicated to Archduke Rudolph. Finally, in 1832 Seyfried published a volume devoted to Beethoven's studies in thorough bass, harmony and composition. While, in the case of the Beethoven volume, his contribution can be shown to have been faulty or fanciful, taken together the three publications provide a substantial compendium of musical pedagogy in Vienna in Seyfried's lifetime mingled with some interesting anecdotal asides. Seyfried wrote nearly 150 entries for Gustav Schilling's six-volume dictionary, *Universallexikon der Tonkunst – Encyclopädie der gesammten musikalischen Wissenschaften*, published in Stuttgart between 1835 and 1843, mainly on his Viennese contemporaries such as Diabelli, Franz Krommer, Schubert and Stadler, and occasionally on composers from earlier epochs such as Johann Joseph Fux and (quite unexpectedly) Domenico Scarlatti. As well as several articles for the Viennese *Allgemeine musikalische Zeitung*, Seyfried wrote for the widely influential *Cäcilia* (published by Schott in Mainz) and Schumann's *Neue Zeitschrift für Musik* (Leipzig, Breitkopf & Härtel).

Seyfried's arrangements of Mozart's music

In addition to the early opera *Drei Väter und drei Kinder*, the recitatives for the German version of *La clemenza di Tito* and the quodlibet *Rochus Pumpernickel*, no fewer than eighteen further works by Seyfried are linked, in various ways, with compositions by Mozart. No other composer attracted comparable compositional attention from him and for so much of his working life (that is, 1798–1837). Works linked to Mozart are listed in Table 8.1.

Ten works in Table 8.1 are items of liturgical music that reflect two common practices of the day: adding additional instruments to an existing work that is otherwise unaltered, or providing a sacred text to an operatic or instrumental movement to form a new work for the liturgy; in the case of 'Justus ut palma' and 'Populi, timete Sancti Nomen' the two practices are combined. For liturgical performances of Mozart's Requiem, Seyfried pro-vided a setting of 'Libera me Domine', to be sung after the Mass and before the absolution of the corpse.[12] It is a skilfully complementary addition to Mozart's work, both in sonority and in thematic material. It is set in the same home key as the Requiem, D minor, and the accompaniment is a *Harmonie* consisting of most of the wind instruments used by Mozart – two basset-horns, two bassoons, two trumpets and two trombones – plus timpani and a supporting double bass (violone); when the liturgical text reiterates two clauses from earlier in the Requiem, 'Dies irae, dies illa' and 'et lux perpetua luceat eis', Seyfried quotes Mozart's music, respectively the beginning of the 'Dies irae (bars 1–4) and the end of the 'Requiem aeternam' (bars 44–8). An arrangement for male voices only was sung at Beethoven's funeral on 29 March 1827. At a requiem service for Beethoven in the Augustinerkirche on 3 April, Mozart's Requiem was performed together with Seyfried's 'Libera me', presumably in its full scoring.[13]

The largest, most ambitious work in the Mozartian catalogue is a three-act opera that is entirely based on music by the composer, *Ahasverus, der nie ruhende*. The libretto, most likely prepared by the composer's brother Joseph von Seyfried (1780–1849), tells the story of Ahasverus, the wandering Jew who, having taunted Christ as he carried the cross to Calvary, is condemned

---

[12] 'Libera zum Gebrauche bei Aufführungen des Mozart'schen Requiem's. In Musik gesetzt von Ign. Ritter von Seyfried... Wien, bei Tobias Haslinger...' Score and parts: complete exemplar in GB-Lbl, H.3269.a.

[13] Contemporary accounts of Beethoven's funeral and memorial services are sometimes contradictory in their details. The clearest one is by Haslinger (the publisher of Seyfried's 'Libera me'), printed as a preface to the following: 'Trauer-Gesang bey Beethoven's Leichenbegängnisse in Wien den 29. März 1827'. Exemplar in GB-Lbl, H.2430 (10). The listing of the 'Libera me' in von Seyfried, *Ignaz von Seyfried* (pp. 485–7) is misleading. It is given as two separate works: the arrangement for male voices and trombones as XV/4, the original as XV/5; as an incipit for XV/5 four bars of the first bassoon part (a harmonic line) are given.

Table 8.1 Seyfried and Mozart's music

Date	Work	Bettina van Seyfried Work Number (BvS), or page reference	Publisher	Notes
1798	*Drei Väter und zwei Kinder*	IV/2		Lost. Music by Seyfried, Mozart and Hoffmeister.
1801	Instrumental recitatives (in German) for *La clemenza di Tito*	V/4		DWJ: BvS associates these with the Italian performances at the Burgtheater in 1804; the German performances at the Theater an der Wien in 1801 are more likely.
1809	*Rochus Pumpernickel*	III/3		Quodlibet; includes the aria 'Se vuol ballare' from *Le nozze di Figaro*.
1812	Fantasy in C minor for orchestra	IX/1	Breitkopf & Härtel [1812]	Orchestration of Fantasy (K. 475) and Sonata in C minor (K. 457).
1813	Fantasy in F minor for orchestra	IX/2	Breitkopf & Härtel [1813–14]	Orchestration of first and second movements of Piano Quartet in G minor (K. 478) and Fantasia in F minor (K. 608).
1821	*Davidde penitente* (K. 469)	Deest		DWJ: performance in Prague used first movement of Seyfried's Fantasy in C minor (= K. 475) as overture. See Angermüller, p. 533.
1823	*Ahasverus, der nie ruhende*	III/10	DWJ: libretto in D-Mbs, Sig. Hr 43	'Romantic drama' in three acts using music from the following works: K. 309, K. 331, K. 387, K. 406, K. 464, K. 475, K. 478, K. 497, K. 516, K. 521, K. 531, K. 560, K. 593, K. 594 and K. 614.
1823	Concertino in C	IX/3	André, [1824/5]; dedicated to Constance Nissen	Orchestration of Sonata in C for four hands (K. 521).
1825–6	Keyboard reduction of Mozart's Requiem (K. 626)	p. 528		Lost.
1825–6	Te Deum (K. 141); additional instruments	p. 528		Lost. DWJ: possibly the same as the anonymous additional instruments published by Haslinger in 1827; see Weinmann, *Haslinger*, p. 3.

Date	Title	Publisher	No.	Notes
1825–6	Mass in F (K. 192); additional instruments		p. 528	Lost.
1827	Libera me Domine	Haslinger [1827]	XV/4, 5	'To be used in performances of Mozart's Requiem.' Score and parts.
1830	*Der hölzerne Säbel*		III/12	One-act opera. DWJ: uses music from K. 233, K. 387, K. 421, K. 448, K. 465, K. 479, K. 493, K. 497, K. 517, K. 524, K. 539, K. 542, K. 551 and K. 597.
1834–7	Equale for three trombones		p. 528	Lost.
1834–7	Mass in C		p. 528	Lost. DWJ: additional instruments for K. 258 or K. 259?
1834–7	Mass in D		p. 528	Lost. DWJ: additional instruments for K. 194?
1837	Gradual: 'Justus ut palma'		XVIII/7	Contrafactum of the chorus 'Che del ciel, che degli Dei' from Act 2 of *La clemenza di Tito*.
?	Concertante Symphony in C		IX/4	DWJ: second orchestration of K. 521 (see IX/3), for different forces and with the addition of the slow introduction from K. 497 (transposed from F to C).
?	'Populi, timete Sancti Nomen'		XVIII/8	Contrafactum of 'Tradito, schernito dal perfido cor' from Act 2 of *Così fan tutte*. DWJ: introduction by Seyfried.
?	'Quis te comprehendat'		p. 528	Lost contrafactum. DWJ: possibly the same as anonymous contrafactum of third movement of K. 361 published by Mathias Artaria (1825) and Diabelli (1833), (KAnh. 110; K. 6 Anhang B.371). See Weinmann, *Diabelli*, p. 304.
?	'Ave verum corpus' (K. 618)		p. 528	Lost. DWJ: with additional instruments?

Information is mainly drawn from Bettina von Seyfried. *Ignaz Ritter von Seyfried. Thematisch-Bibliographisches Verzeichnis. Aspekte der Biographie und des Werkes* (Frankfurt, 1990). Amended and additional information is prefaced DWJ. Other cited sources include: Rudolf Angermüller, *Mozart 1485/86 bis 2003. Daten zu Leben, Werk und Rezeptionsgeschichte der Mozarts*, vol II (Tutzing, 2004); Alexander Weinmann, *Verlagsverzeichnis Anton Diabelli & Co. (1824 bis 1840)* (Vienna, 1985); and Weinmann, *Vollständiges Verlagsverzeichnis Senefelder, Steiner, Haslinger*, vol. II (Tobias Haslinger) (Munich, 1980).

to his fate until Christ's second coming. A popular story from the sixteenth century onwards, it was usually entitled 'Der ewige Jude' ('The eternal Jew') in Germany.[14] Composed towards the end of Seyfried's association with the Theater an der Wien, it was not only his most ambitious Mozartian project but his most ambitious stage work altogether, one in which the romance and drama of the plot is supported by a resourceful, often ingenious use of Mozart's music, mainly keyboard music and string quartets. The opening of the C minor Fantasia (K. 475) is heard several times across the three acts, evoking the constant restlessness of Ahasverus. Indicative of Seyfried's undoubted skills as a word setter and orchestrator is the conclusion of Act 1, where the subsiding of a dramatic storm, which had begun with music from K. 475 (bar 36 onwards), is marked by a full setting for voices and orchestra of the finale of the String Quartet in G major (K. 387), a juxtaposition of counterpoint and tunefulness that is very much in the spirit of *Die Zauberflöte*.[15] Following its premiere at the Theater an der Wien on 29 April 1823 the Viennese correspondent of the *Allgemeine musikalische Zeitung* was fulsome in his praise: 'a veritable national celebration, a burning homage to a glorious hero', a work 'received with enthusiasm, from the first to the last chord'.[16] For Seyfried himself, this was the highlight of a lifetime of devotion to Mozart and his music, but *Ahasverus* never achieved the popularity of other stage works by him, especially *Zum göldenen Löwen* and *Rochus Pumpernickel*. After the initial run of seven performances in 1823 it was not revived in the composer's lifetime.

Fantasy in C minor and Fantasy in F minor

Of all the compositions by Seyfried based on music by Mozart, these two substantial orchestral works achieved the greatest prominence during his life, including through publication by Breitkopf & Härtel and documented performances in Berlin, Leipzig, Prague and Vienna. According to Seyfried's memoirs, the desire to orchestrate the Fantasy in C minor (K. 475) and the associated sonata (K. 457) was borne of his memory of the composer playing them on the piano during his boyhood visits. There was a complementary motive too, revealed in correspondence between Seyfried and the editor of the *Allgemeine musikalische Zeitung*, Johann Friedrich Rochlitz.[17]

By the end of the first decade of the nineteenth century Seyfried had consolidated his reputation in Vienna as an effective composer and adapter

[14] For a standard history see George K. Anderson, *The Legend of the Wandering Jew* (Providence, RI, 1965).
[15] Autograph: A-Wn, Mus. Hs. 3270.

[16] *Allgemeine musikalische Zeitung*, 25 (1823), cols. 365–9, at col. 365. (Hereafter *AMZ*.)
[17] Strebel, 'Der Briefwechsel', pp. 224–79.

of German operatic music, but he was irked by some of the dismissive and occasionally inaccurate comments that his theatre pieces received in the *Allgemeine musikalische Zeitung*, which he also saw as thwarting a wider reputation. Although a capable pianist, Seyfried had never been a professional performer and could not underpin a career as performer–composer in that way. Tellingly, apart from a few dances, he never wrote a single note of original piano music. Indulging his enthusiasm for Mozart and propagating his memory by orchestrating one of the composer's major works was a particularly novel way of broadening and refining his reputation.

In March 1812 Seyfried sent a manuscript score of his orchestration of K. 475 and K. 457 to Rochlitz, together with a lengthy letter outlining his dissatisfaction with the criticism he had received in the journal and suggesting that Rochlitz himself, as editor, should comment on the work.[18] Seyfried would have known of Rochlitz's enthusiasm for Mozart, one repeatedly demonstrated in the columns of the *Allgemeine musikalische Zeitung*.[19] His response was positive: Rochlitz himself had begun work on an orchestral arrangement of the fantasy but had put it aside; he was, therefore, naturally interested in Seyfried's proposal and recommended that the work be published by Breitkopf & Härtel.[20] This was a significant endorsement. It placed the work on a par with major orchestral works by two Viennese composers with significant reputations for large-scale orchestral works: Beethoven (Symphonies Nos. 5 and 6) and Anton Eberl (Symphony in D minor). More specifically Seyfried's work sat in Breitkopf & Härtel's catalogue alongside the complete edition in progress of Mozart's music, the *Oeuvres complettes,* which was a defining representation of the composer's legacy at the turn of the century; the C minor Fantasy and the C minor Sonata had appeared in volume six, published in 1799.

The first performance of Seyfried's Fantasy in C minor was given in Leipzig on 29 September 1812. The subsequent report in the *Allgemeine musikalische Zeitung* was generally positive, 'the whole has such ardour, majesty and delicacy', but there was also a sense that it was too much of a good thing, that it might have been better to arrange only the fantasy or, had Seyfried wanted an additional movement, to use the first or last movement of the sonata; the middle, slow movement of the sonata made the work too long and weakened the total effect.[21] A second performance, in Berlin on

---

[18] Strebel, 'Der Breifwechsel', pp. 227–31, 253–9.
[19] On the doubtful reliability of many of Rochlitz's writings on the composer, see Maynard Solomon, 'The Rochlitz Anecdotes: Issues of Authenticity in Early Mozart Biography', in Cliff Eisen (ed.), *Mozart Studies* (Oxford, 1991), pp. 1–59. For

Rochlitz's comments on the Requiem, see Simon P. Keefe, *Mozart's Requiem: Reception, Work, Completion* (Cambridge, 2012), pp. 16–19, 44–8.
[20] Strebel, 'Der Briefwechsel', pp. 231–2.
[21] *AMZ*, 14 (1812), cols. 719–20; the precise date of the first performance is taken from Strebel, 'Der Briefwechsel', p. 232.

3 January 1813, shortly after its publication by Breitkopf & Härtel, elicited a more uniformly enthusiastic response: 'Herr von Seyfried has earned himself real merit, in that he has arranged for a large orchestra this already long familiar masterpiece for piano with such expertise. Mozart's spirit hovered above the orchestra.'[22]

For Seyfried the successful early performances of the Fantasy in C minor and its publication by Breitkopf & Härtel gave him the wider esteem that he had sought and, emboldened by this success, he immediately embarked on a second major arrangement. His starting point this time was the Fantasy in F minor (K. 608), originally written for mechanical organ. In a letter of 13 January 1813 to Rochlitz, he indicates that he remembers hearing it several times in his youth in this version and gives an intensely vivid description of the effect of the music:[23]

> The terrifyingly wild Allegro, with its artfully worked out fugal theme, arouses, in my view, close to a thousand varied impressions. At the startling modulation to F sharp minor [bar 57] the listener is numbed, and believes that the ground underneath him is trembling. The extremely tender Adagio [*recte*: Andante] in A flat speaks of the harmony of the spheres; it brings forth tears, comforting tears of heavenly longing. The repeated Allegro hurls us back towards restless human life. The two opposing fugal themes present a striking, grave, forceful image of the strife of human passions. The only goal is peace. Strength is exhausted, the struggles of life are over, and the spirit flees the body. The close points to the hereafter.

Although Seyfried writes about Mozart's original version, the music was much more widely known in an arrangement for piano duet that had first appeared in Vienna in May 1799, published by Traeg, which is when it acquired the title fantasy;[24] a year later it appeared in volume 8 of Breitkopf's *Oeuvres complettes*. It was a substantial work in its own right, in three linked sections, Allegro–Andante–Allegro, lasting over ten minutes, and an orchestration of that work alone would have satisfied those who had found the C minor fantasy too long. But Seyfried was even more daring here. He conceived the F minor fantasy not as an opening movement, rather as a finale. A search for a suitable, complementary first movement in F minor in Mozart's output would have yielded little of consequence since, unlike C minor, F minor is not frequently encountered as a home key. The only instrumental work that might have provided an option was another work for mechanical organ, the slightly earlier Adagio and Allegro (K. 594), but it

[22] *AMZ*, 15 (1813), cols. 48–9.
[23] Seyfried's letter was first published in full in Otto Biba, 'Nachrichten zu Mozart in Briefen seiner Zeitgenossen. Unbeachtete Dokumente aus dem Archiv der Gesellschaft der Musikfreunde in Wien', in Yosihiko Tokumaru et al. (eds.), *Mozartiana. The*

Festschrift for the Seventieth Birthday of Professor Ebisawa Bin (Tokyo, 2001), pp. 618–20. It is given in Strebel, *Der Briefwechsel*, pp. 234–7.
[24] Alexander Weinmann, *Verlagverzeichnis Johann Traeg (und Sohn)*, 2nd edition (Vienna, 1973), p. 25.

would not have offered sufficient contrast to K. 608, in particular for the symphonic dimension that Seyfried sought. His solution was a radical one. He preceded the fantasia with two movements from the Piano Quartet in G minor (K. 478), the opening Allegro transposed down a tone and the Andante in its original key of B flat major. Conveniently these two movements, like K. 608, had appeared in the *Oeuvres complettes* (volume 13, 1802), so Seyfried's composite work once more had the broader imprimatur of that project behind it.

The first performance of the F minor fantasy was given by Seyfried's orchestral colleagues from the Theater an der Wien on 3 April 1814, the opening work in a mixed programme of readings, tableaux vivants (including a representation of Raphael's 'Deliverance of St Peter') and ending with Handel's 'Hallelujah' chorus from *Messiah* (in Mozart's arrangement). Predictably, as Seyfried would have seen it, the anonymous Vienna correspondent was grudging rather than lavish in his praise: 'the entire symphony is arranged once more with much unity and the instruments were deployed with effect'.[25] A week later on 10 April there was another benefit concert at the Theater an der Wien, when Seyfried took the opportunity to present his C minor fantasy, almost certainly the first performance of the work in Vienna.[26]

The early reviews of the two fantasies referred to above are typical in not offering extensive commentary on Seyfried's outlook as an arranger. Undoubtedly the two works had widespread appeal, but before probing the nature of that appeal it is appropriate to look at some of their characteristic features as arrangements.

Both works are scored for forces never found in a Mozart symphony: strings, pairs of flutes, oboes, clarinets and bassoons, four horns, two trumpets and timpani, plus one trombone in the C minor fantasy. Works in the minor key from the Classical period, including by Mozart, frequently have four horns rather than two in order to optimize the number of notes available from the natural instruments when the music moves from the tonic to the relative major. But many tutti sonorities in both fantasies consistently employ all four instruments, thus providing, with the woodwind choir of eight instruments, a heavily weighted sound; the closest sonority in Mozart occurs not in a symphony but in individual numbers such as the overture and the finales of the two acts of *Die Zauberflöte*, a work Seyfried knew intimately.

Expanding the range of sonority, and with that the internal contrasts of Mozart's originals, has consequences for many of the tempo markings and associated descriptors. As conceived by Mozart, the C minor fantasy

---

[25] *AMZ*, 16 (1814), cols. 353–4.   [26] *AMZ*, 16 (1814), cols. 355–6.

Table 8.2 Tempo markings in K. 475 and K. 457: Mozart and Seyfried

Original bar nos.	Mozart	Seyfried
	K. 475	
1–25	Adagio	Molto adagio
26–35	–	Larghetto
36–85	Allegro	Allegro molto
86–124	Andantino	Andantino grazioso
125–60	Più allegro	Un poco più moto
161–76	Primo tempo	Tempo primo
	K. 457	
1–185	Molto allegro	Allegro spiritoso
1–157	Adagio	Andante sostenuto
1–319	Allegro assai	Allegro assai

contained four changes of tempo within the frame of an Adagio opening and closing section, while the sonata embeds an Adagio slow movement between two Allegro movements. As Table 8.2 and Examples 8.1a–d indicate, Seyfried takes a different view of some of these internal contrasts, enhanced by contrasts in tone colour. The framing Adagio in the fantasy section is a slower Molto adagio (Example 8.1a); for the ensuing lyrical section in D major (bars 26–35, Example 8.1b) he pushes the tempo on a little, Larghetto, to emphasize the new lyricism and the change of scoring. The third section is brisker, Allegro molto rather than Mozart's Allegro (Example 8.1c), while for the fourth section Seyfried adds a qualifying 'grazioso' to Mozart's Andantino (Example 8.1d). There are two working principles: to widen tempo contrasts (fast music can be faster, slow music slower) and, where appropriate, to be more specific about the mood of the music. The most radical change, however, is also one that goes against the first principle while using the second to mitigate its effect. In the slow movement of the sonata Mozart's 'Adagio' is changed to 'Andante sostenuto', a wholly different conception that is emphasized by a re-barring of the original, from common time to 2/4. The effect is to minimize the contrast of tempo between the slow movement and the surrounding allegro music while, at the same, offering a different contrast of character, a stronger foregrounding of the gavotte rhythms of the music at the expense of the Alberti figuration. Seyfried would have known that an adagio marking for a central movement in an instrumental work by Mozart is much less common than andante and would have realized that the composer's choice of the slower marking in this work enabled the rich keyboard fioriture to make maximum effect. No orchestra could match this eloquence, so, rather brutally, Seyfried brought the movement into line with Mozart's customary practice, including in his four last

Example 8.1a Seyfried, Fantasy in C minor, first movement, bars 1–4 (from autograph: A-Wn, Mus. Hs 3291/1).

Example 8.1b Seyfried, Fantasy in C minor, first movement (= K. 475, bars 26–9).

Example 8.1c Seyfried, Fantasy in C minor, first movement (= K. 475, bars 36–44)

symphonies (K. 504, K. 543, K. 550 and K. 551), and re-imagined it as an andante. If this was, indeed, Seyfried's train of thought, he would have been disappointed by the reviewer's comment in the *Allgemeine musikalische Zeitung* that the movement was the least successful in the fantasy.

Example 8.1c (cont.)

There are three changes of tempo in the F minor work. In the finale, the central Andante section is changed to Poco Larghetto, the more relaxed tempo allowing Seyfried's carefully considered changes of orchestral colour to emphasize the successive changes in register and texture that characterize the music, prompted in the original by the terraced capabilities of the

Example 8.1d Seyfried, Fantasy in C minor, first movement (= K. 475, bars 86–9)

mechanical organ. The changes in the first movement are more fundamental, substantially upping the emotional temperature. Mozart's 'Allegro' is changed to 'Allegro con fuoco', a tempo marking unknown in the composer's oeuvre. At the coda (bar 224) Seyfried adds an impetuous 'Più mosso' to drive the movement home.

Here, as elsewhere in the two fantasies, dynamic markings are altered to exploit the orchestral resource: Mozart's marking is *f*, Seyfried has *ff*. In the climactic exchange of material between piano and strings that ends the development section of the first movement (bars 133–40), Seyfried stings each competitive entry with a *sf* marking, leading to a *ff* at the arrival of the recapitulation. In the C minor fantasy, for the repeated imperfect cadences in B minor that precede Example 8.1b, scored for strings, Seyfried takes the dynamic level down to *ppp*, a dynamic indication never found in Mozart.

One of the main challenges facing Seyfried were those passages, such as bars 73–85 in K. 475, where the figuration is conceived wholly in pianistic terms, usually in the manner of an improvisation and often traversing the full range of the five-octave fortepiano. His solution usually involves the retention of the harmonic framework that underpins such passages and the invention of neutral thematic material that sits consistently in the same register.

In K. 475 and K. 457 this kind of challenge was an occasional, easily accomplished one, but in choosing the first movement of the G minor piano quartet for the first movement of his fantasy in F minor it became more frequent, since pianistic figuration is integral to the thematic weave of the entire movement, often working in conjunction with the martial two-bar motif that begins it. The symphonic persistence of this antecedent motif, and its easy realization in orchestral terms, were central reasons for choosing this movement, but the following two bars, a consequent bravura scale passage

Example 8.2a Mozart, Piano Quartet in G minor, K. 478, first movement, bars 1–8.

for piano that descends through an octave and a half (see Example 8.2a), was not so easily or effectively reproduced in orchestral terms. (Mozart's most familiar antecedent-consequent beginning to a symphony, that of the 'Jupiter', posed no such problems because it was entirely conceived in orchestral terms.) Seyfried's solution was a thoroughgoing one (see Example 8.2b). He maintained the middleground of the harmonic framework (tonic to dominant), the voice leading in the bass (mediant to supertonic) and the supporting rhythmic punctuation (the three-crotchet anacrusis), but changed Mozart's descending scale through the tonic chord to a descending arpeggio. To give additional direction and shape to the four-bar phrase, Seyfried alters the initial *f* for piano quartet to an arresting *ff* for

Example 8.2b Seyfried, Fantasy in F minor, first movement, bars 1–8
(from autograph: A-Wn, Mus. Hs 3291/2).

Example 8.2b (cont.)

the full orchestra and adds a decrescendo to the consequent part of the phrase, making explicit what is implicit in Mozart's original. With this solution, Seyfried committed himself to replacing all the semiquaver passagework in the movement that derives from this bravura consequent with other material. The result is the most consistently detailed reworking of Mozart's music in the two fantasias.

As this root and branch change suggests, Seyfried did not balk at making big decisions as he converted music conceived for fortepiano (plus violin, viola and cello in K. 478) or mechanical organ into a version suitable for performance by an early nineteenth-century orchestra of forty or more players. Inevitably, the expansion of resource led to an intensification of the drama or, put more subtly, to a different kind of dramatic intensity, no longer taut and inward but flamboyant and assured. Further consequences of this changed nature of expression are the modifications that Seyfried made to the conclusion of many of the movements.

At the end of the first movement of the sonata portion of the Fantasy in C minor, Mozart's unwinding of the tension is extended by three bars, ending with a sustained tonic chord for full orchestra, *pianissimo*. In the following movement (Adagio in the original, Andante sostenuto in Seyfried's arrangement), the repeated cadential progressions that end the movement lead, in Seyfried's version, to an additional declamatory tonic chord, *ff*, that subsides quickly to a tonic, *pp*. (Modern listeners may be reminded of the similar ending to the Allegretto in Beethoven's Seventh Symphony, a work exactly contemporary with Seyfried's fantasia.) At the end of the following movement – which also represents the end of the work as a whole – Seyfried extends the coda by twenty-one bars so that he can engineer a crescendo from *pp* to *fff*, with a good deal of dominant–tonic re-iteration and powerfully sustained wind chords. Nine bars are added at the end of the first movement of the Fantasy in F minor, again highly rhetorical in its orchestration but at the same time including a climactic reference to the descending dotted arpeggio that Seyfried has consistently substituted for Mozart's semiquavers. Seyfried's orchestral realization of the slow movement of K. 478, the second movement in the F minor fantasy, sees him at his most sensitive; it is imaginatively and beautifully coloured throughout and requires only one additional bar, a *pizzicato* confirmation of the final two chords, *ppp*. The finale of the F minor fantasy was the least challenging movement of the seven to orchestrate. The piano duet version from which Seyfried worked had no dynamic indications, but they are easily inferred (because of the origins of the movement as organ music), and the four-part fugal writing that is incorporated into the outer sections transfers readily across to the orchestra. Only towards the end of the movement does Seyfried begin significantly to expand its expressive scope. At the stretto section beginning at bar 205, the former legato phrasing is replaced by articulated statements of the head motif, marked *ff*, perhaps a conscious influence of the similarly articulated climatic re-iterations of the main motif in the coda of the 'Jupiter' symphony. To end the work, Seyfried adds fourteen bars of his own. They seem to be making their way to a grandiose conclusion, in the manner of the C minor fantasy, until the very last cadence when a diminuendo down to *piano* accompanies a wholly unanticipated *tierce de picardie*. This would seem to be an authentic realization of Seyfried's own reported response to the conclusion of K. 608: struggle followed by the life hereafter (see Example 8.3).

Stylistic fidelity, fantasia and Mozart's spirit

Although both fantasias were borne out of fervent admiration for Mozart's music, it would be equally fair to say that the results are, for the most part, quite un-Mozartian: they are not circumspect exercises in pastiche orchestration. Everything from the size of the orchestra through to the many inflated gestures of the arrangements contributes to an experience that is, stylistically, an anachronistic one by some twenty years or more. If Mozart provided the raw material and the inspiration, then the composer who seems to lurk behind Seyfried's undeniably resourceful and skilful arrangements is someone else, namely Beethoven. The orchestral forces, the tempo markings, the exaggerated dynamics, the bold juxtaposition of contrasting sonorities, the *sforzando* accents, the forceful use of measured tremolo in thematic writing for first and second violins, the exaggerated signalling of a recapitulation and the ardent sound of the minor key are all redolent of that composer. Seyfried had first-hand experience of hearing three notable works in C minor by Beethoven. The venue for Beethoven's 1803 benefit concert was Seyfried's Theater an der Wien, where the resident composer had turned pages for the composer–pianist in the first performance of the C minor piano concerto.[27] Beethoven's 1808 benefit concert was again at the Theater an der Wien and included two compositions in C minor, the Choral Fantasia and the Fifth Symphony. Other works in C minor that Seyfried may have known were two piano sonatas (op. 10 no. 1 and op. 13, 'Pathetique'), a piano trio (op. 1 no. 1), a sonata for piano and violin (op. 30 no. 2), a string trio (op. 9 no. 3), a quartet (op. 18 no. 4) and the *Coriolan* overture. Seyfried's first fantasia may be seen as a fashionable response to this flow of C minor works; for the modern commentator it helps to cement the familiar historical

---

[27] Seyfried's account of his experience is given in *Thayer's Life of Beethoven*, ed. Elliot Forbes (revised edition, Princeton, 1967), pp. 329–30.

Example 8.3 Seyfried, Fantasy in F minor, third movement, bars 228–46
(= K. 608, bar 216, continuation by Seyfried).

Example 8.3 (cont.)

Example 8.3 (cont.)

Example 8.3 (cont.)

narrative that links Mozart's C minor (as found in his C minor concerto as well as in K. 475 and K. 457) with Beethoven's C minor.[28]

F minor, the key of the second fantasia, also has a Beethovenian pedigree (albeit with fewer works) that may have encouraged the popular reception of Seyfried's second fantasia: two piano sonatas (op. 2 no. 1 and op. 57, 'Appassionata'); one quartet (op. 95); the overture and Clärchen's song 'Die Trommel gerühret' from the incidental music to Goethe's *Egmont*; and the orchestral introduction to Act 2 of *Fidelio*. Works in that key by Beethoven were particularly well received in 1814: on 25 March at a benefit concert in the Kärntnertortheater he directed a performance of the *Egmont* overture; *Fidelio* was given its first performance at the Kärntnertortheater on 23 May; and sometime in the same month the F minor quartet, the 'Quartetto serioso', was premiered. In the middle of this sequence of performances, Seyfried's F minor fantasy received its first and second performances (3 and 6 April).

None of the contemporary reviews of Seyfried's fantasies points out the stylistic incongruity of his arrangements; neither do they mention Beethoven's name. On the contrary, it will be recalled that the *Allgemeine musikalische Zeitung* reviewer of the Leipzig performance of the C minor fantasy wrote that 'Mozart's spirit hovered above the orchestra'. This is the contradiction that lay at the heart of their appeal: the works were successful because they were perceived as Mozartian and contemporary at the same time. Far from opportunism, this represented a position of integrity, one that Mozart, appropriately, would have appreciated.

The concert on 3 April 1814, at which the F minor fantasy received its premiere, began with that work and concluded with the 'Hallelujah' chorus from *Messiah* in Mozart's orchestration. Along with *Acis and Galatea*, *Alexander's Feast* and the *Ode to St Cecilia* this was one of four works by Handel that Mozart had orchestrated between 1788 and 1790 at the behest of Gottfried van Swieten. In all cases Mozart expanded the orchestration, making resourceful use of flutes, clarinets, bassoons, horns and trombones, revised the trumpet parts, and added or altered dynamic marks and occasionally tempo markings too. In imposing a new stylistic order, Mozart often rode roughshod over Handel's aesthetic, but making the work suitable for a new age was the prime motivation. As a congratulatory comment in a letter to Mozart that is attributed to van Swieten put it: 'He who can clothe Handel so solemnly and tastefully that he pleases modern fashion, on the one hand, and, on the other, shows him in his sublimity, has felt his worth, has

---

[28] See, for instance, Joseph Kerman, *The Beethoven Quartets* (London, 1967), pp. 70–1; and Michael Tusa, 'Beethoven's "C-minor Mood": Some Thoughts on the Structural Implications of Key Choice', *Beethoven Forum 2*, eds. Christopher Reynolds, Lewis Lockwood and James Webster (Lincoln, NE, 1993), pp. 1–27.

understood him, has penetrated the source of his expression, from which he can and will draw with assurance.'[29] *Alexander's Feast* and *Messiah*, in particular, had a sustained performance history in Vienna, forging a distinctive posthumous presence for Handel and Mozart in the musical life of the city, as the pages of the 1813 *Wiener musikalische Zeitung* reveal. It was as part of this cultural aesthetic linking historical status with contemporary relevance that Seyfried prepared his two fantasies. It helps explain why what may appear to us to be the inappropriate influence of Beethoven was of no consequence to Seyfried or his audience. To alter van Swieten: 'He who can clothe Mozart so solemnly and tastefully that he pleases modern fashion, on the one hand, and, on the other, shows him in his sublimity, has felt his worth.'

Mozart's spirit in the two fantasies for orchestra has other forward-looking aspects, which tie in with the slowly emerging sense of the composer's symphonic legacy at the turn of the century. Within a year of the composer's death, the three last symphonies were already acquiring an image of unsurpassed musical excellence; with continued performances in later decades, there was a developing view that they, alongside some of Haydn's symphonies and the ones that were being composed by Beethoven, constituted the benchmark for the genre.[30] As a musician who was familiar with this music, Seyfried was able to promote three aspects of Mozart's music in his two fantasias, aspects that enabled him to contribute posthumously to Mozart's symphonic legacy. With two works in a minor key, C minor and F minor, Seyfried expanded the tally of Mozart's symphonies in the minor to three (the early symphony in G minor, K. 183, was at that stage a forgotten work). Second, choosing the first movement of the G minor piano quartet and overcoming the particular challenges it posed for the orchestrator enabled one of Mozart's most motivically focused movements to sit alongside those in Haydn's 'London' symphonies, including the first movement of No. 95 in C minor, which exploits a similarly terse motif, and the first movements of Beethoven's symphonies, most obviously that of No. 5. Finally, the fugal sections in the third movement of the F minor fantasy provided a link with the finales of the 'Jupiter', 'Clock' (No. 101), 'Drumroll' (No. 103) and *Eroica* symphonies. While Seyfried himself was never going to join the emerging symphonic triumvirate of Haydn, Mozart and Beethoven, the two fantasias did help to define some of the key components of excellence in the symphonic genre and, conveniently for the emerging historical narrative, to underline Mozart's prescient, unfulfilled awareness of them.

[29] MDL, p. 296; MDB, p. 337.

[30] See Jones, *The Symphony in Beethoven's Vienna*, pp. 15–17, pp. 121–9.

Although Seyfried's two works were often casually referred to as 'symphonies',[31] the autographs of both works and, following them, the Breitkopf & Härtel publications very deliberately use the term 'Fantaisie'.[32] While this was an acknowledgement of the main sources of the two works, the Fantasy in C minor for piano and the Fantasy in F minor for piano duet, and the desire of the arranger and publisher to profit from that association, it did sideline the five movements that were not fantasias, namely the three movements of the sonata (K. 457) and the two movements taken from the piano quartet (K. 478). The choice of 'Fantaisie' rather than 'Sinfonie' conveniently masked an uncertainty about whether the movement patterns of both works fitted general understandings of what a symphony was in the second decade of the nineteenth century since, with some exceptions, four movements in the sequence fast, slow, minuet/scherzo and finale were now very much the norm. Seyfried's C minor fantasy had four movements, but in two stages, comprising the fantasia proper and then a three-movement sonata that was itself a coherent whole. The F minor fantasia had three movements and, thanks to the G minor quartet, began with a movement in sonata form followed by a lyrical slow movement; however, the finale with its comparatively static, block-like structure did not fit any current symphonic practice. Using the all-embracing term 'Fantaisie' allowed the idiosyncrasies of the structures to stand. More positively it linked well with the changing resonances of the term at the time.

Beethoven wrote four works with the word 'fantasia' in the title: the two piano sonatas of op. 27, the Fantasy in G minor (op. 77) and the Fantasy for piano, orchestra and choir (op. 80). Many more works by him reveal the influence of fantasy as a mode of performance or of composition. In a revealing exploration of the nature of such works composed by Beethoven in 1809, Elaine Sisman has untangled a web of interacting traditions and interpretations that informed usage of the word: fantasia as a rhetorical device, as the product of improvisation at the keyboard, as a topic, and as an evocation of an image, a poetic idea or a tale. One of her most striking observations concerns the first of these, fantasia as a rhetorical device:[33]

[31] As in Seyfried's own letter of 13 January 1813 to Rochlitz concerning the F minor work, Strebel, 'Der Breifwechsel', p. 234; and reports of the performances of both works in Vienna in April 1814, in *AMZ*, 16 (1814), cols. 353–5.

[32] Autograph: 'Fantaisie en ut mineur c mol de W. A. Mozart, Arrangée à grand Orchestre par le Maître de Chapelle Ig. de Seyfried 1812' (A-Wn, Mus. Hs. 3291/1); 'Fantaisie en fa mineur F-mol tirée des oeuvres de W. A. Mozart, et arrangé à grand Orchestre par le

Maître de Chapelle Ig. de Seyfried 1813' (A-Wn, Mus. Hs. 3291/2). The Breitkopf & Härtel editions described them as a 'Grande Fantaisie'.

[33] Elaine R. Sisman, 'After the Heroic Style: *Fantasia* and the "Characteristic" Sonatas of 1809', *Beethoven Forum* 6, eds. Lewis Lockwood, Glenn Stanley, Mark Evan Bonds, Christopher Reynolds and Sisman (Lincoln, NE, 1998), pp. 67–96, at p. 88.

> In a *fantasia*, the speaker or composer uses an image to make an absent thing appear to be present, to call an experience vividly to mind, to bring the audience along into the world of the speaker or composer in order to sway them, move their passions, feel the desired feelings. The *fantasia* has another important function: it serves an image of the *composer's* experience for his or her own use, it becomes a *locator* in memory, helping to retrieve both this and other experiences for use as thematic material.

Seyfried's 'images' are the musical works that form the content of the two fantasias and the 'absent thing' that is revealed is 'W. A. Mozart', as described on the autographs and on the title pages of the Breitkopf publications. Having captured the imagination of the listener, Seyfried is able to capitalize on the expectant emotional state of that listener and, since this was very much a public experience, it generated a sense of shared values. More personally, the fantasias had unlocked Seyfried's own memories of Mozart, memories he then proceeded to indulge for his own expressive purposes.

As a reader of the *Allgemeine musikalische Zeitung*, Seyfried may have recalled reviews of two of Beethoven's symphonies in which the music is likened to a fantasy. The first public performance of the *Eroica* had elicited probably the most frequently quoted criticism of any work by the composer: 'This long composition, exceedingly difficult to perform, is actually a very broadly expanded, bold, and wild fantasia.'[34] The tone of the review as a whole is one of incomprehension rather than hostility and describing the work as a 'fantasy' was, in part, meant to facilitate understanding rather than to damn it outright. Similarly, following an early performance of the *Pastoral* symphony in Leipzig, the *Allgemeine musikalische Zeitung* again suggested that 'rather than a symphony, this composition would much more appropriately be called the fantasies of a composer suggested by those topics that Beethoven mentions'.[35] Both works deal with evoked memory, respectively of a hero and of the countryside, and, more important, the impact of that memory. Seyfried's would-be symphonies, too, were about a hero, a musical one, and Seyfried's enthusiastic response. His decision to call them a fantasy was a shrewd, honest and apposite one. It suggested a stance for the listener and pre-empted criticism that they were not true symphonies.

Concerts spirituels: 6 December 1821

Alongside the Gesellschaft der Musikfreunde, the Concerts spirituels were a major force in Viennese musical life in the 1820s and beyond. They were

---

[34] Wayne Senner, Robin Wallace and William Meredith, *The Critical Reception of Beethoven's Compositions by His German* *Contemporaries* (Lincoln, NE, 1999), vol. I, p. 168.
[35] *Ibid.*, vol. II, p. 95.

founded in 1819 by the ambitious Kapellmeister of the Augustinerkirche, Franz Xaver Gebauer (1784–1822), who replaced the weekly rehearsal of liturgical music between October and May with a *Übungs-Konzert*, that is, a fortnightly public rehearsal of liturgical music plus a run-through of a major orchestral work, typically a symphony but never a work that required an instrumental soloist, encouraging a confluence between the sacred and the secular that affected the reception of both.[36] Sacred and secular works by Seyfried and Mozart were regularly heard, including Seyfried's two fantasias.

In 1821–2,[37] the first concert of the season consisted of Seyfried's Te Deum, alongside Beethoven's Mass in C and a Symphony in B flat by Haydn (probably No. 98, possibly No. 102); the last concert included Seyfried's F minor fantasy alongside an 'Allelujah' by Albrechtsberger, the Gloria from Cherubini's Mass in F and Beethoven's 'Pastoral' Symphony. During the season, two German liturgical works by Mozart, both contrafacta, were rehearsed: 'Heiliger, sich gnädig' (KAnh. 124) and 'Preis dir! Gottheit' (KAnh. 121). More adventurously, during Lent, when orchestrally accompanied music did not feature in church services, Gebauer and his underemployed musicians took the opportunity of presenting Mozart's oratorio, *Davidde penitente*. Two symphonies by Mozart, one in C (probably the 'Jupiter') and one in D (probably the 'Prague'), were also performed that season.

The most striking *Übungs-Konzert* was the fourth in the season, given on Thursday 6 December 1821, the day following the thirtieth anniversary of Mozart's death, more particularly the thirtieth anniversary of his funeral. It was a carefully planned commemorative concert with five items: a cantata by Friedrich August Kanne entitled 'Mozarts Grab' ('Mozart's Grave'), the Symphony in G minor (K. 550), the offertory 'Misericordias Domini' (K. 222), Seyfried's Fantasy in C minor, and the 'Kyrie' and 'Dies irae' from the Requiem. This was an extraordinary programme, almost entirely in the minor key, one that began with images of Mozart's non-existent grave and ended with his evocation of judgement day, with the intervening items likewise emphasizing the sombre, the tense, the melancholy and the darkly theatrical. For the participants and the audience the *spirituel* element was one of Catholic remembrance, but in the Landständischer Saal, the location of the concert, it led to a particularly fervent mixing of the sacred and secular, the mortal and the divine.

[36] Jones, *The Symphony in Beethoven's Vienna*, pp. 184–9. For a discussion of the relationship between choral music and the symphonic repertoire in Vienna in the first decades of the nineteenth century, see Nicholas Mathew, '"Achieved is the glorious work": *The Creation* and the Choral Work Concept', in Mary Hunter and Richard Will (eds.), *Engaging Haydn: Culture, Context, and Criticism* (Cambridge, 2012), pp. 124–42.

[37] The works performed during the season are listed in *AMZ*, 24 (1822), cols. 359–62.

Kanne, like Seyfried, was a composer and writer, but of an altogether more extravagant kind.[38] His text and music, written in only fourteen days, was described as a 'Cantata for the funeral day of the blessed hero of music' ('Mozart's Grab. Cantate zum Begräbnisstage des verklärten Heroen der Tonkunst'). It consisted of three numbers, an aria and two choruses (with preceding recitatives), and had unmistakeable Christian overtones of death and ascension as it moved from contemplating Mozart's grave to the final fugue: 'Praise, Honour and Glory to him who triumphs transfigured in ethereal clouds' ('Preis, Ehr und Ruhm Ihm, der verklärt in Ätherwolken jauchzet').[39] Following this image of Mozart as a musical god, the audience heard a performance of the Symphony in G minor and then a work for the Catholic liturgy, 'Misericordias Domini'. In 1775 the text of the offertory ('Of the Lord's mercies I will sing forever') had elicited a penitential rather than a laudatory setting by Mozart, but there were additional, exclusively musical reasons for including the work in this commemorative concert. It had clear links with the final work in the programme, the two movements from the Requiem; the key is the same, D minor, and both works feature the same opening contrapuntal motif. In the middle of this heady mix of interweaving images, Seyfried's Fantasy in C minor was performed, a remarkably potent context in which to ponder the glory of Mozart's music and the glory of his spirit.

[38] For an account of his career, see two complementary articles by Hermann Ulrich, 'Friedrich Kanne (1799–1833). Leben und Umwelt', *Studien zur Musikwissenschaft*, 29 (1978), pp. 89–154; and 'Friedrich August Kanne (1799–1833). Das Schaffen', *Studien zur Musikwissenschaft*, 30 (1979), pp. 155–262. The cantata is discussed in the latter, pp. 224–5.

[39] The full text was printed in the Viennese *Allgemeine musikalische Zeitung mit besonderer Rücksicht auf den österreichischen Kaiserstaat (AMZÖK)* six days after the concert; AMZÖK, 5 (1821), cols. 781–4. A keyboard reduction of the aria, 'Der Wasserfall, wie sanft er rauschet', appeared as a music supplement to the final issue of 1821; no other musical sources have survived. Kanne had previously written a six-verse poem with the same title, 'Mozarts Grab', published in AMZÖK, 2 (1818), cols. 196 7.

9   Mozart, song and the pre-uncanny

Emily I. Dolan

Uncanny musicology

The uncanny is something of a messy musicological leitmotif. It is invoked to describe performances; whole pieces and specific passages; textures and harmonies; and composers' talents and intuitions. The musical uncanny keeps company with a handful of related themes: technology and mechanization, death and morbidity, darkness, the supernatural, freedom and control. For Carolyn Abbate, the uncanny in music is almost primal: it is bound up with the act of singing and traceable to the macabre image of Orpheus's severed head, afloat and giving forth a song. Singing is a form of enthralling re-animation and stands for, according to Abbate, 'the deadness implicit in any object that has been animated by music'.[1] In operatic performance, singers become inert vessels 'forced into motion by something operating from behind or beyond their bodies'.[2] Music is an ersatz life force. Abbate's vision ultimately addresses the discipline and power involved in all forms of musical performance: to submit to musical works is to give up a large measure of autonomy.

Abbate's argument inverts more typical discussions of the uncanny in music, which often accompany talk of performing or talking automata. Mladen Dolar, for example, takes up the examples of the too-perfect singing of E. T. A. Hoffmann's mechanical Olimpia and the strange sounds emitted by Wolfgang von Kempelen's speaking machine. While Abbate heard the singing voice as uncanny because it made people resemble machines, Dolar reversed the direction: 'There is an uncanniness in the gap which enables a machine, by purely mechanical means, to produce something so uniquely human as a voice and speech. It is as if the effect could emancipate itself from its mechanical origin and start functioning as a surplus—indeed, as the ghost in the machine.'[3] One can also, of course, speak of uncanny listening

---

[1] Carolyn Abbate, *In Search of Opera* (Princeton, NJ, 2001), p. 5.
[2] *Ibid.*, p. 42.

[3] Mladen Dolar, *A Voice and Nothing More* (Cambridge, MA, 2006), p. 7.

experiences separate from the actual sound or the performer: many sounds when heard under particular conditions can produce an uncanny experience. The introduction of sound film, as Robert Spadoni has argued, caused viewers to navigate new configurations of presence, absence and the mechanical: sound, speaking and singing unsettled and alarmed audiences who were accustomed to the conventions of silent film.[4] Brian Kane's recent history of acousmatic sound repeatedly invokes the uncanny to describe different experiences of hearing sounds while being unsure of their source or how they are produced.[5]

Mozart is often described as uncanny: his seemingly effortless talent, his ability to absorb and assimilate other styles, his knack for plumbing the depths of human emotion. This has a long history, stretching back to Hoffmann's famous invocation of the intimations of infinity, melancholy, dread and purple shimmers in the music of Mozart.[6] Lurking behind much of Mozart's uncanniness is the question of Mozart's own humanity. In *Mozart's Grace*, Scott Burnham asks why the combination of Mozart's 'unerring mastery' and his fundamental humanity are not 'disturbingly uncanny, or supremely off-putting'.[7] To ask such a question is, perhaps inevitably, to suggest the opposite; indeed, throughout the book Burnham often zeroes in on moments that he describes as uncanny: from particular harmonies and contrapuntal treatments, to Mozart's combinations of the expected and the surprising, to the way in which Mozart navigates thresholds between the human and the transcendent. We are, Burnham tells us, nothing less than haunted by Mozart and his 'uncanny intimations'.[8]

Of course, the uncanny has a history of its own; many of the elements that we might identify as uncanny in Mozart today would not have seemed so to his contemporaries. As Annette Richards has argued, the young Mozart was sometimes viewed as a kind of wondrous automaton: the Swiss physician Samuel-Auguste Tissot, after witnessing Mozart in 1766, suggested that Mozart was at once part divine and part machine, 'an instrument ... composed of strings harmoniously put together with such skill that it is impossible to touch one without all the others being also set in motion'.[9] Yet there is no horror or recoil in Tissot's description. That came later: when

[4] Robert Spadoni, 'The Uncanny Body of Early Sound Film', in *Uncanny Bodies: The Coming of Sound Film and the Origins of the Horror Genre* (Berkeley, CA, 2007), pp. 8–30.
[5] Brian Kane, *Sound Unseen: Acousmatic Sound in Theory and Practice* (New York and Oxford, 2014).
[6] E. T. A. Hoffmann, 'Review of Beethoven's Fifth Symphony', in *E. T. A. Hoffmann's Musical Writings: Kreisleriana, The Poet and*

the Composer, Music Criticism, trans. David Charlton (Cambridge, 1989), p. 238.
[7] Scott Burnham, *Mozart's Grace* (Princeton, NJ, 2013), pp. 2–3.
[8] *Ibid.*, p. 116.
[9] Samuel-Auguste Tissot, *Aristide, ou le Citoyen* (11 October 1766), p. 189, quoted in Annette Richards, 'Automatic Genius: Mozart and the Mechanical Sublime', *Music & Letters*, 80 (1999), pp. 366–89.

Maynard Solomon drew on instrumental imagery to describe Wolfgang as
Leopold Mozart's zealous creation – 'a living instrument in the form of a
little boy to labor in God's service, producing things of beauty' – the
technological metaphor became distinctly more sinister.[10] In this chapter,
I want to consider, as it were, the *proximity* of the uncanny to late
eighteenth-century music. I also want to attempt to focus the uncanny
on the music itself, as much as possible. What might it mean to speak of
music that is, irrespective of performance and environment, uncanny? By
uncanny, I mean not merely spooky, like a horror movie soundtrack, but
rather music that somehow conjures or takes the form of unsettling
memories.

Like Terry Castle's seminal work on the eighteenth-century uncanny, *The
Female Thermometer*, my inquiry here takes up themes introduced in
Freud's 1919 classic essay on the uncanny. The departure point in Freud's
essay is his dissatisfaction with the general understanding of the uncanny
and in particular with Ernst Jentsch's 1906 study *Zur Psychologie des
Umheimlichen*. Jentsch had argued that things are uncanny when they are
novel and unfamiliar, and cause intellectual uncertainty. Plumbing the
etymological depths of the idea of *Heimlich*, Freud examined the ways in
which the idea of *Heimleich* 'merges' with its antonym *Unheimlich*. 'The
uncanny (*das Unheimliche*, "the unhomely")', Freud posited, 'is in some way
a species of the familiar (*das Heimliche*, "the homely")'.[11] Castle has pointed
out that this etymological unmasking already marks Freudian uncanny as
'itself a sort of phantom, looking up out the darkness'.[12] Freud famously
turned to E. T. A. Hoffmann's tale *Der Sandman*, but not to dwell on
Nathaniel's strange obsession with the wooden doll Olimpia. Indeed,
Freud repeatedly dismissed this as 'quite irrelevant' to the more 'potent
example' of the uncanny lodged within the tragic story. This is Nathaniel's
childhood trauma at the hands of his father's visitor, Coppelius, and the
deadly return of those deeply imbedded fears with the appearance of Italian
optician Coppola. For Freud, the *Un-* in *Unheimlich* is an 'indicator of
repression'. The uncanny is the return of that which had been repressed,
something secretly or strangely familiar.

Castle finds the uncanny *avant la lettre* in the Gothic literature of the
eighteenth century. It was this period, she argues, that 'invented the
uncanny', which she sees as lodged in the shadows of the Enlightenment, a
kind of 'toxic side effect' of the Age of Reason.[13] Castle leads her readers

---

[10] Maynard Solomon, *Mozart: A Life* (New York, 1995), p. 6.
[11] Sigmund Freud, *The Uncanny*, trans. David McLintock (London, 2003), p. 154.
[12] Terry Castle, *The Female Thermometer: Eighteenth-Century Culture and the Invention of the Uncanny* (New York and Oxford, 1995), p. 7.
[13] *Ibid.*, p. 9.

directly into those shadows and into the realms of the carnivalesque, phantasmagoric and the spectral. In the present chapter, however, I do not delve into these ghostly places. I am not interested in thinking about the uncanny in relation to musical works that overtly invoke the supernatural or extraordinary. Instead, I want to consider the ways in which more ordinary musical material – lyrical melody, song – becomes a potential bearer of uncanniness. I argue that by the early nineteenth century, song, shaped by the discourses and practices surrounding the musically familiar, had the potential to mirror the basic structures of Freudian uncanny. The music of the late Enlightenment offers not the uncanny per se, but rather its necessary pre-conditions. For this nascent state, I offer the idea of the *pre-uncanny*.

The combinatorial Enlightenment

The idea of familiarity runs through Enlightenment discourses on music. Recent scholarship on eighteenth-century music has seen an embrace of the everyday, the superficial and the rote. On many levels, the music of the Enlightenment was built around ideas of familiarity and recognizability. That this is being recovered reflects the ways in which these elements have been incommensurate with the Romantic ideals of music making and inspiration that prize singularity, individuality and deviation. But while the eighteenth century was not without its unexpected turns, those turns were themselves comprehensible. Consider, for example, Robert Gjerdingen's path-breaking study *Music in the Galant Style* (2007), which makes visible the common language and procedures that underpinned music of the eighteenth century. These were the schemata: the flexible and adaptable figures that formed musical building blocks, which musicians acquired through extensive practice at the keyboard. In delving into these schemata, Gjerdingen not only recovers the compositional practices of the period, but also courtly listening habits. These habits, in his words, 'seem to have favored music that provided opportunities for acts of judging, for the making of distinctions, and for the public exercise of discernment and taste'.[14] The publication of Wye Jamison Allanbrook's exquisite Bloch lectures is likewise a powerful reminder of the power of the *superficial*.[15] Allanbrook deftly outlined the ways in which the Enlightenment musical style drew upon a treasure trove of stock characters that were easily recognizable.

[14] Robert O. Gjerdingen, *Music in the Galant Style* (New York and Oxford, 2007), p. 4.
[15] Wye Jamison Allanbrook, *The Secular Commedia: Comic Mimesis in Late Eighteenth-Century Music*, ed. Mary Ann Smart and Richard Taruskin (Berkeley, CA, 2014).

The power of topoi – as explored by Allanbrook, Leonard Ratner and Kofi Agawu – lies in their familiarity.[16]

Recognizability also operated on the level of instruments: I have argued that the power of the orchestra in the late eighteenth century stemmed in part from the powerful expressive associations of the various instruments. The complaints that began in the 1790s against the misuses of the characters of instruments – typically wind instruments – reflected their vivid associations and their potential abuses.[17] Like musical topics, these were not deep or secret meanings, but palpable qualities that resided on the surface of the music.

It is helpful to think of the music of this period as a display of combinatorial prowess. That is to say, the richness and expressive power of this style was directly tied to a proliferation of things that could be drawn upon, transformed – like, as Allanbrook suggests, the polyps that fascinated natural historians – and combined. Seen in this light, the musical games and methods for automatic composition that proliferated in this period, easily enough dismissed as mere novelties, appear to embody the basic musical principles of the period.[18]

Both Mozart and Haydn excelled at this combinatorial and transformative 'game' in which familiarity functioned as both an anchor and a compass for their listeners. In Ignaz Theodor Ferdinand Arnold's series of biographical sketches of famous composers, he described Haydn's music as follows:

> His music enters our ears quite smoothly, for we have a sense that we are hearing something that is easily grasped and already familiar to us. But we soon find that it is not that which we had thought it was or which we thought it should become. We hear something new, and we marvel at the master who knows so cleverly how to offer us, under the guise of the well known, something never heard before. Precisely this endearing popularity gives his compositions – for all their harmonic extravagance and instrumentation – an inexhaustible clarity, general intelligibility, and comprehensibility so that we grasp the most difficult things with ease.[19]

---

[16] See Kofi Agawu, *Playing with Signs: a Semiotic Interpretation of Classic Music* (Princeton, 1991); Wye Jamison Allanbrook, *Rhythmic Gesture in Mozart: 'Le Nozze Di Figaro' & 'Don Giovanni'* (Chicago, 1983); Leonard G. Ratner, *Classic Music: Expression, Form, and Style* (New York, 1980).

[17] See Emily I. Dolan, *The Orchestral Revolution: Haydn and the Technologies of Timbre* (Cambridge, 2013).

[18] On these games and methods, see Neal Zaslaw, 'Mozart's Modular Minuet Machine', in Lászlo Vikárius and Vera Lampert (eds.), *Essays in Honor of*

László Somfai on His 70th Birthday: Studies in the Sources and the Interpretation of Music (Lanham, MD, 2005), pp. 219–35.

[19] Ignaz Theodor Ferdinand Arnold, *Gallerie der berühmtesten Tonkünstler des achtzehnten und neunzehnten Jahrhunderts* (1810; reprint, Buren, 1984) pp. 109–11. As quoted and translated in Mark Evan Bonds, 'Rhetoric versus Truth: Listening to Haydn in the Age of Beethoven', in Tom Beghin and Sander M. Goldberg (eds.), *Haydn and the Performance of Rhetoric* (Chicago, IL, 2007), pp. 109–28, at 115.

Here, familiarity played an essential role in giving the listener a starting point from which his music departs and which helps guide and clarify the twists and turns taken within the music.

The combinatorial and transformative power of Mozart's music resides less in the thorough working through of a confined set of musical ideas, and more in what we might describe as Mozart's thematic generosity. His music strings together diverse themes in dramatic forms – as demonstrated in Ratner's classic analysis of the first movement of Mozart's Sonata in D, K. 284.[20] In mixing themes and registers, Mozart also made it possible to mix modes of listening. Indeed, a familiar trope in Mozart scholarship is that of the genius who navigated two musical registers, speaking at once to the connoisseurs and a broader, less refined listening public. One is a register of easy access, suggestive of passive listening and enjoyment; the other gestures towards intimate knowledge and fuels musicological inquiry.[21] The tension is dramatized through Leopold Mozart's repeated requests to his son to compose in an accessible style (begging him, for example, when he was in Paris to talk to an engraver and to produce something that was 'short, easy, and popular'[22]); Wolfgang's eventual 'solution' is to compose works – his piano concertos of 1782–3 – that are positioned 'at the mean between what is too difficult and what is too easy', thereby pleasing both the *Kenner* and the *Nichtkenner*.[23] In May 1789, Adolf von Knigge published an extended discussion of Mozart and Da Ponte's *Le nozze di Figaro* in his journal *Dramaturgische Blätter*. The portion on music – presumed to be by Bernard Anselm Weber – begins:

> It is what was to be expected of Mozart: great and beautiful, full of new ideas and
> unexpected turns, full of art, fire and genius. How we are enchanted by beautiful

[20] Leonard G. Ratner, 'Topical Content in Mozart's Keyboard Sonatas', *Early Music*, 19/4 (1991), pp. 615–19.

[21] Adorno famously heard in Mozart's music the last moment in which the 'popular' and the 'serious' registers could co-exist within a single work: 'after *The Magic Flute*', he writes, 'it was never again possible to force serious and light music together'. The suggestion that there was some sort of unusual mixture in *The Magic Flute* potentially masks the prevalence of such combinations throughout the late Enlightenment style. He denounced combinatorics in the popular music of the twentieth century. For the 'regressive listeners . . . a kind of musical children's language is prepared [. . .] it differs from the real thing in that its vocabulary consists exclusively of fragments and distortions of the artistic language of music'. See Theodor W. Adorno, 'On the Fetish-Character in Music and the Regression of Listening', in *Essays on Music; Selected with Introduction, Commentary, and Notes by Richard Leppert*, trans. Susan H. Gillespie (Berkeley, CA, 2002), pp. 290, 307.

[22] 13 August 1778 (MBA, vol. II, p. 444; LMF, p. 599).

[23] MBA, vol. III, p. 245; LMF, p. 833 (translation following Elaine Sisman). Sisman has unpacked the different ways the Kenner and Nichtkenner distinction was invoked in the Mozarts' correspondence, showing the ways in which these might be invoked to make a point about audiences and also the relationship to the performative difficulty. See Sisman, 'Observations of the First Phase of Mozart's "Haydn" Quartets', in Dorothea Link and Judith Nagley (eds.), *Words About Mozart: Essays in Honour of Stanley Sadie* (Woodbridge and Rochester, NY, 2005), pp. 33–58, especially 36ff.

charming song; now we are made to smile at subtle comic wit and fancy; now we admire the naturally conceived and superbly executed planning; now the magnificence and greatness of Art takes us by surprise . . . Mozart is gifted with the happy genius that can blend art with nature and song with grace.[24]

For Weber, Mozart's music offered a cornucopia of admirable qualities, one after another, from the charming to the comic to the magnificent. Mozart's ability to surprise his listeners with the unexpected was itself an expected quality. Here, Mozart's greatness and magnificence does not necessarily exist on a higher plane, to be appreciated through a different mode of listening. Rather, it is made possible by Mozart's combination of other expressive registers.[25]

The lyrical familiar

Alongside the development of this 'combinatorial style' was the notion of folk music; the values and valences of each might appear – at least initially – to be opposed to one another. In 1782, the composer, music teacher and theatre director Johann Schulz (1747–1800) published a collection of songs: the *Lieder im Volkston* (which might be translated as 'folk style' or 'folk-tone').[26] In his preface, he writes:

> In all of these songs it is and remains my intention to sing more in the *folk* than in the *art* style, so that even untrained lovers of song, as long as they are not completely and totally lacking a voice, should be able to sing them and learn them. To this end, I have chosen only the texts by our best song-poets, which seemed to me to be made for this folk-singing, and I have made the melodies themselves with the greatest simplicity and clarity. Indeed, in this way I sought to imbue them with the *appearance of familiarity*, because I know from experience, how helpful, indeed necessary, this appearance is for the folksong for its swift acceptance.[27]

---

[24] MDL, p. 301; MDB, pp. 344–5.

[25] This echoes similar arguments made in particular about Haydn's late style: James Webster, for example, argues for the co-dependency of the 'sublime' and 'pastoral' modes in the late oratorios. Lawrence Kramer likewise suggests that the power of Haydn's *Creation* lies in its recall; see Webster, 'The Sublime and the Pastoral in *The Creation* and *The Seasons*', in Caryl Clark (ed.), *The Cambridge Companion to Haydn* (Cambridge, 2005), pp. 150–63 and Lawrence Kramer, 'Recalling the Sublime: The Logic of Creation in Haydn's *Creation*', *Eighteenth-Century Music*, 6 (2009), pp. 41–57.

[26] On the idea of *Volkston*, see Matthew Gelbart, *The Invention of 'Folk*

Music' and 'Art Music': Emerging Categories from Ossian to Wagner (Cambridge, 2007), pp. 266ff. On the status of Schulz's song in the Enlightenment, see Wilhelm Schulte, 'J.A.P. Schulz, a Protagonist of the Musical Enlightenment: Lieder Im Volkston', *Music Research Forum*, 3/1 (1988), pp. 23–34.

[27] J. A. P. Schulz, Preface to *Lieder im Volkston, bey dem Clavier zu singen* (Berlin, 1785), p. 2. 'In allen diesen Liedern ist und bleibt mein Bestreben, mehr *volksmäßig* als *kunstmäßig* zu singen, nemlich so, daß auch ungeübte Liebhaber des Gesanges, so bald es ihnen nicht ganz und gar an Stimme fehlt, solche leicht nach singen und auswendig behalten können. Zu dem Ende habe ich nur solche Texte aus unsern besten Leiderdichten gewählt, die mir zu diesem Volksgesange

Example 9.1 J. A. P. Schulz, 'An die Natur' from *Lieder im Volkston* (Berlin, 1782; 2nd edition 1785).

This appearance is, Schulz claims, the 'secret' of the entire folk style. What does it mean to *appear* to be familiar? Within the collection one finds a series of strophic songs, simple melodies that are straightforward to sing, texts (which often praise the beauties of nature) that are predominantly set syllabically, graceful dotted rhythms and regular phrases (see Example 9.1). Schulz's simplicity and clarity reflect both the ease of vocal performance and the ways in which the songs are a simplified version of the kind of music that proliferated in the courtly musical style of the late Enlightenment. In contrast to music that drew together a multiplicity of topics and registers, song could stand in for the unartful. In some sense, musical culture of the late eighteenth century suggested the same relationship between music and song that Gary Tomlinson argued for, when he imagined shifting the discipline of musicology towards cantology, and to think of music 'as a song-ish thing'.[28] For Tomlison and Schulz, song appears as something originary and whole.

gemacht zu seyn schienen, und mich in den Melodien selbst der höchsten Simplicität und Faßlichkeit beflissen, ja auf alle Weise den Schein des Bekannten darinzubringen gesucht, weil ich aus Erfahrung weiß, wie sehr dieser Schein dem Volkliede zu seiner

schnellen Empfehlung dienlich, ja nothwendig ist.'

[28] Gary Tomlinson, 'Vico's Songs: Detours at the Origins of (Ethno) Musicology', *The Musical Quarterly*, 83/3 (1999), pp. 344–77, at 343.

Matthew Gelbart has argued that the late eighteenth century witnessed the co-formation of the concepts of what he calls 'folk' and 'cultivated' music.[29] Not only were these categories co-dependent, but they also, Gelbart suggests, helped to give rise to a new notion of 'art' music, one that he ties to Kantian notions of genius. The art music of the late eighteenth century, in its originality, was the product of genius minds whose productivity mirrored the organicism and naturalism that were associated with folk music. There is fundamental circularity in this chain of influence: the *sound* of folk music and its concomitant associations with naturalness were being actively shaped by the composers of 'art' music.

The most powerful support for Gelbart's argument lies outside his book. One of Haydn's more delightful self-quotations occurs in *Die Jahreszeiten* (1801; Example 9.2). In springtime, the farmer Simon cheerfully tills the fields while whistling the main theme from the slow movement of Haydn's Symphony No. 94 in G major ('The Surprise').

Simon, 'Schon eilet froh der Ackersmann,' from *Die Jahreszeiten* (1801)

Schon eilet froh der Ackersmann	The ploughman is already hastening
Zur Arbeit auf das Feld,	merrily to the field;
In langen Furchen schreitet er	he strides down the long furrows,
Dem Pfluge flötend nach.	whistling behind the plough.

One might read this simply as a joke – and certainly there is something lovely about the image of Simon the farmer tootling Haydn. But it is the recognizability of this tune that allows us to know that Simon is whistling; indeed, using a melody from a beloved slow movement was a necessity for this moment to be effective, all the more since Simon does not literally whistle the tune with his lips, but rather through the orchestra. Haydn's quotation both points to the popularity of his music and draws on the folk-like quality of this melody in its original construction. As I have argued elsewhere, part of the musical force of the slow movement of Haydn's Symphony No. 94 'The Surprise' (1791/92) lies in the astonishing transformation he creates between the simple opening tune and its grand apotheosis at the end of the movement.[30] Ultimately Haydn's quotation is rather bold: it invites us to hear the melody of the slow movement of the 'Surprise' symphony not as having been written by Haydn, but having existed forever, transcending authorship. As Charles Rosen put it, 'to discuss the influence of folk music on Haydn's style is to the set the matter on its head'.[31]

---

[29] Gelbart, *The Invention of 'Folk Music' and 'Art Music'*.
[30] See Dolan, *The Orchestral Revolution*, pp. 142ff.
[31] Charles Rosen, *The Classical Style: Haydn, Mozart, Beethoven* (New York, 1972), p. 329.

Example 9.2 Joseph Haydn, 'Schon eilet froh der Ackersmann', from *Die Jahreszeiten* (1801), bars 1–20.

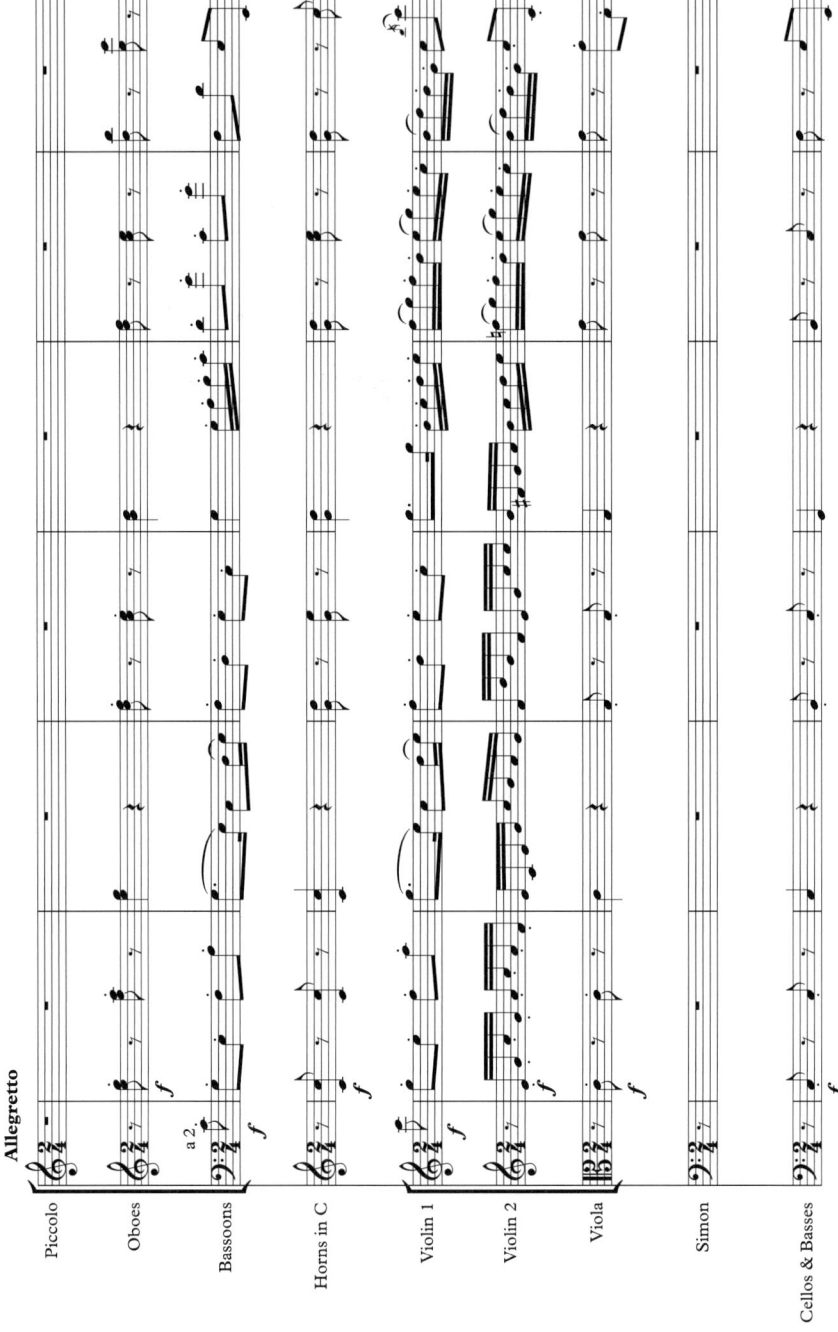

Example 9.2 (cont.)

Example 9.2 (cont.)

Example 9.3 The Starling's Tune.

Starling

We might see Mozart's music, in contrast, as more indirectly conjuring a folk style through feigned familiarity, in a way that invokes the 'Schulzian' folk. On 27 May 1784, Mozart made an entry in his expense book: 'Starling bird. 34 kreutzer'.[32] This was Mozart's beloved pet; as is well known, when the bird died, three years later, he buried the creature with much ceremony, including reading a versed epitaph. When Mozart entered the expense, he also included a tune in the book, with the remark that 'Das war schön!' (Example 9.3).

This is, of course, the melody of the finale of Mozart's Piano Concerto No. 17 in G major, K. 453 (Example 9.4), or at least a modification of it. The starling added an odd fermata and an unexpected G#. Mozart had completed this concerto a month before he acquired his avian friend, on 12 April 1784, which his student Barbara von Ployer performed in Döbling in June 1784. That Mozart's starling sang this melody has raised all sorts of questions; had Mozart not recorded the completion of his concerto in the catalogue of works over a month before the entry into his expense book, it might be tempting to think that Mozart acquired his theme from the bird. Some have speculated that Mozart bought the starling because it could sing the melody.[33] Starlings, however, are enthusiastic mimics, and have been known to pick up and repeat phrases of speech and song, even after a single hearing. Once starlings and bird-men enter the picture, it is difficult not to hear melodic echoes.

There is a certain appeal to the notion that the bird sang it first, perhaps because the contredanse melody has a folk-like and natural quality. (Girdlestone described it as one of 'Mozart's most ethereal concertos, with a pastoral strain'.[34]) Mozart's fondness for the bird and his distress at its passing invites the comparison between this melody and that of Papageno, when he makes his first entrance with the aria 'Ein Vogelfänger bin ich ja' (Example 9.5). Any direct connection cannot be proven. (Allanbrook, for example, dismissed such a connection as 'purely prospective'.[35]) But no

[32] MDL, p. 199; MDB, p. 225.

[33] 'It was its song, no doubt, that endeared the bird to Mozart and made him buy it . . . This concerto is therefore placed, as it were, under the patronage of those feathered folk of whom Mozart was so fond.' Cuthbert Girdlestone, *Mozart and His Piano Concertos* (New York, 1964), p. 252.

[34] Girdlestone, *Mozart and His Piano Concertos*, p. 239.

[35] Wye Jamison Allanbrook, 'Comic Issues in Mozart's Piano Concertos', in Neal Zaslaw (ed.), *Mozart's Piano Concertos: Text, Context, Interpretation* (Ann Arbor, MI, 1996), pp. 75–105, at 99.

Example 9.4 Mozart, Piano Concerto No. 17 in G major, K. 453/iii, bars 1–8.

Example 9.4 (cont.)

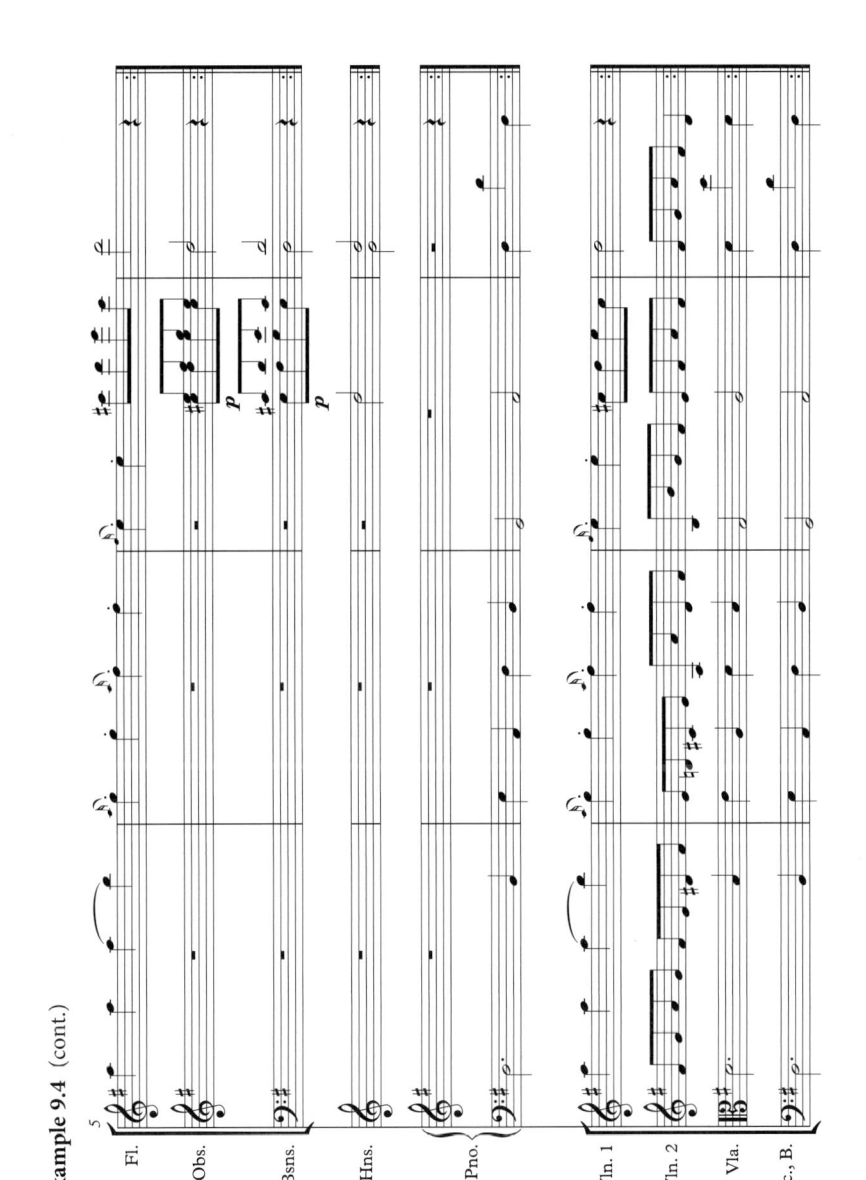

Example 9.5 Mozart, 'Ein Vogelfänger bin ich ja', from *Die Zauberflöte*, bars 27–34.

Example 9.5 (cont.)

proof is really needed: this tune, like the melody of the finale of the piano concerto, possesses the quality of sounding familiar. The desire to hear a connection between the two melodies says more about power of 'familiar-sounding melodies' than it does about their musical similarities. These songs – with their catchy lyricism – have the potential to sound remembered even at first hearing.

It is here that we return to the notion of the uncanny. In the music of Schulz, Mozart and Haydn, song took on the status of what I am calling the *pre-uncanny*. Song – as the sound of the folk, of nature – existed as part of music's memory; it was always already familiar. This is not to suggest that lyrical song was something inherently disturbed or repressed. Nor is it to argue that Mozart, Haydn or Schulz conceived of their folk-like melodies as unsettling. But in standing for something from the past, song could haunt its listeners.

The uncanny potential of song is akin to that of the wondrous eighteenth-century automata that could play instruments, write and draw, such as Vaucanson's flute player or the Jaquet-Droz keyboard-playing musician and writer. As Adelheid Voskuhl has so keenly demonstrated, these machines were not seen as unsettling; rather, they were virtuosic pieces of technology that embodied and performed the elements of sentimental selfhood.[36] These machines combined and recombined familiar behaviours to the delight of their viewers. It was only later, in the early nineteenth century – in particular in the imagination of E. T. A. Hoffmann – that these machines were recast as disturbing. It is difficult for us today to see the Jaquet-Droz musician perform – heaving her mechanical bosom and rolling her eyes – without thinking back to poor Nathaniel and his Olimpia.

Like automata, song could easily transform into something else. Song stood at many different thresholds. It could, for example, easily become bound up with its seeming opposite: the mechanical. For Abbate, Papageno's music hovers between the human, the natural and the mechanical. Though his music has been celebrated for its 'happy simplicity' and the 'cyclic force of elemental nature', there is also a hint of something darker: when paired with his magic bells, Papageno also has the potential, she suggests, to be unnatural and machine-like.[37] This slippage between natural song and mechanical in part reflects the technology of the day: musical clocks were popular pieces of furniture in this period. Though automatic organs could produce 'superhuman' music (as Annette Richards argues about Mozart's F minor Fantasie

[36] Adelheid Voskuhl, *Androids in the Enlightenment: Mechanics, Artisans, and Cultures of the Self* (Chicago, IL, 2013). On the later reception of Enlightenment automata, see chapter 6 ('The Enlightenment Automaton in the Industrial Age').

[37] Abbate, *In Search of Opera*, p. 77.

K. 608, written in 1790[38]), these machines were typically programmed with popular tunes. Even without the mechanizing effects of Papageno's bells, his tunes themselves – in their popularity – were bound up with mechanical music.

But thinking about the special status of lyrical song can also provide an analytical angle for later music, offering a way to approach lyricism in, for example, Franz Schubert's instrumental works. Schubert's lyricism has traditionally presented a challenge to musicological analysis. Tovey unhesitatingly praised Schubert's lyrical gift, while criticizing what he believed to be Schubert's inadequate formal techniques.[39] Schubert's beautiful melodies too easily separate from their formal context; Carl Dahlhaus described the second theme of the first movement of Schubert's *Unfinished Symphony* as having entered 'the bourgeois stock of musical quotations'.[40] Of course, for Dahlhaus, the 'problem' posed by lyricism was its assimilation into large-scale form. While lyricism tends towards stasis and stability, large-scale form draws its coherence and power from the dynamic relationships between all parts.[41]

In Schubert's instrumental works, his lyricism is often marked by instability: the heartbreakingly beautiful E flat major theme in the first movement of the String Quintet; the quivering theme of the slow movement of Schubert's String Quartet in G major, interrupted by pained sforzando chords. When introduced into larger instrumental forms, song takes on the quality of being, I argue, strangely familiar. Like Coppelius/Coppala, song enters uneasily. And just as Hoffmann's tormented Nathaniel was driven to violence, so too is Schubert's music. Take for example, a moment where Schubert draws on a pre-existing song as the basis for a movement: the Andante con moto movement of his String Quartet No. 14 in D minor, variations on his song 'Der Tod und das Mädchen' (1817).

The theme, in its first presentation is homophonic; it is texturally and harmonically stable, even unusually so for Schubert. With each repetition, this stability disintegrates. In the first variation, the rhythmic accompaniment in the second violin and viola speed up; the first violin plays continually off the beat, lending fragility to the theme. Each successive variation adds more turbulence leading to the obsessive and pervasive dactylic rhythm of the third variation. By the second half of this variation, the movement reaches its most volatile state as the violin and cello exchange chords that

[38] See Richards, 'Mozart and the Mechanical Sublime'.
[39] Donald Francis Tovey, 'Franz Schubert', in *Essays and Lectures on Music* (Oxford, 1949), pp. 103–33, see especially pp. 117–18.
[40] Carl Dahlhaus, *Nineteenth-Century Music*, trans. J. Bradford Robinson (Berkeley, CA, 1989), p. 153.
[41] On the 'problems' of analysis, see Suzannah Clark, *Analyzing Schubert* (Cambridge, 2011).

feel both weighty and violent. After a moment of repose in the fourth, major-mode variation, the urgency returns in the last variation, leading to the climax of the movement beginning at bar 118. By bar 131, the energy begins to diminish. The final coda (bar 151) returns to the original homophonic texture. The theme, now in major, sounds not only sweeter, but also exhausted.

Hugh Macdonald, in his now classic essay, identified what he called Schubert's 'volcanic temper'. For him, this is the 'darker side' that is 'remote from the more familiar lyrical Schubert'.[42] Schubert's pairing of the violent and the lyrical has direct precursors in the slow movements of Haydn's late symphonies, which were built around sonic contrasts and which alternated lyrical material with opposing, often violent sonorities. In Haydn's movements these violent outbursts draw their effectiveness largely from the ways in which they are unexpected and surprising. Schubert's violence, when compared with Haydn's, appears less remote. Schubert's lyricism and his violence often exist in close proximity; Schubert's tendency to imbue his lyricism with restlessness and urgency suggests that his violent outbursts grow directly out of this strange lyricism. If we think of Schubert's lyricism through the lens of the uncanny, then the violent outbursts reflect the pain and recoil inherent in the unsettling presence of song that does not fully belong.

The idea of familiarity – and its strangeness – has been a central theme within Schubert studies, usually recast as the question of memory.[43] Much of the scholarship on memory focuses either on the relationship between Beethovenian and Schubertian approaches to form or else on Schubert's own techniques of memory within his works. (Schubert, Burnham states evocatively, 'leads us to no Beethovenian vision of what we could be, but finds us time and again in that hallowed terrible place where we remember what we are'.[44]) But perhaps our point of comparison should not be Beethoven, rather Mozart and Haydn. Schubert's ability to create the lyrical uncanny grows directly out of the special status given to song, lyricism, and the familiar in the late eighteenth century.

[42] Hugh MacDonald, 'Schubert's Volcanic Temper', *The Musical Times*, 119/1629 (1978), pp. 949–52, at 949.
[43] See, for example, the special issue of *The Musical Quarterly* devoted to memory in Schubert's instrumental music (84/4, 2000) and Benedict Taylor 'Schubert and the Construction of Memory: The String Quartet in A Minor, D.804 ("Rosamunde")', *Journal of the Royal Musical Association*, 139/1 (2014), pp. 41–88.
[44] Scott Burnham, 'Schubert and the Sound of Memory', *The Musical Quarterly*, 84/4 (2000), pp. 655–63, at 663.

Index of Mozart's works by Köchel number

Index of Mozart's works by genre

General index